A Flower with Roots

A Flower with Roots

The Story of Mary D. Jesse and Shokei Girls' School

ROBERTA LYNN STEPHENS

Afterword by Komei Sasaki

WIPF & STOCK · Eugene, Oregon

This book is dedicated to Shokei Gakuin in Sendai, Japan, and to all those there who have continued to urge me on to finish this book.

Mary D. Jesse

Contents

Preface | *ix*
Acknowledgments | *xi*
Abbreviations | *xii*
Introduction | *xiii*

1   From the Beginning | 1

2   Not Just An Ordinary Teacher (1911–1919) | 12

3   Divine Guidance—Visible and Invisible (1919–1926) | 28

4   Hopes for a New Start (1926–1930) | 50

5   Interlude (1930–1937) | 67

6   Clouds on the Horizon (1938–1941) | 91

7   Engulfed in the Storm (1941–1947) | 108

8   Welcoming Free And Brighter Days (1947–1950) | 136

9   Destinations and New Beginnings (1950–1952) | 160

Afterword by Komei Sasaki | 183

Appendix 1: Glossary of Japanese Words | 187

Appendix 2: Alphabetical List of Letters/Annual Reports
            and their Origin | 190

Appendix 3: Missionaries at Shokei | 199

Bibliography | 207
Index | 211

Preface

I did not begin writing with the idea of publishing a book. My journey in research and writing began as part of a research project for the editorial committee of *Shokei Jogakuin's 100 Year Anniversary History Book*. Shokei, pronounced "show-kay," is located in Miyagi Prefecture in northeast Japan along the eastern seaboard about three hundred sixty miles from Tokyo. As the American Baptist missionary representative on this Japanese Christian school committee, I was assigned to research the period of school history from 1921–1929, when American Baptist missionary Mary Daniel Jesse served at the school. Born in 1881, Jesse's missionary career began in 1911 and spanned more than forty years. As I researched and wrote, Aiko Kouchi—the alumna representative on the committee and a former student of Jesse's—began translating my writing into Japanese for the committee and connected me to more primary information.

Research of that period assigned to me not only revealed an interesting story of this woman's life, but showed that she had great influence before 1921 and certainly in the twenty years following 1929. By this time, the editorial committee began to realize that Mary Jesse had been a major but forgotten figure in the growth and development of the school, so they encouraged me to research "the rest of the story." In 1991 and again in 1996, the committee allowed me to gather materials at the American Baptist Historical Society (ABHS) in Valley Forge, Pennsylvania (currently in Atlanta, Georgia). ABHS houses the largest collection of historical records from missionaries and Baptist churches in the United States and around the world. From the time of my first visit, the staff at ABHS played a major role in supplying documents and guidance in research and writing. After both visits, I returned to Japan with a large cardboard box full of articles copied from mission magazines from 1910 to 1953, and pertinent correspondence from the personal files of Mary Jesse and other missionaries serving with Jesse.

Although we are looking back in time from a present-day vantage point in this book, I wanted to try to see Shokei School and Jesse not only through her own eyes (fifty personal letters are specifically cited in this work), but through the eyes of the other missionaries. I discovered the intricate and sometimes very emotional heart and spirit covering four decades of leadership in the school. We can see how varying degrees of American and Japanese spiritual leadership, decisions of a foreign denominational mission board, economics of two countries, generosity of American Baptist churches and, of course, the diverse personalities of the school's American and Japanese staff affected the development and character of the school. It is this kind of drama that needed expression in a longer work than a few paragraphs in an anniversary book. So, I continued to do research, and the resulting book, *Nezuita Hana,* or *A Flower with Roots,* was finally published in Japan in 2003. There was a time gap between the 2003 publication in Japanese and this publication. Delay allowed me to find additional valuable material, aided by the internet, that would have been impossible before.

This book will be of interest to anyone who is interested in Japan, development of education in a Christian (mission) school, a denominational mission board's efforts in women's education on foreign soil, the life of missionaries in a past era, the effects of the Pacific War on a Japanese Christian school, or the movement of God in the lives of individuals.

Although this book has been translated and published in the Japanese language, Japanese words set off in italics are used when the translation leads to awkward wording in English. These words are defined when they first occur and in a glossary at the end.

Throughout the book, the names referring to the school vary. Sometimes the name reflects a status given to it by the government. At other times, it is a name used by missionaries, the Japanese, or by a name known to the American Baptist churches' membership during that time period. The following terms refer to the school in various eras: Ella O. Patrick Home, Sendai School, Shokei School, *Jogakko,* Shokei Girls' School, and Shokei *Jogakuin* (*jo* = female, *gakkou* = school, *gakuin* = private school); and lastly, since 2003 the school's name became Shokei Gakuin, because male students were added to the school, so the word "jo," for "female," needed to be removed.

Acknowledgments

Many people have helped me write this book. First and foremost are the many people in Japan at Shokei Gakuin who encouraged me and continued to provide resources for additional research. I recall Reverend Akihiro Shishido (Chancellor of Shokei) and his office staff at Shokei's administration offices who endlessly typed and retyped the material on word processors. Alumna, including Aiko Kouchi, as a resource and translator into Japanese, and Junko Tsuruma, who gave me the final impetus to get the Japanese version published. Professor Mochizuki, Budget Director of the Board of Managers of Kanto Gakuin provided the data for converting yen mentioned in the book into current values. Rev. Yoshio Oshima has been advising and patiently teaching me Japan Baptist history. While these people were busy helping me in Japan, friends at the American Baptist Historical Society were of invaluable help in teaching me how to write and do hands-on research. They include Beverly Carlson, Executive Director and Betty Layton, Archivist. Carlson's successor in the initial research phase, Deborah Van Broekhoven along with Layton read the manuscript and suggested revisions for more clarification in the later phase. Many others helped with formatting and word changes: some of them are Ashley Whitaker, David Kelley, Dr. Paul Aita, the late Dr. Robert Fulop, Ron Schlosser, and Rev. Dr. Reid Trulson.

For the newest section, chapter 1 of the English version, many thanks go to Mary Beth Brown of the Western Historical Manuscript Collection of the University of Missouri as well as the staff and volunteers of the Mary Ball Washington Museum of Lancaster, Virginia for their invaluable help with information on Mary Jesse's family and the geography of her birthplace.

Abbreviations

ABFMS	American Baptist Foreign Mission Society
ABHS	American Baptist Historical Society
ABMU	American Baptist Missionary Union
BIM	Board of International Ministries
IJEC	*International Journal of Early Childhood*
IM	International Ministries
UCC	United Church of Christ
WABFMS	Woman's American Baptist Foreign Mission Society

Introduction

This book is about a very special person in history, Mary Daniel Jesse, whose passion it was to create a fine Christian educational institution in Japan through which girls could reach their full potential, becoming poised young women and followers of Jesus Christ. Her capability, determination, and faith in God were assets which saw her through times of adversity and intense anguish. This book is also about a special school, Shokei Gakuin. With Christ as its model, "living together in peace with others" has always been its base and motto for educating not only the intellect, but the inner spirit and heart. The school has repeatedly gone through the cycle of growing, falling, and rebounding, but its top priority has always been the students. However, this story is not limited to only these two themes. It is a keyhole view of a period of history (1911–1952) in which two different cultures converge to make one story. The story is a combined effort of many heroines, not just one. They are missionaries who had a passion for living, a passion for telling others about their faith in Jesus Christ, and a passion for educating Japanese young women. Their desire was to plant a flower with roots that would keep blooming year after year. It is from their letters and reports that we can see both the raw human and the divinely inspired sides of their personalities. I focus mainly on Shokei Gakuin during the period that Mary Jesse served as missionary-principal, teacher, and president. Before proceeding, I would like to briefly describe the sending organization, Woman's American Baptist Foreign Mission Society, and how its staff related to the missionaries they sent out from such a great distance. This description will be helpful to understand why problem-solving was so exasperatingly difficult before there were telephones, fax machines, and the internet! How were missionaries supported? How did their organization develop and what impact did it have on them, personally? The answers are important to understanding this unique story.

A Bit of Organizational History. In the 1700s, scattered Baptist churches were always wary of organizing for fear of losing the autonomy of the local church. However, Adoniram and Ann Judson, who left the United States as Congregational missionaries in 1812, became Baptists before they arrived in India, and were baptized by William Carey prior to fleeing to Burma. Their colleague Luther Rice shared their compelling story far and wide. This gave the impetus to the formation of the Triennial Convention or the General Missionary Convention in 1814, and was the first nation-wide Baptist missionary-sending body to form in the United States. This organization was the predecessor to the American Baptist Foreign Mission Society, or the current International Ministries of the American Baptist Churches of the United States. The tumultuous years before the Civil War also affected Baptist churches. The Free Baptist Missionary Society broke off and organized independently in 1843, and soon after, in 1845, the Southern Baptist Convention was formed. Also in 1845, the Triennial Con-vention was renamed the American Baptist Missionary Union (ABMU). It continued to manage the well-being of missionaries and funding for work in foreign countries. The Missionary Union was independent of any Baptist church denominational structure, and therefore did its own fundraising for missionary couples and single men, but not single women. Its Board of Managers governed the sending and funding of missionaries for nearly one hundred years before becoming affiliated with the new Northern Baptist Convention established in 1907.

There was considerable resistance to the appointment of single women missionaries, and few were sent until the formation of the Woman's Ameri-can Baptist Foreign Mission Society (WABFMS) in 1871. Eventually, two regional societies were established, with headquarters in Boston and Chi-cago, and later a third in 1874 in San Francisco. When communication and transportation in the United States had greatly improved, all three societies merged into one society in 1913. Their governing board (here referred to as the "woman's mission board" or "mission board") was separate from the ABMU. The woman's mission board made its own appointments subject to approval by the ABMU, and administered its funds by mutual agree-ment. In 1908, the ABMU reorganized and adopted the name American Baptist Foreign Mission Society (ABFMS). In 1955, the WABFMS officially merged with the ABFMS. On a practical level during the intervening years, the couples, single men (ABFMS), and single women of the WABFMS served side by side in their respective country, but after the merger they served under a unified organization. The mission boards were dependent on mission offerings from American Baptist churches in the United States to pay the salaries of missionaries and fund the schools overseas.

By 1900, ABFMS and WABFMS boards, through their missionaries, managed nearly one thousand one hundred forty schools worldwide with the help of indigenous people. Shokei Gakuin was one of these, and one of multiple mission schools in Japan. The investment in schools around the world was truly great. Shokei was dependent on funds from US churches for over fifty years. When economic conditions in the United States wavered, or when Americans became hostile toward foreigners because of immigration or war, offerings in churches for foreign missions decreased. These events had a crippling effect on Shokei and other schools like it.

Relating to State-Side Management. Resources for the material of this book, to a large degree, came from correspondence between the missionary in Japan and the secretary on the home board in the United States, sometimes referred to as the Foreign Secretary (currently called "Area Director"). The corresponding secretary for the WABFMS was the bridge between the missionary and the mission board. She was responsible for corresponding with the missionaries about their needs, problems, and desires, and even reprimanding them when the missionaries' actions or attitudes warranted it. She also had the difficult job of interpreting board policy and advocating for the missionary. During Mary Jesse's tenure, she corresponded with Mabelle Rae McVeigh, Minnie Sandburg (later, Mrs. Charles H. Sears), Grace Maine, Ethel M. Humphreys, and Hazel Shank, all of whose names will appear in this book. Because Jesse corresponded with each foreign secretary in such detail, it was possible for me to knit together the details she wrote about along with Shokei's recorded history, revealing a more complete and personal story of how Shokei journeyed toward becoming a healthy, reputable school.

With the financial burden of so many schools and other work around the world, a topic often discussed in letters between missionary and corresponding secretary was finances. As the number of educational institutions increased and funds decreased, mission administrators at the home office in the United States began to encourage the missionaries to help the institutions become financially independent and cut back on costs. Yet, the board wanted the missionaries to stay involved enough in the school administration to keep an eye on spending and investments in buildings and programs so that they did not fail because of poor management. Jesse often got two contradictory messages from her foreign secretary: guard the finances of the school, and take less responsibility for administration. But she never could understand how to do both at the same time successfully. Guarding the mission board's investment in the school meant having to be involved in the management of the school. Both resulted in the school's dependence on American money and the presence of missionaries. The home board's resources were often stretched to the breaking point while the school remained tied to the apron strings of its benefactor.

Relating to the Mission Organization in Japan. In 1873, Jonathan and Eliza Goble and Nathan and Charlotte Brown were the first Baptist missionaries to arrive in Japan. From that time until 1901, nearly eighty American Baptist missionaries (couples and singles) spent time serving in Japan. They did not have a formal organization amongst themselves except for purposes of fellowship. They would continue as a family with close-knit ties with each other. But they were each directly responsible to their home board. By 1900 it became necessary to begin to coordinate the work in relation to each other, because their work became interconnected with the formation of a growing Japanese Christian denomination. The Reference Committee was formed as the unifying force. It had subcommittees, including a women's committee which dealt exclusively with women's issues and the girls' schools. Then, in 1922, the All-Japan mission meeting was hailed as opening a new era with the establishment of the Joint Committee. More and more Japanese were becoming Christians, and leaders were emerging who needed experience in management. The Joint Committee gradually took over many duties of the Reference Committee. It was made up of six American missionary men and six Japanese men. The women, however, resisted giving over responsibilities for their schools to the Joint Committee, because it meant that men would have too much power over the girls' schools. Boards of Trustees in the schools were gradually given more and more responsibility for the schools, but until that time, issues regarding women missionaries and girls' schools were handled by the women's committee and the Reference Committee.

Shokei Gakuin. The school marks its official beginning in November 1892 with the arrival of Miss Annie S. Buzzell. But prior to Buzzell's arrival, four missionaries in rapid succession had done the groundwork for a girls' school by taking seven little girls into their home. These girls became Christians in the thoroughly Christian atmosphere, receiving their grounding in English while attending a public school. They became a tremendous help to these new, inexperienced missionaries. In particular, Miss Lavinia Mead (1890) incorporated a thorough training program to teach the Bible, singing of hymns, and prayer to the girls, and they in turn accompanied the missionaries to the outskirts of town, where they assisted in Sunday schools and home visitation, because the foreign missionaries lacked language and cultural sensitivities. Although this practice did not originate in Sendai, what these girls did became known as the work of Bible Women who eventually underwent specialized education and became salaried workers.

Mead, who is considered the founder, preceded Annie Buzzell by only two years. Discussion continues today as to whether she or Buzzell should be considered the first principal, but the two worked together side by side, differing in their philosophy, at times, as to whether the girls should be given a general Christian education or should be educated specifically as Bible Women. Buzzell won out. In 1901, Mead left to work in another part of Japan and eventually founded a woman's seminary in Osaka to train Bible Women exclusively. The first official government recognition of Shokei school came in 1896 with the construction of the first missionary residence/school building. The inclusion of a foreign religion as a regular subject in the curriculum prevented the little school from gaining any higher status, but missionaries were not willing to relent on this point. Buzzell worked hard to make it an excellent school. When the Bible was removed from the official curriculum, and the period of study was increased from four years to five years in 1910, the school received accreditation from the Japanese government. The staff continued to teach Christianity and study the Bible through other methods, such as through their residential dormitory program. It was not until 1942 that it became an educational institution with legal standing under Japanese law.

The name "Shokei" was created early on by Buzzell. The origin lies in Chinese characters meaning a plain linen cloth coat which covers a beautiful kimono to conceal its beauty. In simple words, "rich on the inside but modest on the outside." Buzzell thought that this idea matched the Bible verses in 1 Peter 3:3–4: "Your beauty should not come from outward adornment, such as braided hair and the wearing of gold jewelry and fine clothes. Instead, it should be that of your inner self, the unfading beauty of a gentle and quiet spirit, which is of great worth in God's sight" (NIV). This concept and the scripture remain with Shokei Gakuin to the present day.

Now meet Mary Daniel Jesse, who envisioned the role education could play in raising the status of young women who would understand that inner beauty is of great value in the sight of God. Embark on a journey with me to another era and another world to experience the passion of many women giving their lives to planting seeds of faith with prayers that the roots would grow deep to produce a flower of unfading beauty.

1

From the Beginning

Epping Forest—Mary Ball Washington & Mary Daniel Jesse's Birthplace (courtesy of Judy Jesse McCarthy- Dexter Press, Pearl River, N. Y.)

In the bulb there is a flower; in the seed, an apple tree;
In cocoons, a hidden promise: butterflies will soon be free!
In the cold and snow of winter there's a spring that waits to be,
Unrevealed until its season, something God alone can see.

—NATALIE SLEETH[1]

We left Kilmarnock, Virginia, on that sultry Sunday heading north on Highway 3, known in years past as the Kings Highway of the Northern

1. Sleeth, "In the Bulb There is a Flower."

Neck of Virginia. Our tour bus was filled with Japanese high school girls, and we were on a pilgrimage of sorts. I think I was the only one whose heart was beating rapidly out of excitement rather than the oppressive heat!

The driver turned left onto a gravel road. I asked the bus driver to stop so that we could read the large white sign standing at the edge of the road. It said, "The Historic Home of Mary Ball Washington," then in smaller letters, "The Mother of President George Washington." Although it was truly a privilege to visit the birthplace of the mother of the first president of the United States, we were looking for another "Mary" whose name was not written on the sign. This was also the birthplace of Mary Daniel Jesse, the second Missionary-Principal of Shokei Girls' School (Shokei Gakuin) in Sendai, Japan.

As we drove deep into the large tract of land called Epping Forest, we were surrounded by acres of maturing corn. Looming in the distance was a large white colonial frame house surrounded by scattered oak and cedar trees. In the background a thick forest wrapped itself around the edges of the cornfields.

Could it be true that after eleven years of research I was finally able to pinpoint this grand house and meet Mary D. Jesse's relatives? Furthermore, was it not a dream to be able to share this moment with students who were experiencing the very legacy left by her at the mission school where she poured out her heart for forty years, planting a flower with deep roots? Today, in honor of her, the students changed into their bright summer kimonos and gave a concert in front of this grand old plantation house. The time was too short to explore, but it was the start of another pilgrimage for me to find out what the early years of "this Mary's" life might have been like.

NAMESAKE

We are all made up of the stuff that has come before us. And so it was with Mary. She was born of tough but elegant Virginia stock. Although her mother and grandmother were both named Mary, her namesake was different. Not only was she named after Mary Ball Washington, she was born and raised in the same house and, according to tradition, born in the very same bedroom as Mary Ball.[2] Parents hope that we will live up to our namesake, and surely this was true for Mary Jesse.

2. Hisayoshi Saito, "Jesshi Sensei To Watakushi," *Mutsumi no Kusari*, Special Edition, 28–29.

Mary Ball Washington's grandfather, Colonel William Ball, was a seventh generation Ball. He emigrated from England sometime between 1646 and 1649.[3] From 1677 and 1693 he acquired some adjacent parcels of land between the Rappahannock River and Chesapeake Bay, and it was referred to as "the forest," "Forest Plantation," and "Forest Quarter" in various documents. William deeded his lush piece of land to his American-born son, Colonel Joseph Ball, where Joseph built a plantation house that has lasted over three hundred years. Sometime between 1799 and 1826, Epping Forest was the name used for the area.[4] The landowner during that time, possibly Rawleigh Downman, perhaps felt nostalgic for the similarly named forest in England. The name Epping Forest came from a large piece of woodland historically used by kings and queens in Essex County, England, for hunting.[5]

Mary Ball was born in ca. 1707/1708, but only lived in this house for her first three years. After her father died, her mother remarried and moved about fifteen miles away. In 1721, upon her mother's death, she inherited two horses and a plush side saddle. Because the house and land remained in the Ball family for many years, according to tradition and local folklore, she often returned to Forest Plantation and nearby White Chapel to visit her mother's grave, most likely on horseback. Some surmise that she also participated in many a fox hunt. There would have been no better place than in "the Forest." Perhaps it was the image of being the belle of Northern Neck that she portrayed as she rode, that caused people to refer to her years later as "the Rose of Epping Forest,"[6] even though during her years there the land was not called Epping Forest. We truly will remember her as the wife of Augustine Washington, married in 1731, and the mother of George Washington, born February 22nd, 1732 at Wakefield.

MARY D. JESSE'S ROOTS

Mary D. Jesse's ancestors, like the Balls, had also emigrated from England. The two-hundred-forty-one-year-old plantation was sold to Mary's grandfather, William T. Jesse, in 1844. William T. and his wife, Mary, began a life

3. Custer and Ehley, "Custer Family Genealogy," http://www.angelfire.com/tx4/custer/ball.html.

4. Mary Ball Washington Museum Library, "Epping Forest Files."

5. "Epping Forest," http://en.wikipedia.org/wiki/Epping_Forest.

6. Wayland, *The Washingtons*, 15–30.

and legacy in Epping Forest which would last at least another one hundred years. Like other places in that area, the Epping Forest plantation house in the first half of the nineteenth century was a welcoming place of rest for travelers passing through. These Virginians were known for their hospitality and eagerness to hear news from travelers outside their immediate area. And plenty of news there was, with the slavery issue being at the top of the list.

During this era, all plantations and citizens with adequate means were dependent on the labor of enslaved Africans and African Americans. However, William T. was among the plantation owners who leaned favorably toward the Union and was against secession.[7] He and other leading citizens were of the increasingly unpopular opinion that slaves should be racially separated from whites, and that they should be returned to Africa and freed there, rather than being declared free people in the United States. The American Colonization Society promoted these ideals. In addition to opposition from abolitionists, who thought that this was a slaveholder's scheme to keep blacks from being put on equal footing in America, the colonization societies experienced financial difficulties and lamented the continuous news of problems of the newly colonized slaves in Liberia.

Part of their thinking was the notion that the new country of Liberia could provide the Christian influence needed in Africa and be a launching pad for sending missionaries deep into the continent. Although the American Colonization Society was a secular body, in 1821, they joined in a partnership with the General Missionary Convention (predecessor to the American Baptist Foreign Mission Society [ABFMS]), and the Richmond African Baptist Missionary Society to send former African-American slaves Lott Cary and Collin Teague to Sierra Leone and Liberia as missionaries. Through their own labor, both Cary and Teague had managed to purchase freedom for themselves and their families. This relieved the financial burden of these three groups tremendously. But in the end, there was just not enough support in Congress to sustain the colonization venture.

Hopes Dashed. Up until a month before the Civil War began with the bombardment of Fort Sumter, the Jesses (along with the State of Virginia) maintained this stance. Surely there was hope in the words of Abraham Lincoln in his inaugural address that he "had no intent to invade Southern States."[8] But after the fall of Fort Sumter, Lincoln seemingly breached his

7. Severance, *Richard Henry Jesse*, 5.

8. Lincoln, "First Inaugural Address," http://avalon.law.yale.edu/19th_century/

promise and called for the troops to invade the south. The war between the northern and southern states had become a reality, causing William T. and his sons to cast both their hearts and their financial resources into the support of the Confederacy.[9]

During the next four long years, the Jesses used all their resources in support of the Confederate troops as they passed through on their way south to Richmond. Mary Jesse's father, William H. Jesse, was only sixteen when he graduated from the Virginia Military Institute, then joining the Confederate military service. The rest of the family, as well as a number of household servants and slaves, stayed at Epping Forest to carry on with the production of produce and livestock for the Cause[10] and the goals of the Confederacy. At the end of the war, the area was left ravaged, and the people left with no hope. The slaves had been freed, so all the work of this large plantation operation was left to father William T., mother Mary, and the five Jesse children. Mary Jesse's father, William H., and uncle Richard took

> the place of the negro men in plowing the land, in planting the corn and the cotton, in cultivating the crops, in husking and shelling the corn, in plucking the cotton, in raising the vegetables in the garden, in caring for the oxen and stock, in chopping wood in the forest a mile away and in getting up wood for the fireplaces and for the cook stove.[11]

Of course, the domestic work of the house fell to the women, who now had to do all the cooking, laundering, and other housework.

Years of Recovery. In the 1860s, was it the faith of this and other Virginian families that kept them going? Mary Jesse's great-grandfather was a Baptist minister, the Reverend Richard Claybrook. He had a strong influence on this family and the surrounding community. Daily Bible reading and prayers were a part of their weekdays, and of course, no work or play was allowed on Sundays when the family gathered for worship. Occasionally a leisurely stroll was allowed.[12] This was also a society where women were held in high esteem, and where deference and courtesy was paid them

lincoln1.asp.

9. Severance, *Richard Henry Jesse*, 5.

10. Ibid., 6.

11. Ibid., 6.

12. Ibid., 4.

by the menfolk. There was harmony in the homes and there was plenty of frankness and honesty, goodwill and loyalty toward one another.[13]

Education and religion were taught side-by-side in Virginia. The Jesses built a schoolhouse on their plantation across the road where the oldest daughter, Molly, became the teacher of William H.[14] and the other three siblings until Richard H. moved on to Hanover Academy in 1870, then on to the University of Virginia. Eventually he served as president of the University of Missouri from 1891–1908. William H. stayed on at Epping Forest, married yet another Mary, Mary Hampton DeJarnette, in 1879,[15] and began raising his family.

Younger Days. Mary Daniel Jesse, the subject of this book, was the second child of eleven siblings born to the Jesses, on November 16th, 1881. From that time until leaving for college at age twenty-one, little is recorded regarding these years. However, from the facts we have learned about the previous generation, and from her family's ancestry record, one can develop a fairly accurate profile.

Mary was born into an industrious family that had to work hard to maintain a plantation without the benefit of slave labor. But because of their hard work, the Jesses had risen to moderate wealth by the time Mary was born, and she was raised with the typical genteelness of Virginians of her time. According to personal stories she told Shokei alumnae, she learned faith from her mother and societal working skills from her father.[16]

She was raised by a woman who, in the language of the era, she called a "black mammy."[17] This suggests that household servants were present, this time as paid employees. She was homeschooled, perhaps attending the same school established on the Jesse property a generation earlier. While we think of a person of Mary's caliber leaving home between the ages of sixteen and eighteen, for some reason Mary waited until she was twenty-one. She was the oldest daughter, and likely had additional duties in helping to raise her siblings and be a part of their education, just as her aunt had taught her father and his siblings.

13. Ibid., 187.

14. Ibid., 4.

15. https://www.ancestry.com/family-tree/person/tree/18840207/person/721021357/story; see also https://www.geni.com/people/Mary-Hampton-Jesse/6000000037786971837.

16. Henshū Inkai, *ECHO no Hibiki*, 14.

17. Ibid., 14.

The 1890s must have been a tragic decade for the Jesse family, as they had much grief to deal with in losing three of the little ones, one in 1890 and two in 1897.[18] Surely the responsibilities were greater for her in times like these. Were economic hindrances to blame as well for her delay in leaving for college? Did her own private studies to get into a university take longer because of her family situation? Any number of these circumstances could have been the reason for delaying her college education.

College at Last. In 1902, Mary Jesse began at the University of Missouri. It might have been a foregone conclusion that she would go to this institution, because her uncle Richard Henry Jesse was the current president of the university. Thirteen nieces and nephews frequented his home when they were pursuing their studies.[19] She entered the geology department.

We can only see brief sketches of what had transpired during those eight years of study that would lead us to ask, again, why did it take that long? We are given some hints regarding Mary's involvement at the university. According to *The Savitar* yearbooks of the University of Missouri, there is evidence that Mary was particularly interested in playing basketball. While women's athletics are not mentioned in the yearbook of 1902–1903, the 1903–1904 album mentions her as being on the university's basketball team as a freshman in the "goal" position.[20] In the 1904–1905 album, her sophomore year, *The Savitar* reports that she acted as the business manager of the team instead of being a member of the team.[21] In a review of the Class of 1906 as they finished their junior year in 1905, the "gems of the class" theme is developed in an article:

> Then there were the girls, gems indeed, distinguished as basket ball [sic] players and students, enthusiastic in the various activities of college life. The girls who composed the basket ball [sic] team in the spring of 1903 were: Mary D. Jesse, Mary Sears, Carolyn Jesse, Hally Prentiss, Ella Seymour, Lotta Kelley, and Eula McCune."[22]

18. Paliden1952, Leaves, Trees & Nuts, Ancestor Family Trees. See Nanette, http://trees.ancestry.com/tree/9767217/person/-747158888; Julia, http://trees.ancestry.com/tree/9767217/person/-747158891; and Joseph, http://trees.ancestry.com/tree/9767217/person/-747158892.

19. Severance, *Richard Henry Jesse*, 202.

20. "Savitar," 196, line 20. 1903 yearbook.

21. Ibid., 101, line 22. 1904 yearbook.

22. Ibid., 32, line 6. 1905 yearbook.

Again, in the same 1905 yearbook, "Mary D. Jesse" is listed as a guard on the sophomore team.[23] Little did she know how much guarding she would need to do many years later in her career as a missionary! In the yearbooks of 1906 to 1909, Mary does not appear in any sports club list or in any other section of the yearbooks. A "Mary Jesse" is mentioned in the rolls of the YWCA, holding the office of devotional chairman on the 1906–1907 committee.[24] This is more likely Mary's cousin and daughter of President Jesse, Mary Polk Jesse. For reasons unknown at this time, Mary did not graduate with her class in 1906, but actually graduated in 1910. Whether she continued in school in the intervening years or not, we do not know for sure. In 1908, her father, William H. passed away at Epping Forest in a logging accident. It is possible that she had to help her family out in some way for a period of time.

In *The Savitar* yearbook of 1909, Mary D. Jesse is shown in a group picture of the first ever Woman's Council of the University of Missouri as its president and senior member. This newly formed council had the aim of securing "more uniform and individual representation in student activities; to promote larger social interests among university women; and to foster a living school spirit."[25] Women students were cautiously allowed to enter the University of Missouri in 1867. By 1871 there were forty-two women students.[26] However, it was a rather shaky start for the University. The women were only allowed to undertake teacher preparation courses. They were restricted in their movement on campus. But when the university saw that no harm was being done by their presence, they were allowed to attend some other classes "providing always they were to be marched in good order, with at least two teachers, one in the front and the other in the rear of the column as guard," according to the 1873 university magazine.[27]

Their liberty came slowly, as they continued to have to wear uniforms and stay in a special "retiring room" between classes.[28] By 1909, women were likely moving around the campus with much more freedom, but it was found that a governing body was needed to help them learn to socialize and

23. Ibid., 132, line 22.

24. Ibid., 190, line 18. 1906 yearbook.

25. Ibid., 143, line 3. 1909 yearbook.

26. Mizzou Alumni Association, "No Manner of Harm," 10–11. https://hdl.handle.net/10355/54845.

27. Ibid., 10.

28. Ibid., 10.

participate more openly in campus activities and to set rules for behavior (as in 1910, when the council set an evening curfew for the women[29]). Mary Jesse undoubtedly wanted a part in lifting the burden from the shoulders of women who had been traditionally sequestered in this man's world of academia. Even though she only had responsibilities on this council for one year, this kind of work became her life passion as she lifted the yoke, a world away, off the shoulders of young Japanese women who were sequestered to the back kitchens of Japanese homes.

She graduated in 1910 with a Bachelor of Science in Education and with a license to teach at the high school and college level. With an additional year of study, she received a second degree in earth sciences at the age of thirty.[30]

Becoming Rooted. Although Jesse became a Christian and was baptized in 1898 in Litwalton, Virginia, while at the University of Missouri, she was able to solidify her faith. In addition to working part time, she became involved in The Student Volunteer Movement,[31] a college student organization formed to spread mission awareness on college campuses and encourage commitment to mission service overseas. With its beginnings in 1891, quadrennial conventions took place in major cities around the United States. It is likely that Jesse was a delegate at the 1906 Nashville Convention. In the report of the Executive Committee to this convention, the delegates were reminded of the purpose and challenge:

> (1) to lead students to a thorough consideration of the claims of foreign missions upon them as a life-work; (2) to foster the purpose of all students who decided to become foreign missionaries, by helping to guide and to stimulate them in mission study and in work for missions until they pass under the immediate direction of the mission boards; (3) to unite all volunteers in an organized, aggressive movement; (4) to create and maintain an intelligent, sympathetic, active interest in foreign missions among the students who are to remain on the home field in order that they may back up this great enterprise by their prayers, their gifts and their efforts.[32]

---

29. Ibid., 11.

30. Henshū Inkai, *ECHO no Hibiki*, 14.

31. For further information, see "Student Volunteer Movement," http:/en.wikipedia.org/wiki/Student_Volunteer_Movement.

32. Student Volunteer Movement, "The First Two Decades," 4.

These conventions had a powerful impact on all who attended. Her involvement in this movement on her campus gave her a keen awareness of the human dilemma around the world, and as she studied the problem of the world and world religions, she decided that she didn't want to become just a regular teacher, but wanted to be a teacher who taught the way to God through the medium of education. God planted in her heart the desire to become a missionary.[33] This desire was very soon to take root.

So, what is a call to be a missionary? Most Christians would agree that "a call to serve God" is the first experience a prospective missionary must have. This is a gut-level feeling in one's heart that God is telling or urging the person to go to a different culture to tell people about the good news of Jesus Christ. How did a person become a missionary in the first place? What kind of an organization sent them? Having received this call, the person would then apply to a denominational foreign mission society. In the case of our story, it was the Woman's American Baptist Foreign Mission Society (WABFMS). An officer of the society's board arranged an interview during which time several members of the Board inquired about the truth of an individual's call and assessed the skills, personality, and education of the candidates. If there was an appropriate opening, the candidate might proceed directly to the country assigned or get further education before leaving her country.

Sometimes country assignments were changed on short notice if a sudden vacancy occurred in another location. Since missionaries were needed to help promote the cause of evangelism overseas, they were required by the Board to come back to the United States to promote mission education in churches. This was called "furlough" or, currently, "home assignment." In the earlier years, a missionary stayed seven years or longer in the assigned country before returning for more education, generating interest in foreign mission by reporting on their work, and resting. Gradually the terms of service abroad were shortened to five years and then to four years or less with the duration of time at home varying depending on length of time in the field and the needs of the missionary. Current practices of sending out missionaries vary greatly from what is described here, including the addition of parachurch organizations and single churches as sending agents; this change has expanded opportunities in the modern era of missions.

Mary Jesse had received a call, and would shortly join this selection process. She applied to the Woman's American Baptist Foreign Mission

33. Henshū Inkai, *ECHO no Hibiki*, 14.

Society (WABFMS) and was formally appointed at age thirty. Although the specific details are missing, Jesse's dream had always been to go to China as a missionary, but for some unknown reason she was designated to Sendai Japan on April 21st, 1911.

Shokei Gakuin Choir Visits Epping Forest Mansion in 2003
(courtesy of Norio Takahashi)

2

Not Just An Ordinary Teacher
(1911–1919)

Mary Jesse at Graduation (1911)
(courtesy of American Baptist Historical Society)

Unless the Lord builds the house,
They labor in vain who build it;
Unless the Lord guards the city
the watchman keeps awake in vain.

PSALMS 127:1 (NASB, 1975)

Mary Jesse left by ship and arrived in Japan on October 4th, 1911.[1] After spending some time with missionaries in Tokyo, she traveled north by train and arrived in Sendai on October 23rd as an energetic but mature young woman with many talents. She was full of enthusiasm, and determination, and had a good imagination. Her diplomacy, decisiveness and organizational ability were characteristics that would guide Shokei Girls' School (Shokei Jogakuin) into its third decade. But before she could do this, she herself had to discover the place where her gifts could best be utilized. Moving from one job to another might seem unfortunate to some people, but Mary Jesse saw these first experiences as God at work in the opening and closing of doors, until she settled in at last as Shokei's principal. A school with a history and a principal with tenure preceded her installation. She was not, however, held back by cumbersome tradition, but immediately plunged into the work. She learned quickly and left her mark on its history.

IN SEARCH OF SELF

Every person needs a chance to settle in when a new job begins. This was also true for Mary Jesse because her work assignment was not specified in the beginning. As she studied the language, she took her time to find out what kind of person she could become in the Japanese cultural and educational context. Her first few years were spent learning what this meant for her life.

Groundwork. Her first trip to Sendai was memorable:

> The first time I arrived in Sendai it was at night in a fall rain. I arrived after leaving in the AM and traveling about 12 hours by train. At the station Hughes sensei and 15 or 16 students were there to meet me. We hailed a jinrickshaw [sic] and went from the station to Nakajima-cho [location of the school]. I can't forget the sight that night. There was a small river running on one side of the road. The lanterns in the vehicles along the road sparkled in

---

1. Missionary Register Cards, "Mary D. Jesse." This information comes from the Board of International Ministries, Archival Collections of American Baptist Historical Society, Valley Forge PA (hereafter "BIM, Archival Collections of ABHS"). These cards recorded missionary data upon registration, missionary movement, and assignment overseas.

their reflection in the river. It looked like we were going through a flower garden of light.[2]

She arrived while American Baptist missionary Annie Buzzell was on furlough, and while Miss Grace Hughes was acting principal. Almost at the same time, young Miss Helen Topping arrived in Sendai. Topping was born of missionary parents who served in Morioka and Tokyo. She had just graduated from Denison College in the state of Ohio, and the two of them became good friends until Topping left in January 1913.[3] Topping returned to Japan later to teach the Bible in Japanese at the Tokyo Kindergarten Teachers' Training School, a post-secondary school for training kindergarten teachers that her mother started, and later worked with Toyohiko Kagawa.

A missionary's daily life was not just random. Guidelines were set up many years before Jesse arrived to help structure the life of American Baptist missionaries, and now hers, by a committee called the Reference Committee. The Reference Committee was made up of both men and women missionaries elected from among the American Baptist missionary organization in Japan. About 20 percent of the missionary force was selected by the missionaries to be on this committee. For example, in 1919, nine of the forty-six were on the Reference Committee. They were responsible for the immediate care of the missionaries in areas such as language study, education of missionary children, and personal relationships. They were a powerful group, also responsible for sending missionaries back to the United States for furlough, filling positions in Japan vacated by missionaries who returned to the United States, and the planning and construction of buildings needed by churches and schools related to the American Baptist work in Japan. They also had the power to recommend that a missionary not be allowed to continue working at a certain location. Since the committee members also were employees of the American Mission Board and managed the Board's money in Japan, they were responsible to the ABMU and WABFMS Boards, and their decisions were subject to the Board's approval. From distant Tokyo, the Reference Committee impacted Shokei's management in Sendai, merely by moving missionaries around from one school to another, depending on the needs. After Shokei became financially independent in 1942, the Reference Committee made fewer decisions directly affecting Shokei School than it had in the past, but still managed

2. Henshū Inkai, *ECHO no Hibiki,* 15.

3. Hughes, "Sendai," *Gleanings* 18:1 (Nov 1911) 3.

the work assignment, and the health and welfare of the missionaries. The school boards took over much of the rest of the work.

At the behest of the Reference Committee, Mary Jesse studied Japanese in Sendai, while spending her first five months at Shokei teaching part time.[4] After passing her first language examination, required by this committee since 1912, she moved to Tokyo for one year and resided with the Harry Baxter Benninghoffs at Waseda Hoshien (*hoshien* means "garden of service") as she continued her language study. This move, too, would have needed permission from the Reference Committee. Waseda Hoshien was a dormitory and student center for young men who attended Waseda University, and was started in 1908 by the Benninghoffs. While there, Jesse helped the Benninghoffs in their work in the student dorm. She had high praise for the Benninghoffs, whom she felt were the right people to minister to the Waseda students at the Hoshien center. She saw their dormitory work as a real ministry, meeting a need which she called training of the "social spirit" of these young men. She also expressed her feelings about the importance of the relation between language learning and mission. She realized that a thorough knowledge of the Japanese people was necessary to success in evangelism, and that knowledge of the people would be determined by a person's fluency in the language.

She returned to Sendai in November 1912 just briefly to attend Shokei's twentieth anniversary. Since the nation of Japan was in mourning for the death of Emperor Meiji, the celebration at the school was kept low key with no public events. In a 1913 report she wrote with the eyes of a newcomer about the occasion. Jesse noted that the music was good and the speeches were fine. She was impressed especially by one statement made in Anne Buzzell's account of the history of the school that "the influence of the school was out of proportion to its size." At the banquet, she ate her first fancy box lunch and described the lunch in detail in this way:

> Each one was given a dainty little wooden box, with a top which was tied on. Upon opening the box and removing the bamboo sheath which covered the contents we saw little pieces of boiled octopus, slices of lotus root, bits of egg, etc., with a layer of rice at the bottom. A pair of chop-sticks [*sic*] was tied on each box.

---

4. Mary D. Jesse to Shokei alumnae, *Mutsumi no Kusari* 8 (1915) 3. This publication is the journal of the alumnae of Shokei Jo Gakuin.

The celebrations coincided with the Japanese Thanksgiving Day, so Jesse was also able to report her first impressions of how the Christian church had imparted new meaning into a secular harvest ceremony:

> About two hundred children came, and the service was most in-teresting. Very few, though, came to the adult service. The front of the church was piled with fresh vegetables with the green tops on; and upon inquiry we found that these vegetables had been bought with the money from the Sunday school collections, and that after the service these were to be taken to the poor living near, as a gift from the school.[5]

At the end of 1912, Jesse moved up to Morioka, Iwate Prefecture, to take over the church kindergarten while Helen Topping's parents, Rev. and Mrs. Henry Topping, left Japan for furlough in the United States. With the foundation built by the Toppings and Jesse's hard work, it became a well-respected kindergarten where only the wealthy could afford to send their children.

Originally, the Japanese government borrowed the concept of kin-dergartens from Germany in 1876 as a project connected to the Tokyo Women's Normal School. But due to the high cost and lack of success in training teachers, private kindergartens were encouraged. In 1884, the gov-ernment prohibited preschool children from attending primary schools. Thereupon private kindergartens began to increase. By 1906, there were three hundred sixty kindergartens in Japan, but that population was only 1.4 percent of the five-year-olds. Missionaries were instrumental in begin-ning high caliber kindergartens as an outreach to families with means.[6] The first successful kindergarten teacher training school was started by Mrs. Geneveive Topping in 1896. The following year the first Baptist kindergar-tens in Tokyo began. Topping had studied in Germany before marrying her husband and coming to Japan. Most kindergartens were established by churches, but some by Christian schools in conjunction with kindergarten training courses. Kindergarten education in Japan has always been non-compulsory, although virtually every child attends, and nearly all present-day kindergartens are still private.

The Toppings were transferred to Morioka, and in 1907 Genevieve Topping took over a small kindergarten already in progress when it could no longer support itself. The kindergarten was then held in the mission

5. Jesse, "Sendai Letter," *Gleanings* 19:2 (Jan 1913) 40–41.

6. Matsukawa, "First Japanese Kindergartens," 32.

residence, and later became a highly successful ministry of the Uchimaru church. The wealthy town leaders liked their children to attend there. Six different missionaries who taught at Shokei also served as principal/director of this kindergarten for various periods of time.

There were opportunities for Jesse and the Bible Women on behalf of the kindergarten to do visitation in the homes of these town leaders with no Christian background. Visitation in influential homes was not only beneficial for the financial support of the kindergarten, but was also a chance to plant the seeds of the gospel in homes of the upper class. As Jesse continued to direct the kindergarten, she also continued studying the Japanese language.

Annie Buzzell returned from furlough in 1913. She continued her work at Shokei with the part-time help of Miss Amy Acock. Acock also went outside the city for evangelistic work four days a week. She directed the Bible Women in their work and taught at Shokei two and a half days a week. In early April 1915, Acock was transferred from Shokei to the woman's seminary in Osaka started by Lavinia Mead. With this post now vacant, Jesse was moved back to Sendai. But part of her heart remained in Morioka, where she had sixty children under her care.

She continued to help in the teaching at Shokei and took over some of the training of Bible Women. In her 1916 report, she lists her duties as studying the language, doing evangelism in the country, and teaching at the school. She also reported that she was already able to teach classes in Japanese. Work in the country proved to be quite a challenge to her. She did not particularly like following the customs of the countryside, such as "wearing no shoes indoors" or "sitting on one's heels and sleeping on the floor," but she enjoyed the people because they were simple, honest, hospitable, and kind-hearted. She had difficulty finding places for her Bible Women to meet for their training. The only available place was in a hotel, she noted, but in those days, it was considered improper for young women to go to a hotel. Even with these difficulties, she felt that the work in the distant town of Kesennuma was taking on new life, because a kindergarten had just been opened there. Work in Taira, Fukushima Prefecture, and nearby Shiogama town were also progressing nicely, she thought. Lastly, she reported that the work being done with Sunday schools was especially important.[7]

Even in those first years of teaching at Shokei her students remember her as a person who could explain simple truths using a quaint story. The

7. "Sendai," *Our Work in the Orient* (1916–1917) 161.

following appeared in the alumnae magazine, *Mutsumi no Kusari* ("Chain of Friendship") no. 8 shortly after she arrived back in Sendai in 1915:

> Recently I heard an interesting story. A missionary was telling a class of Chinese girls about Christ, his love, his kindness and helpfulness, when one girl exclaimed, "Yes, I know him, I know that man, he lives in my town." The missionary asked her some questions and found, of course, that she had never seen Christ, but that there was a Christian man in her town who was living, as Christ lived, and this girl, when she heard of Christ, thought that this man must be Christ. There is a deep meaning in this story. There are many who will never know any more of Christ than they see in us, Christians. Many are reading our lives more than they read the Bible. When they see us, do they see the Christ Spirit in us? My earnest wish for you and for me, is, that we may be so kind, so loving, so helpful and sympathetic, that those who know us can say, "I know Christ, He lives in my town." . . . All around us are sad, lonely, suffering hearts, whom Christ longs to help, but He has no body but our bodies, no feet, but our feet, no lips, but our lips, no hands but our hands. I think Christ wants to walk through the streets of Japan helping and serving and blessing, just as He used to walk in Galilee when He was on earth. He wants to live in us and use us.[8]

New Partner in Mission. New missionary Miss Thomasine Allen from the state of Indiana arrived in Japan in 1915. She had just finished two years of language study while living at the Sara Curtis Home-School in Tokyo. There, she was expected to become its principal, taking the place of Minnie Carpenter. However, with four girls' schools now in Japan, the WABFMS found that their budget had been stretched too far, so out of the four schools, they chose to close the Sara Curtis Home-School. Thomasine Allen was reassigned to Shokei in 1915. It was difficult for her to adjust to life there, especially the styles of clothing necessary for the cold weather and rigorous conditions of northern Japan. She recalled, "Here I came, fresh out of college . . . with georgette blouses like we wore then. I nearly froze, but my pride kept me warm. Miss Buzzell said [to me], 'can't you settle down and put on cotton hose, you'll freeze to death!' Silk stockings too, my feet nearly died with chilblains."[9] As with other missionaries, studying Japanese was Allen's main task while she helped out at the school. The language was quite

8. Anne Buzzell to Shokei alumnae, *Mutsumi no Kusari* 8 (1915) 1.

9. Hemphill, "Transcription of Oral History."

challenging to her. In 1959 in an interview for her biography, *A Treasure to Share*, she recalls humorous experiences that she and Mary Jesse had while trying to learn the language during those years:

> Of course I went to Japanese church. At some churches I used to play the organ. One of the first churches I attended bothered me a great deal because they kept using a word that sounded exactly like my first name, Thomasine. This word was "'tamashi." Every other sentence had "tamashi" in it. I thought, my, I don't know how in the world he knows my name [Ta-ma-shi-n], what are they talking about me for? My language school teacher was at church that day and I asked her, "They don't know me, why are they talking about me. What is that word, 'tamashin'? Well, the word means "soul!" It was so near my name, of course, but I couldn't imagine what in the world it could be. Miss Jesse was quite disturbed because the pastor kept saying that "even cats can be saved." He was actually talking about Nicodemus, but Nicodemus pronounced in Japanese is "nekodemo" [actually it should have been pronounced as nikodemo] which means "even cats." Until she understood her mistake, she thought that there was something wrong with the pastor's theology.[10]

In this way, Mary Jesse and Thomasine Allen with limited language skills began a decade of devoted service to Shokei together, adding their deep faith and enthusiasm to the work of the mostly new missionary staff. In addition, their service to the surrounding villages, especially to young children and their mothers, left indelible marks on these villages. Both women became self-assured and broke out of the mold of ordinariness.

Jesse left on her first furlough in May 1917. While there, she studied at a Bible teacher's training school in Boston Teacher's College at Columbia University, and at Union Theological Seminary.[11] She was expected to return in December 1918 after further studies, but due to delays, including illness, she did not return until August 1919.[12] It was during this furlough that she attended Columbia University in New York. On June 4th, 1919, she graduated in Faculties of Education and Practical Arts with a Master of Arts degree.[13] Also, a Diploma in Education was awarded in conjunction

---

10. Ibid.

11. Jesse, "Correspondence," *Gleanings* 24:1 (Nov 1917) 3–4.

12. Missionary Register Cards, "Mary D. Jesse." Mary sailed from Seattle on August 9th, 1919.

13. Annual Commencement, "165th Annual Commencement," 36.

with the Master of Arts degree for Supervisor of Religious Education.[14] Surely this would do her well in the years to come.

Major Changes. She arrived back with a new confidence that was put to the test immediately. She had expected to be assigned to the kindergarten in Morioka again. But some shocking changes had taken place at Shokei. Arrangements had already been made for her to replace Anne Buzzell as principal instead of her working in Morioka.[15] Buzzell had left Shokei on a regularly scheduled furlough, but was never allowed to return to the school again except to pick up her belongings. Unbeknownst to her, there had been a movement by some teachers and missionaries to have her removed from the school, based on what were later proved to be false accusations. The Woman's American Baptist Foreign Mission Society (WABFMS), with the backing of the Reference Committee, gave her a new assignment in the northern town of Tono.[16] In addition to having to leave the school she loved, she also had to leave a new kindergarten she started on campus in the school gymnasium just the year before in 1918.[17] It must have been a difficult period for Buzzell, being falsely accused of impropriety, having to leave her beloved Shokei, which she had raised from infancy. To her, Shokei was like a garden of flowers where deep roots of faith were developing. Without knowing it, she left behind a legacy that would only be fully recognized in future years.

DEVELOPMENT OF EDUCATION AT SHOKEI

As Japan entered the modern world, education went through many stages of development. In the same way, Shokei went through many changes as the missionaries and Japanese teachers kept pushing for higher levels of

---

14. Ibid, 22.

15. Japan Reference Committee and Conference Minutes, 6 June 1918, "VOTED: That Miss Jesse be returned to the Morioka field for evangelism work," Resolution 1650. BIM, Archival Collection of ABHS.

16. Stephens, "Between Heaven and Hell," 1–9.

17. Buzzell to Florence Harris, 11 December 1916, Florence Letter Collection. Buzzell expressed hope of beginning a kindergarten as early as 1916 in a letter. The kindergarten officially began in the spring of 1918 with Miss Buzzell as head mistress. It was approved by the Reference Committee in 1918: Case 1601, 5 February 1918, Tokyo: American Baptist Foreign Mission Office. A graduation certificate was issued in 1918 and license for kindergarten granted in 1919 (Shokei Gakuin Archival Collection).

government accreditation and for higher levels of education in their schools for young women in primitive northern Japan.

As Mary Jesse, Thomasine Allen, and others began service at Shokei in 1919, they became part of a well-oiled machine. The school, as it was getting ready to celebrate its thirtieth anniversary, was ready for something new. Jesse had not been given an orientation by the previous principal. Her knowledge of the past was sketchy.[18] But surrounded by a Japanese staff that had been a part of Shokei's history surely helped her in eventually becoming acquainted with what had transpired up to the present.

At the Very Beginning. In the pre-Shokei years, 1887–1892, the women missionaries held Sunday schools all over Sendai. They found several little girls whose parents would not allow them to attend Sunday school but were not opposed to them living with the missionaries and receiving a western education! Most of these girls became Christians by the time they graduated. With an ongoing Bible curriculum as well as a secular curriculum, the first principal Lavinia Mead trained them as Bible Women who could help missionaries with evangelism, and be prepared to become a Christian wife capable of building a Christian home. The missionaries often played matchmaker and were on the lookout for Christian wives for Japanese pastors. They believed that the church in Japan would not grow without Christian homes. The missionaries had learned from the negative experiences of other mission schools in town that moved too quickly toward full school status immediately after the school's foundation. So they took their time in developing the home-school, because their purpose was different than other schools.

In the pre–Shokei years, the missionaries rented different houses where they lived and taught. Their first school building was completed in 1896 and was used as a missionary residence until 1949. It was known among American Baptist missionaries as "the Sendai School," but its official name became the "Ella O. Patrick Home." The funds for the building were donated by the Patricks in memory of their disabled daughter, Ella, who was a supporter of mission work around the world. Japanese called the small home-school Shokei *Jogakkai*. *Jogakkai* meant a "girls' meeting-place" which did not yet merit the name *Jogakkou*, "girls' school" as it earned later.

---

18. Jesse to C. B. Tenny, June 1923, Kanto Gakuin University Library, Yokohama, Japan.

Efforts Toward Accreditation.[19] What did education look like at that time, and how did Shokei (Ella O. Patrick Home) fit in? Jesse would face accreditation problems later, but for now she learned that in late nineteenth century Japan, education was provided for some children, chiefly boys, up to the fourth grade of primary school. Students could not take exams for schools of higher learning (present-day middle school level) without attending an accredited government school (present-day elementary school level). Since few girls could take advantage of this schooling, there was little possibility of improving the low status of females in society.

Shokei's persistence in teaching Christianity using the Bible as a textbook in the regular curriculum for training Bible Women and Christian wives kept them from receiving government recognition. But as time passed, the "Home" had to change its curriculum in order to become a real school. During the early 1890s, there were several categories of schools: elementary school, middle school, university, specialty schools such as technical and teacher training schools, and "non-accredited schools" (*kakushu gakkou*). By no choice of its own, Shokei fell into the latter type. This category included any school where teaching centered on cultural, non-traditional-type skills such as calligraphy, English, bookkeeping, study of classical literature, handicrafts, and, in Shokei's case, study of the Bible. At the close of the century in 1899, the governmental Department of Education passed the Educational Act (*kunrei-dai-junigou, shūkyou-kyouiku-kitei*), which stipulated that religion could not be taught if graduates of a school wanted to earn the right to enter the higher course (*koutouka*[20]). Of course, Shokei wanted their graduates to be able to apply for higher learning. The school applied to Miyagi Prefecture's Board of Education in 1899 to establish themselves as an accredited *kakushu gakko*. To earn this accreditation, the home-school had to set down basic rules for the school for the first time, including the establishment of entrance requirements. Bible classes were taught in a newly established Bible department for training Bible Women. Their existence as a private school was recognized on November 24th, 1899, and their official name changed from Shokei *Jogakkai* to Shokei *Jogakkou*.

Originally, Shokei was built on the principle of educating students who had no money. The school loaned students the money to go to school

---

19. See the chart on page 27, "Shokei's Educational Diagrams."

20. *Koutouka* refers to education equivalent to present-day junior college. Junior colleges were not introduced in Japan until after the Second World War.

on the condition that they work for Shokei one or two years after graduation to pay back the money lent to them. The money to lend them actually
came from sponsors in churches in the United States. The reality was that
the payback system, and the system of accepting girls with low academic
ability, was keeping Shokei from the next level of accreditation. In 1903,
non-supported students began entering the school through increased efforts of recruiting, and by 1904 none were accepted who needed full scholarships. Missionary-Principal Buzzell wrote:

> We are making progress along the line of self-support; as we have
> ceased to receive girls to support, unless in some rare case we take
> one, being individually responsible. It will take some years yet to
> finish all that we have, but we have taken no new ones for more
> than two years . . .
>
> Our new class (1907) is much smaller than usual, which
> makes us feel more strongly what we have already felt for some
> time, that we must secure government recognition if we hope to
> continue the School with other than supported girls, or those of
> inferior ability [sic], so this is the great question which is before
> us at this time.[21]

The problem worked itself out because by 1910, all students who were
receiving financial help graduated. At the same time, the course for Bible
Women also became unnecessary because there were no applications for it.
The Bible department would not be a hindrance to further accreditation in
the future.

From 1909, the school began preparations to apply to become a recognized middle school where graduates could have all rights to apply to upper
level schools. The reasons were described in the following way:

> Our school is smaller in numbers than it has been for years, owing
> to changes that have been made in the educational department of
> the government, taking away all privileges from graduates of pri-
> vate schools not registered and recognized by the government.[22]

21. Buzzell, "Ella O. Patrick Home, Sendai," *Japan Baptist Annual* (1907–1908) 36,
39.

22. Buzzell, "Missions in Japan: Sendai," *Thirty-Eighth Annual Report of the Board*
(1909) 158.

By the end of the year, the application was finished and included the following permanent changes for the Five-Year Basic Education Course (called *honka*[23]). These changes included:

- Increasing the basic education course from four years and four months to five years[24]—government schools varied, some were five years and some were four years;

- Receiving students from age fourteen rather than beginning from age twelve and/or graduates of sixth grade of government elementary school course—by this time girls' chances for education had significantly increased; and

- Abandoning the Bible department and the money-lending payback system.

They no longer recruited the poor, or students whose objective was becoming a Bible Woman. Bible training would be carried out in the dormitory, and Christian education activities would continue as a part of the non-academic school program.

Buzzell delayed her furlough so that she could finish the application process. The Department of Education recognized Shokei as an official girls' middle school in January 1910.

Dream of Higher Education for Women. Early missionaries were not only concerned with evangelism, but were also concerned with the social problems of the day. Jesse, in particular, believed that training in home economics was the one course that could contribute most toward the uplift of women. How to manage a household and family, providing clothing (sewing), good nutrition (food preparation, etc.) were all areas necessary for women to function intelligently in their homes and society. The school could provide modern, scientific training to the girls not available in the traditional hand-me-down education in the homes.

---

23. *Honka* refers to "basic education" and generally corresponds to seventh through eleventh grade.

24. Buzzell, "Ella O. Patrick Home, Sendai," *Japan Baptist Annual* (1909) 34. The graduation was held in June even though classes were finished in March. The additional three months were used for graduates to prepare their final graduation paper. This situation had become quite cumbersome to the school. The Prefectural Board of Education recommended that an additional nine months be added to the regular course, making it a five-year course. The June graduation of 1908 was thus extended to March 1909 to comply with the Japanese calendar year.

Thus, the change in curriculum in the five-year *honka* course in 1915 was the seed of a dream to begin higher education. An option was introduced where a student could take a two-year basic education course and then enroll in a three-year specialized course in home economics.

Mary Jesse was in the United Stated and not yet the principal when the first challenge to the groundwork of a higher department began. In 1917, a new building was constructed on campus for expansion of this higher department dream under Buzzell's leadership. For reasons that are somewhat unclear, problems—possibly financial—developed among the students in the specialized course in home economics. The problem peaked in 1919 immediately after Jesse became principal. There seems to have been a plan by a breakaway group for the whole home economics department to become a separate school from Shokei with a different name, using a gift of money designated for higher-level training in home economics. But the WABFMS in New York City turned down this group's request, because the donor specified that the gift be used specifically for Shokei *Jogakkou*'s home economics department.[25] In addition, the American Board saw this new separate school idea as being in competition with a new women's college in Tokyo that had been open less than two years. The Women's Christian College (presently known as Tokyo *Joshi Daigaku*) was a joint venture of seven Protestant denominations, including American Baptists, which could not begin institutions of higher learning independently because of the great expense.[26] Included in this new higher-level course was a domestic science department, prepared to receive students from mission schools such as Shokei, that had special training courses above *honka* (basic course). The suggestion of the WABFMS Board was that, instead of a separate school, a department be started within Shokei that would not be competing with Tokyo's Women's Christian College, but would be a feeder school for it.[27]

---

25. WABFMS, Foreign Department and Finance Committee, Expunged Vote #3325, 27 December 1919, BIM, Archival Collections of ABHS. A detailed letter of explanation accompanied the results of this vote. However, the actual situation remains unclear. The comments by the American Board on the issue of changing the name of the school are also included in notes in the Japan Reference Committee, JRC #1927, 9 March 1920, American Baptist Foreign Mission Office, Tokyo (moved to ABHS in 2009).

26. No title, *Japan Baptist Annual* (1919) 17.

27. Explanation for vote of Foreign Department and Finance Committee, Woman's American Baptist Foreign Mission Society, #3325, 27 December 1919. (BIM, Archival Collections of ABHS).

Although Jesse was not in favor of sending Shokei *honka* graduates to Tokyo, the higher department (*koutouka*) concept was nonetheless born in a tangible way, and the Nakajima property across from the main Hachiman campus was purchased with part of the donor's funds. It would be another ten years before a building could be built to house the higher department, but at least a beginning had been made. This proved to be historically significant, because this domestic science department of a different name still exists today, almost one hundred years later.

This latter issue of dealing with the disgruntled breakaway group in an amicable way was the first challenge Mary Jesse met as she began her tenure as principal. Through this crisis and the succeeding years, she had many chances to prove that she was truly not just an ordinary teacher.

Shokei's Educational Diagrams

Until 1908

From age 14~
Course term 4 yrs

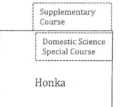

Honka
(Regular Course or
Basic Education)

Previous to 1908, younger
students studied but without
official recognition.

1908~

From age 12~
Course term 5 yrs
years

Honka

Courses consisted of Chinese,
English, history, geography,
math, law, economics, PE

1915~

Honka 5 yrs age 13~
Supplementary 1 year - age 18
(pre-Koutouka)
Domestic Science 3 years
Admission age 12~

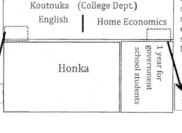

Supplementary
Course

Domestic Science
Special Course

Honka

Students who could only stay 3
years or who academically
could not compete in Honka
studied in a 3-year Domestic
Science course. Supplementary
Course included such courses
as ethics, English, Domestic
Science, flower arranging,
Bible.

1920~

Honka 5 yrs-age 12~
Domestic Science 3 years
Koutouka-Higher Department
3 years-age 18

Koutouka   (College Dept.)

English | Home Economics

Honka

1 year for
government
school students

1 year English elective

1 year Extra Domestic
Science elective

Extra year of study was for
students from government
schools who lacked special
emphasis' given to Shokei
students in English
Domestic Science and Bible

1936~

Senkoubu College Dept.
2 years –age 17
Koutou Jogakubu 4 years-age 13~

Senkoubu (College Dept.)

Domestic | Kindergarten | Commercial
Science | Teacher Training | Training

Koutou Jogakubu
Junior High Dept.

English was eliminated.
Courses: Domestic
Science, Kindergarten
teacher's training,
Commercial training

1950~

Junior College 2 years-age 18~
High School 3 years-age 15~
Junior High 3 years-age 13~

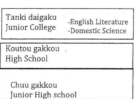

Tanki daigaku
Junior College

-English Literature
-Domestic Science

Koutou gakkou
High School

Chuu gakkou
Junior High school

Post world war II the whole
educational system changed
under MacArthur.
Shokei university replaced
the Junior College in 2004.

3

Divine Guidance—Visible and Invisible (1919–1926)

Principal Mary Jesse Upon Appointment (1919)
(courtesy of Shokei Gakuin)

There is great peace in accepting that we can't do it all,
and that in a very real way we don't need to.

—EDDIE ASKEW[1]

1. Askew, *A Silence and a Shouting*, 20.

T his chapter covers Mary D. Jesse's first five years of missionary service as principal of Shokei. With the exception of a short period after World War II when the Japanese principal suddenly resigned, this was the only period she served as principal. As Jesse led the school, the attraction of the new upper division courses, revival among the students, and a new vision for the future spurred phenomenal growth. Through all these changes, Jesse struggled to make her dream come true of building a reputable school where roots of faith could grow deep. This ultimately led to the reaffirmation of her own faith, which was often reflected in her words, "I believe in Divine guidance."

LAUNCHING NEW VENTURES

When Jesse began as principal, she faced many challenges. But she had a great team of Japanese teachers and missionaries to co-lead with her, and an enthusiastic student body with which to work. Whether the subject was higher department, curriculum, students' health, relief work, or the new school-church,[2] the missionaries and teachers exerted careful planning and great effort on behalf of the students. She continued to learn about the school she was inheriting.

Buzzell's Tenure. Annie Buzzell had served as principal and dreamer at Shokei for twenty-eight years. She came in 1892 as a capable twenty-eight-year-old as an experienced schoolteacher to replace Nellie Fife, and partnered with Lavinia Mead in building up the tiny home school. She led the school through various stages of accreditation and turned it into a school recognized by the authorities near and far. Her influence on its graduates, especially as it related to faith in God, was truly great. Her authoritarian style of leadership worked well with the students, but in the latter half it worked negatively upon missionaries, colleagues, and Japanese staff. Although she did not immediately recognize it herself, it was time for a leadership change for the growth and development of the school.

---

2. A "school-church" refers to a church which is developed on the grounds of the school. Most Christian schools in Japan started one to spiritually guide the large number of students who became Christians. Eventually, most school-churches moved off campus, making it easier for the public who were not alumni to attend. The school-church became a significant part of Shokei in future years.

Mary Jesse as Principal. During the latter years of Buzzell's service, Shokei had gradually slipped behind the times in terms of curriculum content and teaching techniques, but under Mary Jesse's capable leadership and hard work, the school was counted among the leading schools again. She brought a sense of dignity and pride to the school. She was a good communicator and sensitive to the needs of those working with her, but she held strongly to her own views. She took her responsibilities seriously, often worrying about the consequences of the Mission Board's actions and her own. Caution preceded all her decisions.

There are only a few original letters on file written by Jesse between the time she took over as principal in August 1919 and when she left Shokei for an extended period in 1931. A few of her reports appear in summary form in the mission magazines. Letters written by missionaries serving with Mary Jesse provide us with additional insights about her and the school. Personal letters written from America during the 1930s shed the greatest light on the problems of that earlier era. The fact that Jesse submitted letters of resignation to the Board three times between 1919 and 1931 shows that those years must not have been easy ones. Yet according to the public record of mission magazines and private letters from other missionaries, these were golden years for Shokei.

Varied Gifts, One Team. To help in the management and teaching of classes, there was a full staff of missionaries: Thomasine Allen, Gladys Somers, and Ruth Ward. Ruby Anderson and Annabelle Pawley were on furlough in 1921. That missionaries had to leave on furlough and be reassigned when they returned to Japan was an on-going problem. The management of curriculum and scheduling of classes was continually readjusted in response to changes in missionary personnel in any Baptist mission school in Japan. This was an administrative problem, but it was also an opportunity to enrich the lives of the students, exposing them to the varied gifts, personalities and faith of many American women. During this time of transition in and out, missionaries involved in country evangelism had to be brought in to help the school. The school had grown to the extent that each students' classes were now taught by Japanese teachers instead of missionaries, as in the early days. When necessary, missionaries fluent in Japanese taught English and Bible, but this was rare. The others less fluent taught subjects such as English, music, and domestic science.

From 1922–1925, Shokei had its first encounter with a missionary whose profession was health and physical education. Ruth E. Smith had little experience before coming, but brought with her a keen awareness of the physical needs of the students. She felt that most Japanese girls had weak constitutions, flat feet and curvature of the spine, incorrect posture, and many wrong habits and attitudes about health, and she was not shy in saying so. Introduction of western styles of dress, such as leather shoes instead of wooden sandals (*geta*), had been taught without teaching the proper use of these items, she thought. Students could wear *geta* through the rain puddles without getting their feet wet, but they should not wear their new leather shoes in the same way, she reasoned.[3] Smith also introduced a uniform for physical education, including custom-made shoes for exercising. These novel ideas of exercising in clothes other than a kimono and *geta*, and using non-military-style calisthenics not only attracted the attention of neighbors around the school, but schools around the country that sent in orders for the new exercise shoes.

In 1923, the Japanese faculty felt that each student should have at least one subject taught by a missionary teacher because of the positive impact the foreigners were having on students. As a result, and because of the fact that some missionary teachers were away on furlough, all missionaries had to take on more teaching hours. Jesse, in addition to her administrative duties as principal, taught twenty-three hours a week. Smith and Allen, whose actual assignment was country evangelism, also had to teach twenty-three periods a week.[4]

Not Enough Room. The school's greatest problem during those first years was lack of space. With the beginning of the new *koutouka* (upper division), problems relating to classroom and dormitory space were acute. In April of 1920, the Nakajima-cho property (currently called Hachiman) was purchased in faith that there would be a donor to provide funds needed to

---

3. Ruth E. Smith to the WABFMS Board, 4 June 1925, Correspondence File of Ruth E. Smith (hereafter each correspondence file of the missionary will be referred to as "BIM Correspondence File").

4. Sadie T. Ross, "Annual Report," 1923, BIM Correspondence File.

buy it.[5] Further, during the Woman's American Baptist Board meetings in October, the Board decided to use part of the Rockefeller Fund to purchase the land for sixty thousand yen.[6] Based on the cost of living in 2009, this amount is equal to four hundred nineteen thousand yen, or four thousand, four hundred eighty-one dollars!![7] Thus the first step for upper division education had begun, adding hope. Jesse kept busy in conferences all hours of the day with one theme: what to do with so many students. And, in 1922, because of the need for more space, the kindergarten started by Buzzell in 1918 which was housed in the gymnasium in the basement of the chapel had to be closed because the space was needed for the increasing number of middle school students.[8]

In the following article, Jesse expresses to the American Baptist churches the difficulty she experienced in turning down students for admission, many of whom hoped to live in Shokei's dormitory. She compares it to an exciting drama being performed on stage.

If you home friends have never been at some high school in Japan on the day of competitive entrance examination you have missed some excitement. As there are only high schools enough to accommodate about one tenth of those desiring to enter, competition is very keen and excitement runs high.

Early in the morning, before I was out of bed, the jinrikishas [jinrikisha] began coming from the station and soon groups began to arrive walking: fathers, brothers, sisters, mothers with their small children, coming with the girls who were to take the examination. They all came in and waited in the big sewing rooms. At nine the bell sounded, the girls were all marched out and lined up in the halls for roll call to see if they corresponded to the names sent in previously. Then they were divided into sections

5. "Sendai," *Our Work in the Orient* (1920–1921) 87, BIM Correspondence File.

6. WABFMS, "Foreign Department and Finance," 27–29 October 1920, vote #4075.

7. Professor Masamitsu Mochizuki, Budget Director of the Board of Managers of Kanto Gakuin, assisted in converting yen of the era indicated, into goods and services indices for key financial figures to assist the reader in understanding the value of the yen in relation to the dollar for the same amount of money today. Professor Mochidzuki used information from the Consumer Price Index (CPI) in 2009 for calculating figures in this book from the Bank of Japan, "Nihon Ginko," 1986. Other material came from http://www.boj.or.jp/announcements/education/oshiete/history/11100021.html, and http://www.boj.or.jp/en/index.htm/. From here forward the yen/dollar equivalences in 2009 for some items will be noted as they occur in the text.

8. "The Sendai Girls' School" (adapted from Mary Jesse's report), *Japan Baptist Annual* (1921) 34.

and marched to the different examination rooms where teachers awaited them. During the examination, the relatives sat on the mats in the sewing rooms and drank tea. As soon as the papers on one subject were finished they were taken to the teachers' room and graded. The grades were all arranged and the students ranked first, second, third, etc. and the next morning the names of those chosen were posted, so each girl came back with trembling, anxious heart to see if her name was on the list, for we had more than one hundred applicants and had announced that we could take only forty. Such shouts of joy if the name was listed! Others came away with big tears falling for they had failed to get a place and could not go to school.

The second act of the play opened when the especially earnest and persistent ones began to call on the teachers, taking presents and begging the teachers to use their influence with me to take them anyhow even though they were not among the forty best. Fathers, mothers, brothers, called on me urging me to take their girl stating all the special circumstances. It seemed useless to tell them that we were full to the limit, they would not give up. Ten pastors from the country places came requesting that we take their Sunday School children who had applied. We sat hours at a time and discussed. We realized that we owed something to our Christian constituency and to the children of our Christians, even though they could not make the highest grades because the country schools are poor. Well, our forty has grown to sixty and still others are begging and we have no idea what we shall do with so many.

One case yesterday melted my heart. The little motherless girl of fourteen years having heard of our school a year ago, sat in the kitchen after the day's work was done and with key and dictionary studied night after night hoping to enter our school. I just could not send her away.

One to-day [sic] was too pathetic to refuse. The father, a judge, died a few years ago and the mother, an earnest Christian, became a Bible woman and was supporting her girl in one of the public schools of the city. Recently the mother learned that the daughter was not attending church and upon investigation found that the students from the school dormitory could go anywhere they wished on Sunday, except to a Christian church. A few days later the mother received the Bible and hymnbook that belonged to her daughter. The matron had sent them to her as the daughter would not be allowed to keep them in the dormitory. The mother further learned that a shrine had been put up on the school grounds and every child was required to worship there daily. The mother said her conscience would not allow her to keep her daughter there, so she had taken her out, but she could not bear to have her child grow up without education. She wanted her in our school and in our dormitory so that she (the mother) could go on with her work with a happy heart. How hard it is to turn them away!

How we need our new dormitory! How we need more classrooms! With a hundred new girls—we took in about forty in the higher department in addition to the sixty regulars—we are crowded for room. We have such a splendid new lot [Hachiman] all ready for the buildings. The dormitory is our first great need and then if we could get a building for domestic science we could make over our three big sewing rooms, kitchen, and etiquette room into classrooms and thus be provided for a long time.

. . . Does it pay? Our girls are usually Christian before they graduate. All of the classes that graduated this year were Christians. Think what it will mean to have them go back to their country villages Christians! Sixty homes touched by Christianity! Perhaps all of the sixty later to be wives and mothers or teachers or Christian workers! Surely it pays to have such schools.[9]

Dormitory at the Center. A major attractive feature of Shokei during the early twenties was the dormitory. It attracted girls from all over northern Japan and quickly became overcrowded. Jesse took a special interest in it and put a lot of her time and energy into its program and dorm life. The thirty-five-student capacity dorm now housed eighty to ninety students. Study areas were made into sleeping rooms to accommodate the numbers. Due to the generosity of a Mrs. E. M. White, the Stafford Memorial Dormitory for forty students was built and dedicated in July 1922. It only partially relieved the overcrowding but was hailed for its modern conveniences. It introduced the girls to sanitary and hygienic living with proper privacy the missionary teachers thought was needed. Modern plumbing, electric heat under wooden floors instead of *tatami* mats, and cots instead of futon were among the list of "firsts." It was built with the arrangement of rooms to develop self-government and self-support among the girls. Missionaries and faculty thought of the dormitory as a place to create a truly Christian atmosphere. It was the dorm girls who became Christians before those who commuted from their homes. The dormitory was organized like a big family, but at the same time it provided an opportunity for students to develop their leadership skills and learn personal responsibility. Devotions were

9. Jesse, "Sendai Girls' School," *Gleanings* 26:4 (May 1921) 69–71.

held daily and meals were eaten together. The girls eagerly attended Bible studies and other Christian-related activities that were woven into dorm life where girls quickly felt a part of God's family before they became a Christian. Still, many had to be turned away. Until it was closed in 1992, the dormitory continued to be a very important feature at the school.

New Beginnings for Higher Education. Almost as soon as Mary Jesse took over the position of principal in 1919, the school began preparing for the *koutouka* (higher department), which became the seed for the junior college begun in 1950. The *koutouka* received Japanese government recognition as a higher education course by 1921. Northern Japan needed schools for girls that prepared them to enter a university. Shokei answered that need. Several *koutouka* departments were established. The English department, the sewing, and cooking departments had an initial enrollment of sixty-one students.[10] A music course began a year later. As a three-year preparatory course for college entrance, the *koutouka* provided yet another way to reach girls for Christ who entered from government schools, according to missionary philosophy. The missionaries wanted as many non-Christians as possible to be exposed to the Christian gospel. This was the beginning of the practice of purposely encouraging students with no Christian background to study at the school. They had spent years teaching the Christian faith to the *honka* students at the middle school level, some of whom went on to the *koutouka* level. But girls from government schools did not have this Christian background. When they entered the *koutouka*, it gave missionaries and staff another fresh opportunity to share the gospel of Christ through Shokei's program with those who had never heard it. Special entrance stipulations were set based on their previous year's education.

Entrance stipulations for the *koutouka* were set as follows:

- Graduates of Shokei's Basic Education (*honka*) five-year course qualify to go straight into the new three-year English course.

- Graduates of the *honka* five-year course qualify to go straight into the new three-year domestic science course.

- Graduates of four-year government schools are required to take one extra year of English before entering the three-year *koutouka*.

- Graduates of Shokei's *honka* special domestic science department are required to take one extra year in the *koutouka* course to graduate.

10. Jesse to C. B. Tenny, June 1923, Kanto Gakuin University Library, Yokohama, Japan.

The Music Department Conundrum. In 1921, a new music department was established in the *koutouka*. This created the need for missionary music teachers. One of the objects in establishing the *koutouka* was to train music teachers for the public schools. A voice teacher, however, was difficult to find, and the school was unsuccessful in sending out graduates as they had hoped. Ruth Ward, who had received a bachelor's degree in piano from University of Redlands in 1916, was appointed head of the department. In 1921, there were as many as ninety students in the *honka* and *koutouka* who were already learning piano and organ. Ward served until 1924, and then Marguerite Haven succeeded her with "splendid results."[11] Sadie T. Ross, wife of Charles H. Ross, who founded the North Star Baptist Church, taught classes intermittently all through the 1920s.[12] She reported that although there were few graduates of the music department (one student in 1923), the music classes provided a wonderful atmosphere at the basic education level that few other schools could match. Concerts and recitals drew crowds. The instruments were few, but the audiences sat in rapt attention when the Estey organ was played. The faculty dreamed of having a concert piano and organ—oh, for a pipe organ! The "instrument" getting the most use was Mary Jesse's victrola. It was in constant use in a variety of classes, including music appreciation classes, for illustrations or piano lessons, at many little parties, and in worship.[13] Although general music education continued to be a vital part of the curriculum, the *koutouka* music course was closed at the end of 1924. Then in 1927, the *honka* music curriculum was greatly affected by budget cuts and a lack of instruments. The girls took it upon themselves to raise money to buy a piano by giving public concerts and charging admission. Music remained a drawing card for the *honka* up through the early 1930s, with more girls applying to enter than could be accommodated.[14] Haven left for furlough in July of 1930 and Alice Bixby from Hinomoto Girls' School was transferred to Shokei to lead

11. Winifred Acock, "Annual Report," 1924–1925, BIM Correspondence File.

12. Charles H. and Sadie Ross from Pomona, California were missionaries with the ABFMS in Sendai from 1910 to 1929. They lived in a house on the Shokei campus which served thereafter as a residence for principals of Shokei. The Rosses began the North Star (Hokusei) Baptist Church one block north of Shokei in 1926 and when the school-church closed on campus in 1933 because of lack of leadership, many students began going to this church (currently called *Kita-san Banchou Kirisuto kyoukai* of the United Church of Christ in Japan).

13. Ross, "Annual Report," 1923, BIM Correspondence File.

14. Ross, "Annual Report," 1927, BIM Correspondence File.

the music. Through her efforts, music became a vital part of the Christian program at Shokei again.[15] In addition to putting on memorable Christmas programs, Bixby also developed a choir at the school-church. Their community concerts drew the public's attention to the school and its excellence. William Wynd commented, "Bixby is the sort of teacher who inspires in her pupils a love for music and who develops their talents in an unusual way; but she is an evangelist as well as an educator. Her passion for music is exceeded by her passion for souls."[16]

Alice Bixby's contribution to the music program was short-lived, however. In 1934, the Reference Committee made up of elected Japan Baptist missionaries who made decisions regarding missionary personnel voted to move her to Osaka to serve at Mead Woman's Christian Center. At the request of Shokei's principal, Dr. Ukichi Kawaguchi, Mary Jesse (who was in America at the time) wrote a letter to the American Board, asking that Bixby be retained at Shokei, contrary to the Reference Committee's decision. From that letter, we learn a few details of the situation. Bixby had been requested at Osaka for several reasons: 1) her fluency in Japanese was needed in consultation work; 2) Mead Christian Center was in desperate need of a principal—candidate Saburo Yasumura agreed to accept the position of principal at Mead Christian Center on condition that he was given a missionary associate; 3) The Women's Committee, a sub-committee of the Reference Committee, further felt that "for Bixby's own sake she should be moved to a more congenial atmosphere," the implication being that the atmosphere in the missionary residence, perhaps unhealthy personal relationships, were affecting Bixby negatively.

Jesse wrote, giving her reasons for wanting Bixby to remain at Shokei: 1) Retaining a foreign music teacher was a drawing card for the school and advertised the school to the Japanese public since there were still few foreigners in Sendai; 2) Losing Bixby's service would thwart the school's efforts to increase enrollment, especially since the other mission school in town, Miyagi Jogakkou of the German Reformed Church in America, offered even more advantages in music; 3) It would leave only one missionary at the school; 4) Bixby was also greatly needed because she was the treasurer of the Shokei Board of Trustees and school treasurer. Suitable plans

15. Woman's American Baptist Foreign Mission Society, "Sendai," *Sixtieth Annual Report* (1930–1931) 55.

16. Wynd, *Seventy Years*, 110–11.

could hardly be made to fill the responsibility of accounting for mission funds used by the school.

Jesse suggested that Alice Bixby be allowed to change her living conditions within Sendai, but not be moved from the school. Jesse quotes Dr. Kawaguchi's appraisal that Bixby was "absolutely indispensable to our school both in her music and in her noble Christian influence."[17] Jesse's argument proved insufficient to prevent the transfer of Alice Bixby. Missionary placement was beyond the control of the school. However, Bixby would later return to Shokei with a very different experience awaiting her.[18]

Helpful Hands. Despite the many problems that faced the students and teachers at Shokei daily, they still had time to respond to the larger community. September 1st, 1923, a day traditionally known as an auspicious day on the Japanese calendar, the Tokyo-Yokohama area called the Kanto Plain experienced the worst national calamity in its history up to that time. At 11:58 am, the Great Kanto Earthquake struck, causing widespread fires that destroyed most of the residential and business areas of Tokyo and Yokohama. Over one hundred forty thousand people died or went missing. Edward Behr, in his book *Hirohito*, notes that, according to Japanese folklore, a giant catfish thrashing around in the bottom of the sea caused earthquakes when the Japanese race was misbehaving. It so happened that at just this time, Japan was experiencing yet another political crisis in its cabinet. This situation may explain, he says, why the government did not let the outside world know about the disaster immediately. Although the earthquake destroyed all normal means of communication, the government deliberately jammed the radio waves and denied that anything had happened. Royal Navy officers from a warship which had just entered Yokohama harbor learned of the disaster when they found people swimming out to sea to avoid the ensuing fires. As they brought blankets and medicine on shore, they thought that it was incomprehensible that the government attempted to keep this calamity a secret from the world. Rumors spread that Korean immigrants had offended the spirits. Tokyo survivors in some sectors massacred thousands of Koreans while the police and army stood by.[19] American Baptist Missionary, James H. Covell, was on vacation in Nagano Prefecture at the time, but came back to Tokyo/Yokohama to check on

---

17. Jesse to Mabelle R. McVeigh, 15 January 1934, BIM Correspondence File.

18. Bixby returned to Shokei and served from 1939–1941, after which time she was interned in Sendai by the Japanese government.

19. Behr, *Hirohito*, 45–47.

the situation. He commented that "the horrible atrocities committed on the Korean laborers right after the quake makes me shudder."[20]

After the confusion from this natural and human-caused disaster died down, aid from outside the Kanto area began to come in, and that aid would continue for several years to come. However, while the rest of the world was just learning of the disaster, immediate needs could only be met with local resources. Winifred Acock, missionary at Shokei, recounts how many people in the north were affected financially because relatives living in Tokyo had lost everything. This was the situation of at least one student. When the other students heard of her situation, fourteen of her classmates paid her tuition so she could continue to attend school. Other students contributed money for the needs of girls at Soshin Girls' School in Yokohama, where the school was totally destroyed. All the girls were continually sewing and knitting for the students in the distressed areas.[21]

The School-Church. Another concern of Jesse's early on was keeping up with the demand for Christian education and instruction of new converts. There was only one Baptist church in town at that time, and it was quite a walking distance from Shokei.[22] This led to the idea of establishing a church on campus.

In 1919, an official school-church (church inside a school) was established in the school chapel, with attendance being voluntary. By 1923, the attendance by students and neighborhood people had risen to one hundred twenty with an evening attendance of far more.[23] Evening meetings consisted of lectures given by special speakers, both Japanese and American. By 1926, the Sunday school was drawing five hundred children from the community and students from the school itself. The Sunday school teachers were the older students in the *honka* and *koutouka*. Winifred Acock recorded many stories of how work with the Shokei students in Sunday school

20. Watanabe, *Covell*.

21. Acock, "Annual Report," 1923, BIM Correspondence File.

22. Referred to as Sendai (*Daiichi*) Baptist Church and established by Thomas P. Poate in 1880. During the Buzzell era, students attended this church. In 1945, the church building was destroyed by American firebombs. After WWII, the church elected to remain in the United Church of Christ in Japan.

23. The school-church continued until 1934, when it was annexed to North Star Baptist Church (*Kita San-banchou Kyoukai*). Another church inside the campus began in 1949 after Mary Jesse returned to Japan. It was called Shokei Church. In 1972, it moved outside the campus to Nakajima-cho, then to Nakayama, Sendai, and since then has functioned independently of the school.

reaped a harvest during the week at school. Many of these converts were *koutouka* students with no Christian background, who were forbidden by their parents to be baptized.[24] On Sunday afternoons, some students went to the outskirts of town to the poorer communities and conducted neighborhood Sunday schools. Mead and Buzzell started this practice during the first years of the school. After 1926, the school-church took over these neighborhood Sunday schools as their own "missionary contribution," taking on the finances and direction of the afternoon Sunday school where more than three hundred fifty children were benefiting from the teachings of Jesus.[25]

EMBRACING THE FUTURE

Jesse knew early on that campus expansion was the only way for the present and future students to enjoy the unique atmosphere and growth that Shokei could provide young women. Two features of the school's uniqueness in the twenties were the installation of Japanese leadership and the spiritual growth of the students.

Plans for a New Administration and Campus. During the 1920s, government schools were snatching up Shokei graduates as teachers. In 1923, the first graduate was accepted as a teacher at top-ranked First Girls High School. In the missionary's way of thinking, there was nothing more important than being able to place Christian teachers in government schools. Shokei continued to attract the attention of government officials, and that same year the report of accreditation by the Imperial Department of Education was finally received. This was a result of the long hard work of all the teachers.

Until Jesse's furlough in September 1924, she worked to encourage Japanese leadership at Shokei. She was among the earliest Baptist women missionaries to recognize the necessity of putting the leadership in the hands of the Japanese. The first person to recommend this approach at Shokei was, in fact, Annie Buzzell. In 1916, when Buzzell was thinking ahead to her next furlough, she requested that the Woman's Board consider Yugoro Chiba to serve as principal while she was away. The American Board was not ready to put the school fully into the hands of the Japanese. Their response to her request was "Voted: That we inform Miss Buzzell that we are

24. Acock, "Annual Report," 15 July 1925, BIM Correspondence File.
25. Agnes Meline, "Annual Report," July 1927, BIM Correspondence File.

surprised at her statement and hope she has made no such arrangements, since we desire to have an American woman as head of the school."[26] Very few of the other women missionaries at the school shared in Jesse's idea to install Japanese leadership, but by the time she left on furlough, she had at least convinced those at Shokei and the current dean, Dr. Ukichi Kawaguchi, that he should take over the position of principal in her absence.

Although it appeared that life at Shokei was exciting and growth was palpable, Jesse's private letters reveal another point of view. During the two years prior to the beginning of her furlough in 1924, she felt that little progress had taken place at the school. There was a severe shortage of funds from US churches and almost no Japanese support base existed. There was no opportunity for expansion, and, in her own words, she felt she was just "marking time." However, determination and diplomacy kept her emotions in check, and with a kind of cautious haste, she began making plans to execute her new ideas. Before returning to the United States she surveyed every piece of land in and around the campus and drew up a master building plan for a campus that could accommodate kindergarten through junior college. This included the possibility of purchasing the land where Shokei had seen its beginnings from 1892–1896 just north of the school campus. She returned to the United States with new determination to campaign for funds to finance her new plan.

A New Era with Dr. Ukichi Kawaguchi (1924–1935). While Jesse embarked on a long road of deputation in America on behalf of Shokei, the school began a new period in its history under the leadership of Dr. Ukichi Kawaguchi. After more than thirty-five years of leadership by American Baptist missionaries, Kawaguchi was named the new acting principal. His service spanned a ten-year period. The son of a farmer, Kawaguchi went to America for twelve years. He studied first at William Jewell College, then at Rochester Theological Seminary and the University of Chicago. After receiving a PhD in Philosophy, he returned to Japan to teach at the Baptist Theological Seminary in Kanto Gakuin, Yokohama. From there he was called to the position of dean at Shokei. He was well known for his earnest Christian life, scholarly mind, and untiring work. He was greatly respected by both his Japanese and missionary colleagues. The combination of these characteristics helped Kawaguchi lead Shokei through some of its richest years of revival and poorest years in terms of finances. The Great Depression

---

26. Minutes of Foreign Department and Finance, 16 March 1916, vote #812, BIM, Archival Collections of ABHS.

was beginning to sweep across America, affecting the financial situation of churches as well. In addition, there was a strong anti-Japanese feeling in the United States, reinforced by the Exclusion Act of 1921 and the succeeding Quota Immigration Act of 1924, which limited immigration of Asians, but particularly Japanese, into the United States. This attitude inevitably seeped into the churches, where offerings for missions decreased.

Principal Kawaguchi's first task, then, was to begin building a financial base for the school in Japan. This included revitalizing the alumnae organization. They and the Parent-Teacher Association (PTA) shouldered more and more of the repairs and improvements.[27] Even the students themselves raised money for special speakers and janitorial supplies to help combat financial woes. Eventually, the WABFMS Board presented a mandatory plan to Shokei for financial independence. However, the plan did not come to fruition until sometime after Kawaguchi had left Shokei.

A second problem was the rising tide of modern thought among young people in Japan beginning in the mid 1920s and continuing on into the thirties. The Japanese government's long-time neglect of the poor in the countryside, the sweathouse workers of the city, and the unprotected and unemployed created fertile ground for socialism and communism. The government clamped down severely on any group espousing leftist ideology by imposing a stiff penalty of up to ten years in jail for participation in extreme forms of left-wing politics. Missionary Georgia Newbury's reports tell us that the girls avidly read the newspapers and were filled with questions about the new socialist and communist ideology. Lively debates took place everywhere on campus. Kawaguchi dealt with this problem in a very prudent manner. While student strikes were leaving their marks on other campuses, Dr. Kawaguchi left communication lines open between students and faculty, averting any major confrontations. He helped the students to contrast the teachings of Christ on social action issues with godless socialistic and communistic thinking.

The students were quick to notice the differences between the new political thought which took the side of the poor and disenfranchised, the lack of boldness, and lethargy of the church in relation to the social problems. They asked questions like "Why don't Christians insist on the real principles of Christianity to combat socialism?"; "Why does God bring poverty into the world?"; "How can we make a Christian society?"; "How and what shall we do for the socialist to bring him to God's grace?"; and "How can we

27. Kawaguchi, "Shokei Jo Gakko (Ella O. Patrick)," *Japan Baptist Annual* (1931) 78.

improve the inside of the Christian church in Japan?" Kawaguchi skillfully guided the students through this period of unrest without stifling their process of free thought.[28] In the end, only one student was caught up in social uprisings; she was arrested, and later died in a Tokyo jail.

Revival. When the Holy Spirit moves in the hearts of people, they become acutely aware of their sin, feel compelled to believe in Jesus Christ as their Savior, and are baptized in large numbers. People in turn reached out to others with the joy of the gospel. This phenomenon has been recorded in many countries but is not so well-known in Japanese history. At Shokei, in the 1920s, a similar movement began to occur. Many baptisms took place over a period of ten to twelve years. Factors that contributed to this revival were a faculty of dedicated Christians, a large team of American missionaries, and the efforts and spiritual guidance of Principal Kawaguchi. The school encouraged faculty and Christian students to model their Christian beliefs. Revival was also spurred on by special evangelistic meetings held each year, and by the students themselves leading other students to faith in Jesus Christ.

Mary Jesse attributed the fine religious life of the school to several groups: the school-church and the Junior/Senior Young People's Society (Young Women's Christian Association, YWCA).[29] The work of the YWCA, as missionaries called it, is noteworthy here. It was organized in Japan in 1905, and in 1918, Annie Buzzell began a chapter at Shokei. By 1924, it had become a highly-organized group of over two hundred student members. Twelve student officers guided the other student members in spiritual growth and service to the whole school. Their goal was to have a heart as beautiful as the nature that surrounded the school.[30] Each year, these students had planted the seeds of revival through intense prayer for their school and classmates, and through the organizing of Christian activities. In 1922, there were thirty baptisms, and in 1923, with the help of evangelistic meetings held by Saburo Yasumura of Kanto Gakuin in Yokohama and Evelyn Camp of Mead Christian Center in Osaka, one hundred three decisions were made for Christ. Of these, thirty-one baptisms were carried out. Seven YWCA Bible classes were formed, as a result. Girls continued

---

28. Newbury, "Ella O. Patrick Girls' School, Sendai," *Japan Baptist Annual* (1932) 79–80.

29. Jesse, "Sendai Girls' School," *Japan Baptist Annual* (1922) 36.

30. "Joshi seinen kai yori," (From Girl's young people's group) *Mutsumi no Kusari* 15 (1924) 7.

to come every day to the leaders to announce that they wanted to become Christians.[31]

In 1924, Mary Jesse left on furlough, but the teachers continued to gather together to pray once a week. The students were doing the same. They organized morning prayer services at 5:00 AM for dorm students and at 7:30 AM for day pupils. Another group named "Friends of Jesus" met every Sunday morning at 5:30 AM for several years.[32] Six students banded themselves together to pray and work for the school. They called themselves the Robin Club with the motto "Make somebody happy today." They wore a badge secretly and held weekly meetings. Their purpose was to teach Christianity through joy and liveliness, to help the school in any way possible, to keep order and quiet in the halls, and to make money to buy mops, brooms, etc. for keeping the school clean. They sold boxes of bread to the teachers to earn money.[33] This "secret club" and the YWCA cabinet, from which it came, seemed to contribute to the increased spiritual focus on campus, and the beginning of revival.[34] Music teacher Marguerite Haven described the special evangelistic meetings held with a Bible teacher from Shokei's sister school, Soshin, in Yokohama:

> How we wished you might have shared with us the joy and inspiration that the last few days have brought; that you might have been able to go from the class-room [sic] at a time outside regular school hours, to see every girl in her place joining with the others in prayer for a special blessing of God upon our school. For four days these special prayer-conducted meetings were held by the girls themselves. Most of them were conducted by students, and from everyone came the same report, every girl present, *everybody* interested. The great interest manifested came as a result of weeks and months of effort and prayer on the part of a number of earnest Christian girls in the school, the officers and cabinet of the YWCA. After four days of preparatory prayer, Miss [Chiyo] Yamada, Bible teacher of Kanagawa Girls' School [Soshin Jogakkou], visited us for three days and put in every spare minute giving talks to eager listeners and answering questions. After, the large number of inquirers who wished to talk with Miss Yamada was so great that from three-thirty until nearly eight o'clock she was kept busy, except for a few minutes given to a hurried supper. The YWCA

31. *Our Work in the Orient*, 52.

32. Jesse, "Annual Report," November 1927, BIM Correspondence File.

33. Ross, "Annual Report," 1923, BIM Correspondence File.

34. "The Ella O. Patrick Girls' School," *Japan Baptist Annual* (1924–1925) 51–53.

officers who had planned a little reception for her, of their own accord, turned their party into a prayer-meeting . . .

Results cannot be told completely here, but today in the waters of the Hirose River, which flows past our school, 24 girls were baptized.[35]

As the YWCA grew stronger each year, more baptisms were recorded. In November 1927, eighty more students were baptized in the Hirose River, and one week later, an additional fourteen more were baptized. It was not uncommon for conversions to occur among those who had come to observe the baptisms of their friends. Some joined the school-church and some joined other churches in town. Agnes Meline's observations of a baptism were as follows:

We were a little anxious about the girls going into the cold water, so we carried down our blankets to put around them as they came out of the water.

It was an impressive sight to see the girls so courageously express their faith.

A little dressing tent was provided for them by the edge of the stream where they quickly changed their clothes. Immediately afterwards we had them come to our house [the Ella O. Patrick Home], and while they were drying their long black flowing hair around our cheery wood stoves, we served them hot foreign tea.

When asked if the water wasn't awfully cold, [they] said, "we were too happy inside to feel the cold outside." We rejoice with them in their new-found [sic] joy in Christ.[36]

Others made decisions for Christ, but were kept from baptism by opposition in their homes. Good results came from special evangelistic efforts of Saburo Imai, a famous convert and former Buddhist priest from Aoyama Gakuin School, and follow-up work was done by Michi Kawai, the founder of the Japan and Tokyo YWCA of Keisen Girls' School. Also, in early spring of 1927, a group of earnest Christians in the *koutouka* organized some special meetings. Because of pressing schoolwork, they had no opportunity for the meetings, but through planning, prayer, and personal evangelism, won nine of their classmates, who confessed Christ in baptism in the spring. Efforts continued into the fall, as they had such a feeling of responsibility for their classmates. They had planned and prayed all summer and earned

35. Marguerite Haven, "Sendai," *Our Work in the Orient* (1925-1926) 148-49.

36. Meline, "Annual Report," 15 January 1927, BIM Correspondence File.

enough money to invite a speaker in the fall. Organizing prayer bands and workers' groups (evangelistic teams) resulted in more baptisms in the spring of 1928. Prayer meetings continued with newer and older Christians giving a continual testimony as to how Christ changed their lives. These student groups were doing practically all the evangelistic work.[37]

A PILGRIMAGE IN FAITH

In the meantime, Mary Jesse was in the United States, fighting her own battle to trust God when she could not see the outcome. Returning to the United States in September 1924, her one-year furlough turned into an exhausting two-year stay and a brush with death. As she toured a hostile America, trying to rally support for her beloved girls at Shokei, she sensed the futility of it all and saw little for all her work of deputation. She observed patent discrimination against Asian immigrants, both privately and officially through the law, which had been building up for some years. According to legislation of the Naturalization Act of 1790, non-Caucasians were ineligible for US citizenship, but could continue to immigrate. However, now in this post-World War I era, fueled by a biased press, xenophobic fears had been mounting for some time, and Americans began fearing for their jobs. The Immigration Act of 1924 was an attempt to make it easier for Northwestern Europeans to immigrate while restricting Southern and Eastern Europeans. The National Origins Quota of 1924 was particularly aimed at Japanese and Filipinas by restricting the number of immigrants to two percent of those in the United States, according to the 1890 census. On May 26th, the day of the official beginning of the new law, a day of national humiliation was declared in Japan. The debates had succeeded in making more Americans than ever resentful of the Japanese, and this resentment now affected Jesse's appeal for support of the work at Shokei.[38]

---

37. "School Report," *Japan Baptist Annual* (1928) 77–78.

38. The Immigration Exclusion Act of 1924 is often mistakenly called the Japanese Exclusion Act of 1924. The reason is that it was truly aimed at people of Japanese ethnic origin. Asians other than Japanese had already been barred in the Barred Zone Act of 1917. Now any Asian who could not qualify for American citizenship was not to be allowed into the United States. In previous agreements (1907–1908), Japan at least had a small quota, but now there was no quota, thus, also barring all those people of Japanese origin "aliens ineligible for citizenship." (Japanese born in Canada with Canadian citizenship were not allowed to enter the United States either.) This policy continued until 1952, although some exceptions were made. Daniels, "United States Immigration Acts,"

The unresponsiveness of churches in the United States where Jesse spoke caused her to doubt the idea of returning to Japan. Without the necessary funds to carry out expansion of a school bursting at its seams, she felt that she had no further role there. This prompted her to accept the position of YWCA Religious Education Secretary for Washington DC. She felt uneasy about holding that position while still on the payroll of the WABFMS, so she wrote to the foreign mission secretary, Mabelle McVeigh: "I wonder if I should resign to the board? . . . If that is best, please consider this my resignation."[39] The foreign mission secretary was the stateside advocate for missionaries to the WABFMS Board. Jesse felt paralyzed, discouraged, and confused, wondering if going to Japan in the first place was a mistake. If it wasn't a mistake, then why did she feel so strongly that she should quit now? To her, something was wrong somewhere and it all seemed like "just a shameful waste" for her not to go back. Her hopeless cry was, "I can't see a plan . . . Is there such a thing as Divine guidance?!"[40] Did she get an answer to her question?

Divine silence is sometimes a part of divine guidance. If Jesse had not sensed the lack of guidance from God and unanswered prayers, she would have returned to Japan after her one-year furlough. She would not have traveled to Indiana State in October of 1925 to make one last plea for Shokei. And there, she would not have met with such a splendid response at the Indiana Baptist Convention. At the Convention, a minister mounted the platform and gave the executive director, Dr. Carlos Dinsmore, a Scottish Rites diamond ring. He announced that it was to be sold and the proceeds to be used for the school in Sendai. From this gesture, people in the audience, one after another, came up to pledge more than five thousand dollars that night.[41] Within the next month, one by one people began to respond. People donated through no small sacrifice. Some women made their families go without Christmas presents in 1925 and 1926 so that they could have a small share in women's education in Japan.[42] Later in the fall of 1925, a cable arrived for Jesse saying that the Indiana Baptist Convention of churches would like to support her

---

164–65.

39. Jesse to Mabelle R. McVeigh, 7 September 1925, BIM Correspondence File.

40. Ibid.

41. Blake, *Finding A Way*, 116–17.

42. One woman interviewed by the author in Indiana in 1991 recalls being told by her grandmother when she was twelve years old that, the following Christmas, the only presents for the family would be fruit and nuts because money for presents would be donated to missionary Mary Jesse for Shokei Girls School in Japan.

further in her work with the pledge of fifty thousand dollars![43] The funds would be gathered through a fall campaign in the state of Indiana with the help of Thomasine Allen, who was on furlough at the time. It would be at least enough to build the much-needed building for the home economics higher department. What glorious news this must have been!

At the end of December, Mary Jesse faced a life-threatening illness. She wrote to the staff at Shokei that she might not return after the operation, insisting that they install Dr. Kawaguchi as principal of the school in the spring of 1926. The operation was a success, however, and the surgeon told her that if she had been in a small town with inexperienced doctors, it would have cost her life. Her recovery went well. She resigned from the Woman's American Baptist Foreign Mission Board to work as the YWCA Religious Education Secretary while recovering. But when she recovered fully, the Woman's Board "ordered" her back to serve at Shokei. She left for Japan on August 21st, 1926,[44] and arrived two weeks later with a new awareness of the nature of the visible and invisible guidance of God.

43 "Allen: Indiana Baptists Pledge Toward New Building Sendai—Hudson," Hudson, Cables, Incoming Cables, 15 October 1925.

44. One Member, "Jeshii Sensei to Futatabi Oufute," *Mutsumi no Kusari* 18 (1927) 12–18.

Ruth E. Smith (1922–1924)
(courtesy of Shokei Gakuin)

Sadie Ross (1923–1928)
(courtesy of Shokei Gakuin)

Winifred Acock (1924–1926)
(courtesy of Shokei Gakuin)

4

Hopes for a New Start (1926–1930)

Principal Ukichi Kawaguchi and Thomasine Allen
(courtesy of Shokei Gakuin)

Longing for solitude is the longing for God.

—RUTH HARLEY BARTON[1]

When we actually plant something we are liable to claim it as our own,
to be too protective or exclusive.
Yet whether we plant it, or scatter seed in the wind,
it is the Lord who brings it to maturity.

—EDDIE ASKEW[2]

1. Barton, *Sacred Rhythms*, 32.
2. Askew, *A Silence and a Shouting*, 12.

Although there was a long road ahead before anyone would see the new Indiana Building, Mary Jesse returned to Shokei full of new hopes for the future, fully expecting to work directly with students and do no more administrative work. Still, pressure built up day by day, because the new Japanese administration remained dependent upon her for advice. She folded under the pressure and was forced to rest. Because of her convalescence and the absence of other missionaries who were on furlough, new faces and personalities came to Shokei and added to the colorful make-up of the staff.

CONSTRUCTION PLANS THWARTED

Announcements of the promised money from churches in the state of Indiana preceded Jesse. Dr. Kawaguchi got permission from the government to build, and announced to the public via the newspaper that a new building, called the Indiana Building, would be built. In the spring of 1927, thirty-eight students entered the *koutouka* domestic science course with the expectation of studying in the new building, but the funds did not come. Kawaguchi felt embarrassed to meet the public and the press. How could they save face? And worse, he feared "getting in bad" with the government for his empty promises if there was further delay. Jesse felt tremendous pressure again to produce the needed resources.

But she had an idea. In April 1927, she wrote a letter to Dr. Carlos Dinsmore of the Indiana Baptist Convention outlining her plan to build, even though the funds promised were not in hand.[3] This plan is included here because it shows the extent to which Jesse went to get the school out of its precarious position with the government and the public.

In this letter, she first acknowledged Dinsmore's letter in which he promised to have the funds gathered in Indiana and on hand by February 1st, 1928. Jesse presented her plan as follows: she would like to start the new building in June or July 1927, using funds which already had been collected. The WABFMS rules stated that a building could not be built unless all the funds were in hand, but she planned to borrow forty thousand dollars from the Baptist mission that had become available from the sale of mission property in Japan. This would depend on the approval of the

3. Jesse to Carlos Dinsmore, 2 April 1927, BIM Correspondence File.

Woman's Board for release of the funds, of course. Since the money was already earmarked for other purposes, it could be used and then paid back by taking out a loan. Thus, the bills for the building could be paid off in November. She suggested that, if Dinsmore agreed, the Indiana Baptist Convention could borrow money between November and February so that they could pay back money borrowed from the land fund. When the funds from the Indiana Baptist Convention's fall campaign became available in February 1928, the loan could be paid back. According to her thinking, this plan would accomplish several things. It would give the Indiana fall campaign a specific tangible goal. It would relieve the over-crowding at Shokei sooner than anticipated, and most importantly, it would reestablish Shokei's credibility with the public. But for some unknown reason, this emergency plan was not approved, and due to flagging interest of Baptist congregations in Indiana, the campaign was still more than ten thousand dollars short by April of 1928. This led the Indiana Baptist convention to borrow the remainder.[4]

STAFF TRANSITIONS

The latter half of the 1920s was a period of growth in terms of the number of missionaries sent to Japan, but many of them had little experience with the Japanese language, and they needed a lot of guidance. Some came for a season, made their contribution and left, while others stayed longer. Shokei's enormous English and music program required the expertise of native speakers of English. Between 1924 and 1930 no fewer than fifteen missionaries either entered or left Shokei. While Jesse was on furlough, Thomasine Allen did the reporting to the WABFMS regarding Shokei, but when she left for furlough in 1927, Georgia M. Newbury, who had come two years earlier, acted as spokesperson for Shokei until she resigned in 1935. Agnes Meline, Acock, and Allen, who had been full-time missionary teachers at the school, left on furlough and had to be replaced. Missionaries, some new and some who were transferred from other places, helped to cover for them. Neither Acock nor Allen returned to Shokei because of new assignments, so the contributions of the newcomers were very important. At least three of the missionaries who served were missionaries to China sent for only one year until the turmoil in China subsided. Their observations in their letters record details of Shokei school life not found elsewhere.

4. Blake, *Finding a Way*, 117.

New Foreign Staff. Georgia Newbury had the greatest influence on Shokei in terms of English education during this time. Born in Astoria, Oregon, she received most of her education on the West Coast. Before appointment in 1922, Newbury studied at Boston College of Oratory.[5] She served a term in Tokyo before coming to Sendai, arriving before Jesse went on furlough in 1924. According to recollections of Shizuyo Kato, long-time household helper of missionaries, Newbury had a bright personality but she was plagued with arthritis. She had a little dog named Nifty that she dearly loved and took everywhere with her.[6] But she is known most for "making English a living language."[7] In 1926 she was made head of the *honka* English department. Her flourishing pen provided unique descriptions of life at Shokei. Among these articles was her widely read description of a big event in the life of the school, the visit of the representative of the emperor's son, Akihito, in 1925. The following is an excerpt from one of her letters:

> The event of greatest importance to us was the visit of the Crown Prince's representative and personal friend to our school. This was the only girl's school chosen in spite of the fact that there are many very fine High Schools [*sic*] for girls in Sendai. So it was paying a real tribute to mission work in Japan and especially to Christian education . . . Upstairs in the big school Miss Allen with her class of second year youngsters anxiously spending the last precious moments practicing in whispers their lesson about a big fat cook, seven little hungry boys, and a pancake.
>
> Downstairs excitement ran high. There was Miss Newbury wondering if she could serve the ice cream and pour the coffee at just the right moment and without accident or mishap. . . Outside were the girls lined up with care and precision forming two sides of a square.
>
> Look! The police arrive! Then more officials and the street is [*sic*] closed to all traffic! There are breathless moments of suspense, then a military command and all stand at attention. Many autos roll up to the gate then one larger than the others comes to a stop directly across the gate entrance, another command and all bow then stand at attention while our honored guest and his attendants and guards pass up the drive and into the building.

---

5. Missionary Register Card, Newbury, BIM, Archival Collections of ABHS.

6. Suzuyo Kato, interview by author, 13 June 1992.

7. Wynd, *Seventy Years*, 227.

. . . Is there any significance in the fact that that representative should ask to meet the American teachers and eat food that he had been told was prepared by those teachers?

Perhaps this was a step towards bringing together the Kingdoms of this earth. . . . And who can say how much of the Christian atmosphere permeated the halls of our campus of our school that morning.[8]

Newbury was truly dynamic in many ways. As she recited poetry during the Literary Week program, she had Marguerite Haven play the piano in the background. She also taught gymnastics to the students. Here also, Newbury got Sadie Ross to accompany the students' routines on the piano. Missionaries were often known for their interesting use of the Japanese language, often a direct translation of an unfamiliar English phrase into Japanese. When the students were not thinking through an idea as she thought they should, Newbury would say "Is your head just a decoration?" or "*Anata no atama wa kazari atama desuka?*", bringing inevitable snickers from the other students.

Marguerite Haven, another newcomer who came from California, joined the staff to fill in the vacancy left by Ward's return for furlough. She stayed at Shokei for six years. In their reports, other missionaries often mentioned her accomplishments in the area of music. Shokei was put on the map, so to speak, because of her leadership in music. In her July 1927 report, Meline commented about difficulties Haven faced: "More pupils apply for instrumental and vocal training than can be accommodated, for we are handicapped by lack of teachers and instruments and space."[9] She also mentioned that because of the ticket sales from the concerts they gave, the music program had become "self-supporting."[10] One former student recalled how hard Haven worked to get the girls to sing. When their voices would not produce the pace and rhythm of the song, she would exclaim "no-soi, no-soi." This word was apparently her personal creation of the Japanese words *noroi* (lazily) and *osoi* (slow paced)![11] When Haven left in 1930, the immediate arrival of Alice Bixby made it possible for the music program to continue for a few more years. Haven's next assignment was Soshin Girls School, where she was equally admired and continued her valuable work.

8. Newbury, "Annual Report," October 1925, BIM Correspondence File.

9. Meline, "Annual Report," July 1927, BIM Correspondence File.

10. Ibid.

11. Shin Chiba, interview by author, 28 March 1996.

Both Newbury and Haven worked with Allen, while Mary Jesse was away in the United States. Thus, with Jesse's reentry and Allen's departure, these rather new missionaries were the "senior" missionaries during the next few years, which were so difficult for Jesse, and during the time when the movement of short-term missionaries in and out of Shokei was greatest. Fortunately for the school, both Newbury and Haven were very skilled in their own profession, but they were undoubtedly left with the task of orientation of new missionaries to Shokei while being inexperienced themselves. They also had to communicate with the Japanese *honka* staff, despite limited language skills, while Jesse concentrated totally on the *koutouka* and school administration. They found it difficult to relinquish their authority as missionaries and adjust to the new philosophy of management by the Japanese. When management decisions were handed down to them, they tended to assume that Mary Jesse, whom they seldom met, was still making the decisions.[12] These assumptions caused a rift between them and Jesse. However, this stress was offset by the joy they all experienced at being present during the greatest years of Christian revival at the school.

Japanese Staff Enrichment. Shokei was continually adding distinguished Japanese teachers to their teaching staff. In 1927, the addition of three new teachers strengthened the staff. Mr. Yoshinaga Maruyama had just returned with a Master's Degree from the University of Chicago; Jiro Sawano was the son of a Baptist pastor and graduate of Oriental University (Touyou Daigaku); Kei Aizawa was a Shokei graduate who had attended Kobe College, worked in the Osaka YWCA, and taught in a government girls' school in Akita Prefecture. Kawaguchi recognized that delegating responsibilities was essential to Shokei's survival. So, in the same year, he appointed Michie Takano, a graduate of the government higher normal school and a teacher at Shokei for twelve years, as the new dean of the *honka*. Jesse was appointed as the dean of the *koutouka*, and Giichi Kanamori, a graduate of Boston University, assisted her.[13]

TRIAL BY FIRE

The next few years were some of the most difficult years of Mary Jesse's career. Her strength of character was tested as she passed through the heat

---

12. Jesse to Sandburg, 31 May 1933, BIM Correspondence File.

13. Meline, "Annual Report," July 1927, BIM Correspondence File.

of adversity. She appeared weakened by it at first, but years later she showed increased endurance and wisdom because of those difficult times.

Disappointments. Her dream of expanding the physical campus to hold the tremendous numbers of students seeking higher education at Shokei had to be put on hold. Planning for emergency measures to cope with the problem of inadequate facilities prevented her from spending time with students and missionary colleagues, and drained her emotionally and physically. She carried on with the work, often as the only foreigner on staff who could speak Japanese fluently. In 1927, the only two missionaries beside herself who could speak some Japanese were Allen and Newbury. When they were both on furlough, Jesse had to do all the work requiring Japanese. Kawaguchi wanted her to be in all administrative meetings, and he felt that he could not carry on any business without her advice. Kawaguchi, although a very capable leader in his own right, hesitated to make decisions with boldness. He had become far too dependent on Jesse for her administrative and people skills.

In the spring, there were many serious problems. Several missionaries refer to these problems in their letters without being specific as to their nature. However, we do know of the pressures from overcrowding, the refusal of the plan to build the Indiana building ahead of time, and the pressure put on Kawaguchi by the press. In addition, the evacuee missionaries from West China had been assigned to Shokei, having neither cultural orientation nor language training. Florence Skevington, with her sister Gladys from Szechuan, and colleague Emma Brodbeck of Suifu, had been forced to leave China because of an insurrection. All the foreigners in the towns where they served were evacuated, and mission schools had been closed. They spent the first quarter of the new school year at Soshin. Then they came to Sendai in the fall of 1927, where the atmosphere among missionaries was tense. Too many problems regarding buildings and interpersonal relations were coming to a head. In the spring of 1928, when Meline, who had moved to Soshin in Yokohama, became ill and returned to America, Florence Skevington was asked to take her place, making it necessary to return to Soshin for another quarter. Then all three China missionaries returned to China in July 1928.

Exhaustion and Enforced Rest. Jesse had her annual physical exam in August while on vacation. The doctor warned her about overworking. For her to return in good health, he recommended that she should have a two-hour sun bath in the morning, half an hour of relaxation at noon, two hours of exercise in the afternoon, and no work at night! All the pressure of schoolwork and new missionaries coming had taken its toll. In September 1927, Jesse wrote about her physical exam results and then told of discouragement, and a feeling of futility at several levels.

> We have spent hours and hours working on plans to raise money in Japan but the present system of having our Women's work so largely administered by missionaries makes it hard to do anything.
>
> As a matter of fact five of the six of our Board of Trustees live in Tokyo and it would take 150 to 200 yen[14] to bring them up for a meeting and the school just cannot pay for it. There [have] been no meetings of the board at all during the past year, and I think possibly there have been several years since we had a real meeting of the Board . . .
>
> I am troubled about repairs. The property will deteriorate so [sic] if roofs are allowed to leak and drains are not cared for . . . but no money . . .
>
> It is needless to speak of equipment . . . Then the problem of heating. We have no funds for fuel and the old furnace [in the chapel] is broken down again . . . It is too late now to put in heat for the winter. At least it would be very difficult to do it while school is in progress even if we had the funds. I suppose we shall just have to give up the use of the chapel in the cold weather, which will mean the Music [sic] must stop and also that we cannot have chapel exercises, Sunday school or church during the cold months, or the many meetings the girls have, student meetings, YWCA literary [retreat]. This will mean a serious loss to the religious life of the school, but we shall try to do our best with small groups using the chapel. The chapel is used every period in the day and we have no place for the girls. Last winter, Miss Haven had her feet so frosted teaching there that the doctor had to lance them several times. The girls too suffered . . . In their own houses many do not have heat but they sit on their feet and that is very different from having their feet hanging down, than [sic] sitting on chairs.
>
> . . . Perhaps some day before very long it may break through these thick black clouds and bring to us here in the Sunrise Kingdom a Bright New Day. This is my prayer.[15]

---

14. According to Dr Mochizuki, the yen/dollar value in 2009 for train fares was one hundred fifty yen to $7.98, and two hundred yen to $10.64 (see chapter 3, note 7).

15. Jesse to Mabelle R. McVeigh, 4 September 1927, BIM Correspondence File.

Jesse held on until late November of 1927 when she was near total collapse.[16] The Japan Baptist mission voted that she be sent to the "nursing home" at the missionary summer vacation resort village of Karuizawa in central Japan and put under doctor's care. There, she was assigned to stay in bed for two months. She was not even allowed to write letters. Her only freedom was to take her meals in the dining room downstairs. After a month of rest, she began to sleep well at night and to relax. She did write several letters to Foreign Secretary Mabelle McVeigh telling of the problems before coming to Karuizawa and the anxiety she was feeling presently at being away from Shokei. It is best described in her own words.

> Besides the school problems, in Miss Allen's absence I have the evangelistic work [in the countryside], too. We can't leave the school entirely to the Japanese. I thought the Board expected us to keep in touch and have some part in determining policies, rules, constitution, etc. So when they ask me to serve on these numerous committees, or urged me to be present at soudans [consultations] and conferences, I tried to go and do what I could. No one else could do this.
>
> The [women?] are teaching my hours now in addition to their own while I am up here resting. They are glad to do anything, but they can't do Japanese work.
>
> However, it has not been the work so much as the conditions, the disappointments, the embarrassing situation we are in before the public, the financial burdens, the crowded conditions so that good work is impossible, and there is no way day or night of getting out of it all since the house [the Ella O. Patrick Home] is used for school purposes. Then too there is the attitude of the Mission and Board toward us. No one seemed to understand. It is not easy to be in such a place. Every one comes to me with every kind of problem. They expect me to know what to do, to have some plan. I must be advisor, helper, go-between, interpreter and since the house is used for school purposes there is no opportunity of getting out of it all.[17]

Speaking of the problems created by her absence while in the "nursing home," she continued,

> I wish I could do as you suggest and divide responsibilities—the trouble is that no one there can work in Japanese—Marguerite

16. Mary Jesse was reported as ill as early as July 1927 (Cables: Outgoing Cables).

17. Jesse to Mabelle R. McVeigh, 18 January 1928, BIM correspondence File.

Haven while she never studied Japanese, can use a few nouns and verbs and get her ideas across somewhat but she cannot understand a sentence of a soudan [consultation] nor can she understand what is said at teachers meetings. All have had heavy teaching schedules but they can't do the Japanese work or share responsibility. The three China Missionaries know nothing of customs either and of course could not "serve" on committees, etc. You see Miss Allen and Miss Newbury both could share in the Japanese work and I must take their places . . . It is not easy to be tied up this way when there is so much to do.[18]

The inferences to the Board not understanding refer to the fact that the Baptist Foreign Mission Board wanted the school to become less dependent on them for personnel and finances. This was the eve of the Great Depression in America, but years of dependence on the guidance of missionaries made it difficult for the school to begin the process of independent thinking and planning. Yet, to avoid the conflicts concerning to whom the school belonged, the WABFMS desired that policies and administrative guidance be given. Jesse had been caught between a rock and a hard place. Dividing and relinquishing responsibility at school was much more difficult than the Mission Board realized. Jesse, in a sense, was a sacrificial lamb.

All people hoped that with a complete rest, she would feel better by the time she returned to Shokei in late February or early March 1928, but such was not the case. It's unclear exactly what happened in the next year. The missionary staff consisted of Haven and the three missionaries from China. Allen and Newbury were still on furlough. Allen never returned to Sendai, but went on to Morioka for seven years, and then to Kuji to begin pioneer work in that rural area. There she continued until her death in 1976. While Skevington was assigned temporarily to Soshin Girls School in April, Newbury cut her furlough short and returned to Sendai to cover some of Jesse's classes after she returned. Under the direction of the Japan Reference Committee, Jesse was told to curtail her activities until her strength had returned.[19] As might be expected, many duties also fell by the wayside, such as forgetting to use special appropriations from the United States.[20] Jesse found the mission house (the Ella O. Patrick home) unbearable, since it was

18. Ibid.

19. Newbury, "Sendai," *Japan Baptist Annual* (1928) 77.

20. Newbury reported that four thousand yen would finally be used for a new heater in the chapel. Newbury to Mabelle R. McVeigh, 25 April 1928, BIM Correspondence File.

always the center of activity for all the missionaries who lived there, each one having their own ministries. She left early in the morning before the others were up and came back late at night. Sometimes she didn't see the other missionaries for days at a time. Sometime during the next year, she went to live with Charles and Sadie Ross on the edge of campus so that she could be quiet when she wanted.

She continued in her position as dean of the *koutouka* while Newbury took charge of the *honka* English program. In order to relieve the load put on Jesse, Newbury, full of good intention, took all of Jesse's *honka* classes to help her out. Thus, Jesse's contact with the *honka* decreased rapidly. In later years, she looked at this action with resentment, and used it as one of the reasons that a wall had developed between her and the other missionaries.[21] In that same letter, she refers to this period as "a tangle of circumstances." The rift grew wider and it became apparent that there was a big difference between the missionaries' philosophies of management. The following are her comments on the matter in 1933:

> While the others [missionaries] in theory accepted Japanese lead-ership, when it touched them, there was trouble. They could not believe that the reorganization was really in effect—and that the Japanese were doing things. Before, things centered in the mis-sionaries and they were teachers, were in everything, so now the others feel left out—that they had no place, and since they were not running things, I must be the one "running things." They could not see that a new day had dawned and that the central commit-tee—Japanese—was working out the plans telling us what to do . . .
>
> I wish now that something could be done to take the mis-sionaries out of the center of things there, since we have Japanese leadership.[22]

Departure of China Missionaries. As the time drew near for the three China missionaries to return to China, they reflected on their experi-ences: The anti-Japanese spirit they had felt in China soon melted away as they came to love and respect the Japanese they had met in Sendai.[23] They were delighted in filling their time with teaching only, rather than having the disciplinary and administrative duties they were accustomed to in their schools in China. Teaching in the English course of the *koutouka* was es-

---

21. Jesse to Grace Maine, 31 May 1933, BIM Correspondence File.

22. Ibid.

23. J. Emma Brodbeck, "Annual Report," January 1928, BIM Correspondence File.

pecially pleasant, because the students could more easily discuss difficult ideas. "There is a marvelous spirit of evangelism among the Japanese," they said, "and our greatest desire is to be able to lead some to a love and knowledge of the One we are trying so humbly to serve."[24] Their arrival at Shokei seemed to relieve the situation at a time of unprecedented need, and their return to China seemed like a calamity.

Mary Jesse Keeps a Low Profile. The construction of the Indiana Building began in 1928, and was ready for occupancy in the spring of 1929. Although it was a time of rejoicing for most, Jesse felt that she could no longer go on. She saw the building through to completion. Whether from the feeling of exhaustion or loss of direction for the future, she thought it was time for her to step aside. She wrote her letter of resignation to the WABFMS on March 25th, 1929.[25] In the letter she set the date of resignation to be July 10th, 1929. Since she was under contractual obligation to the Board, she said that she would be willing to go to another part of Japan if needed until the contract was fulfilled in 1931, her next regularly scheduled furlough year.

Kawaguchi, upon learning of her letter, wrote to the same board expressing his "immense regret" at the news of Jesse's letter of resignation.[26] He begged the Baptist Board to refuse to grant her resignation because she was "one of Shokei's most valuable members of the faculty." He had not mentioned the resignation to the faculty because "it will cause a serious problem among them." The response from the Board to the resignation is not recorded, but a cable was sent from the Tokyo mission office to the Home Board saying that she had decided to stay.[27] During the next three-year period, Mary stayed somewhat in the background with her activities barely recorded in mission magazines and no record of her correspondence with the home office. We know from letters of other missionaries that her work primarily consisted of helping the *koutouka* to become independent from the *honka* as it moved into the new quarters of the Indiana Building. These policy-determining days paved the way for a smooth transition to the new *koutouka* that eventually became Shokei Junior College. A new curriculum was established along with guidelines of administration. These

---

24. Ibid.

25. Jesse as her "Annual Report," 25 March 1929, BIM Correspondence File.

26. Ukichi Kawaguchi, letter to the WABFMS, 5 April 1929. File of Mary D. Jesse.

27 "Mary D. Jesse Has Decided To Remain—Ella O. Patrick Home School, Sendai," Incoming Cables, 7 June 1929.

were no small feats in and of themselves. Mary kept busy leading several Bible studies with many interested college students outside Shokei. Each week she gave training to Shokei students who were teaching in both the school-church and neighborhood Sunday schools. Perhaps these were some of her happiest days because she could work personally and directly with students and was less involved with overall administration of the school and missionaries, and more specifically involved in development of the *koutouka*.

A BANNER YEAR FOR SHOKEI

While Mary Jesse's heart was still in turmoil over the difficulties of the last few years, 1929 and 1930 were exciting years for the four hundred students and their teachers at Shokei.

Dedication of the Indiana Building. No doubt, a highlight of these years was the opening of the new building named for the state in America from which most of its funding had come. Since it would be a center for training in Domestic Science, it had a well-equipped kitchen and an adjoining dining room, a good laundry room with facilities for dyeing and drying. Classrooms, a sewing room, a teachers' room and offices comprised the first floor. The upper floors held the classrooms for the English course, a small library, and the auditorium. However great the modernization was, it had its problems too. It was too expensive to run all the new electrical equipment they had installed.[28] After all the financial problems involving the churches in Indiana, not being able to use all of the modern facilities must have seemed like the final blow.

The two days of dedication were held on June 27th and 28th. Among several addresses made, the public officials emphasized the need for religion in education and the teaching of the "Golden Rule." On the second day, the Graduates' Association honored teachers who had worked at the school for ten years or more. Graduates and faculty had a dinner in the new building and then enjoyed athletic events in the afternoon, culminating with a concert in the evening. The Indiana building served Shokei well for seventy years.

School Activities and Creative Leadership. The purpose of most school activities was to encourage spiritual growth and service to others. In 1929, the students put on a very touching service on the morning of the Fourth of July for the American missionary teachers. They always tried

28. "Ella O. Patrick School, Sendai," *Japan Baptist Annual* (1930) 45–46.

to keep this event a secret. In this particular year, in the service itself, the students sang "My Country 'Tis of Thee," and a large American flag was let down from the gallery railing at the back of the chapel. Bouquets of flowers were given to each American teacher. It was an emotional moment for the missionaries to see this tribute of appreciation of the work they had done.[29]

The fall term was busy, too. In October, the whole school helped the graduates conduct a one-day bazaar. Classrooms were turned into attractive booths. Short entertainment was also given for those who came to buy things. The proceeds were added to the endowment fund that the graduates had started. Founders Day took place again in November as it had every year. A public literary program was given, including a short Japanese play, an operetta in English with costumes of various countries and periods. A presentation by the English department of "A Midsummer Night's Dream," guided by Georgia Newbury, was another highlight, along with musical performances. At Thanksgiving time in the same month, the school-church brought fruit and vegetables for the poor and gave them to the Sendai orphanage. Several Christmas programs were held, one for the school-church and another for the school itself. Several baptism services took place throughout this year as well, but evangelism efforts were especially rewarded with the baptism of many students on January 1st, 1930.

For several years, Newbury had been developing the innovative oral method of English teaching in the *honka*. Several groups of teachers from local schools visited Shokei in the winter of 1930 and again in April to observe her work.[30]

Tohoku University Professor Tenshi Muraoka and Professor Sakusaburo Uchigasaki of Waseda University, a member of the Imperial Diet and one of the original members of Annie Buzzell's Bible class brought special lectures to the students. Lectures were also given by Shunpei Honma of Yamaguchi Prefecture, who was highly influenced by Shokei girls while listening to their hymn singing and seeing their positive attitude when he lived in Sendai. William Axling, American Baptist missionary, gave two strong addresses on Christianity during a tour of the area.[31]

It was also a big year in terms of changes in personnel. Long-time Japanese teachers Mr. Tatsusaburo Uchimura and Mr. Takeo Kon severed connections with Shokei after several years of stirring up dissention among

---

29. Newbury, "Ella O. Patrick School, Sendai," *Japan Baptist Annual* (1929) 35.

30. "Ella O. Patrick School, Sendai," *Japan Baptist Annual* (1930) 46–47.

31. Kawaguchi, "Shokei Jo Gakko," *Japan Baptist Annual* (1931) 80.

the teachers. Mr. Giichi Kanamori retired, while missionaries Haven and Ross went on furlough. Sadie Ross had taught part-time at the school for many years.[32] Newcomers included Louise Jenkins, who came in September 1928 to replace the China missionaries in the *koutouka* English course. Two years later she returned once again to Hinomoto Girls' School in Himeji where she had come from originally. Jenkins was tall and had very broad shoulders. She always wore a long shawl that reached down to her knees. Her hobby was astronomy, and she enjoyed looking at the stars with her students. Some students, in addition to feeling intimidated by her height, felt uncomfortable with her method of getting them to do their homework. If a student had not learned her lesson, she called the student out of the classroom after class was dismissed, laid her hand on the student's head, and prayed, "May God help you to learn your lesson." In a joking manner, the students passed along the message, "If you don't learn your lesson, you'll be prayed for in the hallway."[33]

Although Kawaguchi was not physically healthy, he found the strength to continue his successful guidance of the school through its many problems stemming from the loss of seasoned personnel and the lack of upfront leadership from Jesse. From 1930–1931, political trouble began brewing again in Japan. A patriotic front determined to squelch human rights and left-wing thinking, began stirring up nationalistic sentiments among the common people and young army officers. Groups espousing this nationalistic thinking attempted to cause confusion in the government through assassinations of liberal politicians supporting western ideas. Although all of this was confusing to the students, Kawaguchi was also able to successfully guide the students' thinking in these matters once again.

The staff was greatly encouraged by the reinforcements who arrived in 1930 and 1931. Dr. Kawaguchi reported that Mr. Yoshio Wajima of Tokyo Imperial University and Mr. Iwao Kawamura of Kyoto University joined the staff teaching history, philosophy, and psychology respectively.[34] With the departure of Haven, Alice Bixby came to help for a time. Bixby had spent most of her years at Hinomoto, but most recently she came from Soshin to help Shokei with its large music program. Her command of Japanese was a tremendous help, according to Kawaguchi. Another missionary who only stayed a year was the quiet but spirited Freda J. Clause. Clause came with a

32. Ibid., 45.

33. Chiba, interview by author.

34. Kawaguchi, "Shokei Jo Gakko," *Japan Baptist Annual* (1931) 77.

background in teaching and experience in library work. Shokei benefited from the help she gave in the rearrangement of the library that had been almost totally managed by alumnae. After a year, Clause went to Tokyo to study the Japanese language for two years. At the end of that period of service, she joined the staff of Tokyo Women's Christian College.[35]

At least there was new hope with the establishment of the *koutouka* in the Indiana building. But as the school moved into the 1930s, hope in the future of the school diminished due to finances, lack of missionary staff, and decreased enrollment. Newbury, however, continued to take time for personal interaction with the students. One way to do this was summer camping. Takayama in Miyagi Prefecture is a spacious camp on the Pacific Ocean about twenty miles northeast of the center of Sendai. It has cabins used by missionaries for rest during the summer. It began in 1889 and was incorporated in 1907. Three missionaries, Nellie Fife, Mr. R. Halsey, and Mr. E. H. Jones from the WABFMS and ABFMS were on the original committee to establish the area for missionaries in conjunction with the local village. Many missionaries over the years from Shokei spent their summer vacations there for rest and relaxation. In the 1932 issue of *Japan Baptist Annual*, she reported that one of the highlights of the year was taking a group of girls camping to this seaside missionary retreat. There, not only did they have discussions and worship together, but learned how to cook over an open fire in the rain![36]

35. Freda Clause to Sandberg, 25 March 1933, BIM Correspondence File.

36. Newbury, "Ella O. Patrick Girls' School, Sendai," *Japan Baptist Annual* (1932) 7–9, BIM Correspondence File.

Missionaries socializing in the Ella O. Patrick Home missionary residence (about 1925). L to R: Thomasine Allen, Winifred Acock, Margaret Haven, Ella Gifford, Georgia Newberry (courtesy of Shokei Gakuin)

5

Interlude (1930–1937)

"Forget the former things;
do not dwell on the past.
See, I am doing a new thing!
Now it springs up; do you not perceive it?
I am making a way in the desert
and streams in the wasteland."

ISAIAH 43:18–19 (NIV)

This chapter is so named to indicate the period of time when Shokei seemed to lose its vision for the future. In the early 1930s when Mary Jesse was absent from Shokei, nothing of significance seemed to be happening at the school, almost as if it were experiencing a "Great Depression" like that in the United States. Although cheerful, capable Japanese and missionary leadership remained at Shokei, their guiding spirit, Mary Jesse, was absent. As Shokei's reputation rose, so did tuition, until Shokei had the highest tuition in the province. The economy of northern Japan was not healthy. There was economic depression and famine everywhere, but not everything was bleak. The students remained active and involved with many service projects. While the Japanese war was accelerating in Manchuria, Shokei's internal affairs began to improve under leadership of a new principal, Mr. Kensuke Ando. For these two or three years, because of the war, the economy had a short period of growth, with Shokei being the beneficiary. The alumnae and parents rallied in support of the endowment fund. As the graduates increased in number and became more active as alumnae, they all reached deeper into their own pockets to help out their school. The school trustees appealed to the churches in America, but the churches there were also trying to feed their own congregations. So, the trustees began cutting costs. These included dismissing high-salaried teachers and cutting into the curriculum. As noted before, the music department was the first to go, along with Alice Bixby.[1]

FORSAKEN BUT NOT WITHOUT HOPE

The school seemed like a microcosm of society at the time. Losses seemed more prominent than gains. However, good news and positive efforts were seldom lacking.

Feelings of Loss. One cannot help but ask why Jesse stayed in the background from the time the Indiana Building was dedicated until her next furlough. The last mention of her activities was in 1929, found in a 1930 issue of the *Japan Baptist Annual*. There she is mentioned as having a Bible class of young men at the Hokusei (North Star) Baptist Church, where several of her students followed Christ in baptism. Mission magazines usually contain reports of missionary furloughs and transfers, but nothing is publicly recorded about her leaving on furlough in 1931. According to her Missionary Register Card used to report missionary data and movement, she sailed from Kobe on July 2nd, 1931 and arrived in New York on September 21st, 1931.[2] A letter from Freda Clause tells us the reason for the extended trip. Jesse left on a regular furlough but took Misao Sato with her. Misao Sato had been at the school from its inception as a small child of seven, and was presently a music teacher there. Starting in Hong Kong, they made their way back through Europe to the east coast of the United States. As a thank-you gift for Sato's years of dedicated service, the alumnae gave her the chance to study at the Baptist Mission Training School.[3]

Now a dispirited school faced both the temporary loss of Jesse and their long-time loyal student and music teacher, Misao Sato. But as we shall see later, the resignation of Principal Kawaguchi in 1935 and the welcoming

1. Wynd, *Seventy Years*, 231.

2. Missionary Register Card, Jesse, BIM, Archival Collections of ABHS.

3. Freda Clause to Minnie Sandburg, August 1931, BIM Correspondence File. The Baptist Mission Training School, founded in 1881 in Chicago, Illinois, was a training school for women who felt called to the ministry and missions at a time when society thought it unacceptable. Many women missionaries had training there before going into service overseas.

of Kensuke Ando, the next principal, ended these few years of real pain. The resignation of Georgia Newbury, the only "veteran" missionary left at Shokei, followed.

Until Newbury resigned, she was so totally engrossed in activity with the students that she hardly noticed that other missionaries were unhappy with her. She always took the needs of the students seriously, but seemed to ignore problems resulting in the breakdown in relationships with other missionaries that her strong personality caused. After Newbury left, several experienced people and one new recruit were sent to Shokei for short periods of service.

Closing of Afternoon Sunday Schools. Even before the foundation of the school, Lavinia Mead and other missionaries had begun Sunday schools on Sunday afternoon in the outskirts of Sendai. From the beginning, students from the school helped with these Sunday schools as part of their own leadership and spiritual development. During the 1920s, the *koutouka* students carried on the work, and beginning in 1930, the student YWCA at Shokei took over the Sunday schools; however, due to the lack of funds, they had to close many of them. Each Sunday afternoon, a room was rented in various areas of town for one yen (fifty cents in 1931). That winter, the students came to Newbury with the problem of finances. In addition to the room fee, money was needed to buy small cards or pamphlets for the children to take home. The students had exhausted their own resources. After consultation, all except three of the Sunday schools were closed down. Newbury promised to help with the deficit when necessary to keep the three schools open. In this way, at least some of this ministry was preserved.[4]

Service, Scholarship, and Celebration. The students' fervor for service never waned during these years. One letter written by Helen Wilson tells of some of the activities of the girls in the YWCA. For Doll Festival Day on March 3rd, the girls planned to give dolls to poor girls confined to hospital beds. They each purchased a doll and together made clothes for them. They gave each doll a name as enthusiastically as if they were choosing their own names. After they admired the dolls and took pictures, they distributed them in a government hospital. This same group made a large scrapbook containing samples of typical Japanese things, and together with silk bookmarks on which they had written their favorite Bible verses, sent

---

4. Newbury to Sandburg, 8 April 1932, BIM Correspondence File.

it to a church in America. A similar scrapbook arrived from America for each of the girls.[5]

Scholarship among the students began to fall. To stimulate scholarship, the Shokei faculty developed a significant incentive. If a student's grades did not fall below the eighty-percentile mark and she maintained a grade average of over 90 percent, half of her tuition would be waived. Three girls in the student body (two of them sisters), who were commuting to school from the local orphanage, reached this goal.[6]

Shokei participated with the rest of the community in observing "Sympathy Week." Students collected money and used clothing, and the girls in the "Y" repaired the donated clothes. As in past years, members of both the *honka* and *koutouka* went to the national YMCA camp at Gotemba near Mount Fuji for their summer biennial conference. Other girls put on a Vacation Bible School for community children. Throughout this year, the Christian students took turns leading the chapel service once a week.[7] The yearly "Special Evangelism Week" was held in January 1933, with Rev. Saburo Imai of Aoyama Gakuin College[8] in Tokyo coming as the special speaker for the week. As a result, twenty-eight girls were baptized.[9]

In December 1933, much to the delight and relief of the Japanese nation, a male heir to the throne was born to Emperor Hirohito. Shokei also joined the larger community of Sendai in celebrating the birth.[10]

From Seeds to Fruit. When bad news is common, good news is welcomed. A certain student named Miss Ito (no first name is recorded) graduated from the domestic science department in 1926 at the time when many students had become Christians. Although a small person in stature, this graduate had a big heart which richly abounded with the spirit of Christ. After graduation, she went to live with her father and taught at a high school in a tiny village north of Sendai. There was no Christian work in the whole district, so she began to invite the children of the primary school to her home. She taught them hymns and told them the story of

5. Helen Wilson, "Shokei Jogakkou, Sendai," *Japan Baptist Annual* (1933) 41.

6. Ibid. This orphanage is presently known as Ikuji-en.

7. A. C. B. (Alice C. Bixby), "Sendai Girls' School" *Japan Baptist Annual* (1934) 23–24.

8. Aoyama Gakuin was founded in 1874 by Methodist missionary Dora E. Shoonmaker.

9. WABFMS, "Miss Anne S. Buzzell," *Sixty-Fourth Annual Report of the Board*, (1934–1935) 72–73.

10. Newbury to Constituency, 5 January 1934, BIM Correspondence File.

Christ. In the spring of 1933, a nurse at the Imperial University Hospital came to Newbury and asked to be baptized. When asked where she first heard of Christianity, she replied that she had attended Ito's class in that small village while in primary school.[11] Graduates sprinkled all over the northeast were quietly exerting their influence as they planted roots deep and watched them grow.

EFFORTS TO SAVE THE SCHOOL

The Woman's American Baptist Foreign Mission Board found that it could not keep up with the needs of the school without them making some changes. Student enrollment for the last few years had dropped drastically, and teacher's salaries were at their lowest. The school and WABFMS took strong measures to save Shokei in these financially difficult years. Totally closing the school was never considered, but drastic cuts were encouraged, while support originating in Japan was demanded by the WABFMS.

Increased Enrollment. In private schools, it has always been the responsibility of the teachers to make efforts in advertising the school by visiting public schools from where students might be applying. The year 1934 opened with a ray of hope when the largest class in five years was admitted. A great deal of time and effort was put into calling in the homes of students who were possible candidates for the domestic science and English courses in the *koutouka*. Both missionaries and Japanese staff with a group of graduates followed up on every lead given to them. They brought in thirty new students. It was a welcome sign after the previous year's enrollment had dropped to a ten-year low.[12] Extra efforts were made to acquaint the community with Shokei. To promote the school, fourth-year students in the *honka* gave a public choral concert in Sendai City. In December, senior students at two local high schools were invited to visit classes, see a musical performance and have a meal at the foreigners' house.[13] All of the efforts by teachers, alumnae, and missionaries contributed toward the increased enrollment.

Reducing Repair Costs. In an attempt to avoid repair costs, there appears to be plans to tear down the Ella O. Patrick building which had been used as a missionary home, dormitory, and classrooms for over forty years.

11. Newbury, "Annual Report," 15 July 1934, BIM Correspondence File.

12. Newbury to Maine, 7 April 1934, BIM Correspondence File.

13. Alice C. Bixby, "Sendai Girls' School," *Japan Baptist Annual* (1934) 23.

When the alumnae heard about this, they were very disappointed. Anne Buzzell wrote from Tono to the alumnae attempting to console them. She reminded them of the rich history of the house, which included several memorable weddings: "its mission fulfilled, its work ended . . . The old shell goes," she said, "but the life that was nurtured there for so many years goes on growing, multiplying, sending out new branches, new influences in every direction."[14] For some reason, the plan was not carried out. But the record shows that in 1934, rooms were rented out to foreigners in Sendai for the purpose of accumulating funds for repairs.[15]

In that same year, a robbery occurred at the Ella O. Patrick building. The burglar stole money and goods from the missionaries. Newbury wrote a lengthy letter about the actual condition of the building and what the police said about the reasons for the robbery.[16] In response to this letter, the Board granted the school money for a fence to be put up around the house and for a few other needed repairs. The home office also suggested that rental money be used for other repairs not covered by this grant.[17] (This iconic building was not taken down until 2013, when a replica of it was built on Shokei University Campus.)

Proposal of Amalgamation with Miyagi Jogakkou. In their attempts to escape their heavy financial burden in foreign countries, the WABFMS made a major proposal. In a letter dated April 3rd, 1933 from Foreign Secretary Minnie Sandburg, we learn that the home boards of American Baptist and German Reformed Church in America under which Miyagi Jogakkou (another mission school in Sendai) existed, had communicated with both the Japanese and missionaries about a plan to combine the two schools. They felt that duplication of departments in these schools was a waste of money. Sandburg writes about her hopes:

> I hope that the Japanese who are interested in these schools will understand fully the attitude of the boards in such a move as this and will cooperate, instead of making it more difficult. We simply cannot continue to provide so much money for education work in Japan, and even if we could, it would hardly seem justifiable to duplicate unnecessarily. I think all of you who are associated with

14. Annie Buzzell, preface, to Shokei Alumnae, *Mutsumi no Kusari* 23 (1932) n.p.

15. Newbury to Maine, 7 April 1934, BIM Correspondence File.

16. Ibid.

17. Acting Foreign Secretary (Grace Maine) to Newbury, 7 June 1934, BIM Correspondence File.

these schools will be able to help the graduates in forming their attitude toward them.[18]

Georgia Newbury was doing the corresponding with Sandburg and was instrumental in relaying the feelings of the principal and faculty. Fortunately, the plans were never carried out.[19] Because of the rivalry between the schools and because the schools' own separate historical identities were so well established, amalgamation would have been unthinkable. This suggestion would have changed the history and character of both schools forever.

Removal of the *Koutouka* Recommended. Pressure from the Mission Board for drastic measures to cut costs continued. Again, in October 1934, Acting Foreign Secretary Grace Maine commented about Shokei's serious condition. American Baptists were already contributing substantially toward the Women's Christian College in Tokyo, she said, and therefore it was not right to also support duplicate courses in Shokei's *koutouka*:

> Certainly the overlapping in the Higher Department should be eliminated, and girls who are ready for college should get their full training at the Women's Christian College. . . There is so much overlapping now in Sendai. . . Sendai Girls' School received this year almost twice the amount that was granted to either the Himeji school[Hinomoto] or the Yokohama school [Soshin]. This must be because of the Higher Department. I hope that it will be possible for [it] to be eliminated, thus reducing the expenses of the school.[20]

Even though few people at that time knew of the Mission Board's desire to eliminate the *koutouka*, many were keenly aware of the severe financial problems. From an historical perspective, we can sense the importance to Shokei of the success of the endowment fund movement to Shokei because it started at the grassroots level. Its success would enable the *koutouka* to continue.

Endowment and Interlocking Issues. As early as 1928, the alumnae established a fund for endowment of the school to help the school become financially independent from the Woman's American Baptist Foreign

---

18. Foreign Secretary (Minnie Sandburg) to Newbury, 3 April 1933, BIM Correspondence File.

19. Newbury to Maine, 7 April 1934, BIM Correspondence File.

20. Maine to Newbury, 3 October 1934, BIM Correspondence File.

Mission Society.[21] They added seven thousand yen[22] to the fund in 1929 and continued adding a little each year until the school could establish a tangible goal.[23] In addition to private donations, proceeds from the annual fall bazaar were contributed to the fund. The Fiftieth Anniversary to be held in 1942 was still eleven years away but the leadership thought it would be a suitable time to celebrate Shokei's independence. An additional fifty thousand yen would still be needed.[24] The alumnae were already in the process of formulating more specific plans for future goals. However, action necessary to reach the goal took more time than the Mission Board anticipated. So, in 1934, while feeling strangled by its own financial burdens, the Mission Board requested that the school become financially independent in four years.[25]

According to Newbury in an August 10th, 1934 letter, when Dr. Kawaguchi received the four-year ultimatum, he wrote to Grace Maine that four years would be impossible in his view. At least eight years would be needed. Newbury thought that even eight years was too short. His plea was declined. However, things changed rapidly when Mr. Kensuke Ando became principal of the school in 1935. A plan was drafted to ask each graduate to donate three sen three rin[26] each day, or one yen[27] per month.[28] It was estimated that by the Fiftieth Anniversary, with the help of teachers, parents, and the Society of Friends and Supporters, not just fifty thousand

21. "Ella O. Patrick School, Sendai," *Japan Baptist Annual* (1930) 47.

22. According to Dr Mochizuki, the yen/dollar value in 2009 of what the alumnae added was 40,180 yen, or $429 dollars (see chapter 3 note 7).

23. Newbury to Constituency, 8 April 1933, BIM Correspondence File.

24. Newbury to Constituency, 25 February 1931, BIM Correspondence File.

25. Newbury to Maine, 7 April 1934.

26. One hundred *sen* = one yen; one thousand *rin* = one yen. The *sen* and *rin* coins were put into circulation in 1871 and taken out of circulation beginning in 1954 ("Japanese Yen," http://en.wikipedia.org/wiki/Japanese_yen#cite_note-11).

27. According to Dr Mochizuki, the yen/dollar value in 2009 was six yen to under one cent (see chapter 3 note 7). Each person then donated less than one cent a day.

28. Kentsuke Ando, "Issen no Kaiin Shoshi ni" ("To the One Thousand Alumnae!"), *Mutsumi no Kusari* 26 (1935) 4.

yen,[29] but one hundred thousand yen[30] could be raised.[31] Enthusiasm and help was generated to the extent that the school reached its goal by September 1940, two years earlier than planned.

The problem surrounding the endowment fund and becoming financially independent from the Board was only one of many interrelated problems. Newbury believed that Kawaguchi was one of the finest Christians one could find, but he did not have the executive ability to handle these present crises. In addition, he was not able to cope with the discouragement of the faculty.[32] They were as burdened as the leadership was over the decline in enrollment, skyrocketing school fees, and cuts being made to save money. Morale was at a low ebb, and he did not know how to restore the enthusiasm of former years.

SHOKEI—ALWAYS ON HER MIND

Between 1931 and 1935, even though Jesse was not physically present at Shokei, her heart and mind were occupied with Shokei. She spent these years reflecting on the tumultuous twenties and early thirties, and then found her way back to Japan with another mission board before returning to Shokei. She wrote numerous letters to the Mission Board, now regarding her ideas and feelings relating to Shokei as if she were still there, active on campus. During her previous term of service, something had not been right. She wanted to find out what it was. By the time she did, the WABFMS could not send her back due to dwindling finances.

Sorting Things Out. As previously mentioned, in 1934 she wrote to the Baptist Mission Board, expressing great dismay at the Reference Committee's decision to take Alice Bixby out of Shokei without discussing the matter with the school.[33] Her many letters to the board secretary, Grace Maine, help to clarify her concerns and feelings about Shokei. She had left on a regularly scheduled furlough, truly wondering if she could ever return. She felt that she no longer had a role to play there. On one

29. According to Dr Mochizuki, the yen/dollar value in 2009 of what they had planned to raise to support the school was 400,500 yen, or $4279 (see chapter 3, note 7).

30. According to Dr Mochizuki, the yen/dollar value in 2009 of what was raised was 801,000 yen, or $8,559 (see chapter 3, note 7).

31. Newbury, letter to Constituency, 10 August 1934, BIM Correspondence File.

32. Ibid.

33. Jesse to Maine, 15 January 1934, BIM Correspondence File.

hand, Shokei desperately needed her guidance, but the board in America had encouraged her to make the school less dependent upon her.[34] She left on the pretense that she now needed to be with her mother who was ill. But before she even reached America, her sister's husband died suddenly, making it possible for her sister to care for her mother.[35] How she spent her first two years in America is made clear, thanks to one letter written to the alumnae and published in their magazine, *Mutsumi no Kusari*. There she says, "Both mother and sister are better, so that I can give my time freely to the things I want to do. I enjoy the garden, reading, and often, too, I speak about Japan in the churches in and around Ashland and Richmond. I spoke three times this week and have four appointments for next week."[36] She also wrote to the WABFMS Board in 1934 that, after her first eight months at home, she realized that she might be unable to return to Japan. At that time, she asked the board to take her off salary. She listed her reasons as follows:

- She was tired of problems and wanted to get away from it all.

- The whole outlook for the work (in Sendai) was discouraging and people generally did not seem to realize it. Churches such as those in Indiana, which had provided strong support, expected a glowing account of the school, and facts did not justify this. She felt that she had little to say that would help, so she did not want to attempt deputation work (later, however, she did do some deputation).

- She was needed at home because of one sister's illness, and later because of the illness and death of another sister.

- She felt that those missionaries who are still working in other countries have bills to pay there. So, they should have all available money. All of those who are home (in the United States on furlough) need to make a sacrifice for them, take cuts in salary, etc., to allow all the work in foreign countries to continue.[37]

Her salary redirected to them would help the financial problems of the American Board.

She could do without salary for a while and was glad to be able to help out, she said. Other missionaries were being detained in the United States

---

34. Jesse to Sandburg, 31 May 1933, BIM Correspondence File.

35. Jesse to Sandburg, 20 April 1933, BIM Correspondence File.

36. Jesse to Shokei alumnae, *Mutsumi no Kusari* 24 (1933) 3.

37. Jesse to Maine, 12 May 1934, BIM Correspondence File.

and not allowed to return to their country of service or were overseas where they were being asked to stay for a year or two longer to avoid having to pay her passage. Jesse wanted to be put on the same basis as other detained missionaries.[38]

In an April 6th, 1933 letter, she tells of investigating the possibility of returning to Japan with the YWCA or a college in Kobe.[39] Later in the same month, Dr. Kawaguchi wrote urging her to return. Someone asked her if she would consider going to Tono following Annie Buzzell's retirement. The Board could not give her any definite answers as to when she could return, so she wanted an opportunity to talk with them in person about her ideas.[40]

People at Shokei were puzzled at her seeming unwillingness to return. Her thinking on this subject is difficult to piece together from her letters. Several unresolved issues seem to surface: First, when the Board handed over leadership of the school to the Japanese in 1926, there had been no clear policy established regarding the role of the missionary, nor the Board and school's financial responsibilities. That was causing endless problems at Shokei, which she felt were not related to missionary personnel problems. Her leaving in 1931 may have relieved the problems at the school.[41] It was now easier to tell who had authority, but how would the bills be paid, she thought, and how could future expansion take place without a crisis occurring with each new project? Secondly, it seems that the Board could not send her back to Japan because of its own financial constraints, but wanted to keep her on the active missionary list until the time that funds became available to send her back. Thirdly, she still could not resolve her feelings of anxiety toward what had happened between herself and the other missionaries and between herself and the school before she left.[42] Regarding this third point, Jesse decided to consult with two different respected psychiatrists about the problems. Both psychiatrists agreed that she was running away from the problems, adjustments needed to take place, and that her return to Japan was absolutely essential. They too agreed that she had taken the situation at Sendai too seriously. However, they differed in opinion as to how adjustments should be made. Lastly, they advised that

38. Jesse to Sandburg, 6 April 1933, BIM Correspondence File.
39. Ibid.
40. Jesse to Sandberg, 20 April 1933, BIM Correspondence File.
41. Ibid.
42. Jesse to Sandburg, 31 May 1933, BIM Correspondence File.

she have frank and objective dialog with the Board, since the situation at Shokei was the Board's responsibility and not hers.[43] Because of the lack of finances of the WABFMS and because of the necessity to solve her problems in Japan, Jesse began looking for a way to get back to Japan through a different organization.

A Way Back—Misunderstood Motives. She investigated the possibilities of a short-term position as a contract English teacher with the Southern Baptist Convention. Although she often found herself thinking of the burdened teachers at Shokei and the heavy responsibility they must bear, she asked Grace Maine about how the Board would view her being "temporarily" lent to the Southern Baptist Convention. She worried about it seeming "disloyal." But "a real need is to me a challenge. I want to help out somewhere; to spend my time usefully."[44]

Accordingly, beginning in June 1934, several letters were exchanged between the Southern Baptist Executive Secretary, Dr. Charles E. Maddry, and Grace Maine regarding "former missionary" Mary Jesse going to the girls' school in Kokura, Japan.[45] In one letter Maine explicitly states that the WABFMS finds it impossible to return Mary Jesse to Japan at that time.[46] Shortly, Jesse wrote to Kawaguchi about going to Kokura in southern Japan. His distress is clearly seen in the following reply that Jesse forwarded to Maine:

> The letter which reached me this morning gives me an intense disappointment. How could you go to a Southern school? We cannot let you go to any other school. We must have you come to this school if it is possible for you to leave home at all. Do please come to us!! . . . We needed you when you were here and we have been in need of you ever since you left us. There is no change in this . . . Soon after I received your letter I spoke to Miss Sato with regard to your letter. She is completely upset over the matter in the same way as I . . . We hope to make this such a school [self-supporting] by the 50th Anniversary in the fall of 1942. To this end we are organizing a Promoters' Association . . . We want you to become our advisor . . . Please come and help make this school stand on its

---

43. Jesse to Sandburg, 20 April 1933, BIM Correspondence File.

44. Jesse to Maine, 12 May 1934, BIM Correspondence File.

45. Charles Maddry to Maine, 8 June 1934, BIM Correspondence File of Mary D. Jesse.

46. Maine, carbon copy of letter to Maddry, 11 June 1934, BIM Correspondence File of Mary D. Jesse.

own feet. This is your school. For this school you gave your best. Please come and give your most matured self for this school which you love so dearly.[47]

He followed this letter to Jesse with a letter to Grace Maine hinting that he felt betrayed:

Ever since she left us three years ago on her furlough, it has been our great wish to have her return to us at an earliest possible date; but to our deep regret, her personal health, the condition in her family and relatives, and some other considerations have retained her in America, and we were of the opinion that these were the main reasons for her stay in the homeland. And yet through her personal letter . . . I understand that some of these considerations have been removed and I learned that she is ready to return to Japan. By this letter, to my intense disappointment and complete surprise, she is considering to accept a call of the Southern Board to work at one of its schools in this country. We feel that it is absolutely impossible for us to let her accept this call of the Southern Board. We are fully convinced that if she were to return to Japan at all, she must come to work with us here at this school . . . If any adjustment in the missionary or in the native personnel is needed to make her return to this school easier, I believe that such an adjustment should be made.[48]

This was followed by a letter to the officers of the Woman's American Baptist Foreign Mission Society from the faculty of Shokei pleading for them to return Jesse to Shokei.[49]

This reaction, of course, distressed her greatly, for she never intended to offend Shokei, but she knew that going to another school and using another board's money was a way of getting to Japan without her board having to pay the bill. She had not officially resigned because she still held on to the slight hope that American Baptists could send her back to Shokei someday. She wanted to be considered as a "loan" to the position of teacher of English for the Southern Baptist Board from the American Baptist Board, thus avoiding the necessity of resigning and reapplying.[50] The exchange of letters

47. Jesse, excerpts of letter to Maine, July 1934, BIM Correspondence File.

48. Ukichi Kawaguchi to Maine, 7 July 1934, BIM Correspondence File of Mary D. Jesse.

49. Members of the Faculty of Shokei School to Officers of the Woman's American Baptist Foreign Mission Society, 12 July 1934, BIM Correspondence File of Mary D. Jesse.

50. Jesse to Maine, 20 July 1934, BIM Correspondence File.

between Grace Maine and Dr. Maddry indicates that the Board approved of the "loan." Dr. Kawaguchi wanted her to do public relations work and fund-raising in the United States for the school, but she wrote to him again, saying that she was not the person to do fund-raising for the school, and that she would consider coming back when the school got back on its feet. "We must be loyal to the Cause, not just to the local work." she wrote.[51] This rather sharp comment likely came from a very harried Jesse. For very soon afterward, in August, with little time for preparations, she left for Kokura, Japan.[52]

NEW LIGHT FOR A DARK AGE

Without the presence of Jesse, Shokei tended to look more inward instead of outward and upward. Key figures came and left, each contributing their own efforts to make Shokei a better school.

Ukichi Kawaguchi's Resignation. The resignation of Kawaguchi and the installation of the new principal, Mr. Kentsuke Ando, during this same school year created great changes for Shokei. The circumstances under which Kawaguchi left were regrettable, but not unexpected. Newbury was the only missionary at Shokei in the first half of 1935, because Bixby and Wilson had left in 1934. She became the chief confidante of Kawaguchi.[53] In her words,

> I can't tell you the hours he has spent either here in my study or the number of times he has called me to his office to pour out his troubles, and disappointments. Etc. etc. . . . While knowing that the trustees were doing what was right and best for the school, I felt that I must be patient and sympathetic with him for after all his [time here] has been a most faithful service.[54]

This statement seems to indicate that the School Board of Trustees asked or urged Kawaguchi to resign.

Ando the Builder. Although the departure of Ukichi Kawaguchi seemed regrettable to many, the coming of Mr. Kensuke Ando was highly

---

51. Jesse to Maine, 29 July 1934, BIM Correspondence File.

52. Jesse to Maine, 28 October 1934, BIM Correspondence File.

53. Newbury to Maine, 13 February 1935, BIM Correspondence File.

54. Ibid.

celebrated. His coming did for Shokei what an intravenous feeding does for a person who is ill. One missionary described it in this way:

> The largest first year class Shokei Jo Gakkou in Sendai Japan has ever had; more of a Christ-like spirit growing among the students and teachers; improvements being made to the buildings and grounds; even a new building being under construction! The cause is a short smiling fatherly-looking man often seen walking around the campus thinking of things that would make it be a better school. You ask him how he has done all this when a year ago it all looked so hopeless? With a light shining in his eyes he will answer, "Faith in God."[55]

Kentsuke Ando was born in a small village, the fourth son in a poor family of ten children. He had to work his way through school but managed to attend a government school in Tokyo. His brother lived with a Christian family in Yokohama who selflessly cared for him. This caused young Ando to wonder what this "new religion" was like. His brother became ill. Wanting to visit him but without the money to do so, Ando set out walking the twenty miles in the hot summer sun. As a gift to the family, he brought a large white radish (daikon) that was about four feet long. Here this ambitious young man was walking twenty miles to see his brother, perspiration rolling from his brow and the leaves of the radish slowly withering under the rays of the blazing hot sun. To his surprise, the family had taken exceptional care of his brother even though his illness made extra work for the family. He attended the family prayers and asked his brother many questions about the new religion. The following year, Ando also began to live with the Ukawa family. One day Mr. Ukawa took him to visit Clara Converse, principal of Soshin Girls' School. Mr. Ando always recalled what she had said to him, "You learn great things in school but the most important thing is to know God."[56] At age twenty-one he was baptized into the Christian faith, and from that time on was filled with the desire to tell the people of Japan about Christ.

Ando came to Shokei having sacrificed an illustrious career. He was a member of Tokyo's Yotsuya Church, where Newbury first met him when she was studying Japanese.[57] Before coming to Shokei, Ando was a teacher in elementary schools in Tokyo. Tokyo Metropolitan Educational Au-

55. Margaret Cuddeback, "Annual Report," October 1936, BIM Correspondence File.
56. Ibid.
57. W. A. (Winifred Acock), "Ando the Builder," *Japan Baptist Annual* (1936) 7–8.

81

thorities knew him for his administrative ability and creativity. After nearly two-thirds of the city, including his school, was destroyed in the 1923 Great Kanto Earthquake, the authorities gave him a large sum of money and asked him to use it in the area where his school had been destroyed. He used part of the money to rebuild the homes destroyed by the quake, and then used the rest to build the best school in Tokyo, in an area where scarcely a building or family had been left untouched by the quake.[58] The new school eventually enrolled one thousand seven hundred students with vocational training for both boys and girls. During this project, the National Department of Education asked him to organize the primary school principals from around the country. They provided him with an assistant principal so he could be released for this new work. He traveled all around the country, helping raise the level of efficiency of these principals and teaching them character-building skills. He never hid his Christian testimony, and sometimes faced strong opposition.[59]

He stepped out of this limelight to accept the job as principal at troubled Shokei. He received one-third less salary with no pension. His goal was to build the best school possible, not based on numbers, but based on Christian character. One of the first things Principal Ando did after arriving was to interview three hundred of Sendai's educators, businessmen, professional men, newspapermen, and heads of families asking for their criticism of the school and their suggestions for future development.[60]

Next, he began to reorganize courses to train the students to fit more precisely into life in the North. Some of these changes included the addition of a kindergarten-training course and commercial courses to the *koutouka*.[61] In the spring of 1936, families were having difficulty affording the five-year *honka* course, so it was reduced to four years. The hardship was due to famine and typhoons that had racked the North.[62] The new courses, however, moved Ando toward his next goal, which was to have a student body of six hundred by 1940. There was also a shift in the names used for each department. "*Honka*" was dropped and "*koutou jogakubu*" now referred to the four-year junior high department. "*senkoubu*" was now

---

58. Cuddeback, "Report," October 1936, BIM Correspondence File.

59. W. A. (Winifred Acock), "Ando the Builder," *Japan Baptist Annual* (1936) 7.

60. Ibid., 8.

61. WABFMS, "Sendai," Sixty-Fifth Annual Report of the Board (1935–1936) 109.

62. Cuddeback to Mrs. Charles Humphreys, 5 March 1936, BIM Correspondence File.

the name used for the higher education department that would eventually become the junior college. Already numbers of applications for the year 1937 had increased. He planned a new building, even though money was tight. He had already set an endowment fund goal of one million yen. In September 1935, he urged all people interested in helping to save the school to join The Society of Friends and Supporters and save one yen monthly for the endowment fund.[63]

Ando and the Faculty. Mr. Ando's care of the faculty was particularly noteworthy. He was known as one who always put others' needs before his own and delighted in providing something special and personal. For example, in 1936, when financial problems were at their worst, bonuses that were typical for Japanese companies could not be afforded at Shokei. Mr. Ando, feeling deeply for the plight of the teachers, gave each of them a bonus from his own pocket. Mrs. Ando brought a special touch to dreary faculty meetings by providing a rare treat of a cup of piping hot coffee for each teacher.[64] Coffee was a luxury that was hard to come by. We can imagine their delight, knowing that a cup of coffee was approximately four hundred fifty times the cost of a cup of green tea.[65] The Andos had a relative in Brazil who occasionally sent the coffee to them.

Despite the excitement that surrounded new hopes for the school, the Japanese teachers watched with consternation as a period of instability upset the missionary community.

Georgia Newbury. Although most Japanese teachers remained on the faculty during the transition, the only missionary to see the differences between the Kawaguchi era and the Ando era was Newbury—albeit only for a short time. Just her presence provided stability during the period of transition and uncertainty. During the first several months of 1935, even with Ando's arrival, Newbury was feeling the sting of criticism from her missionary colleagues from outside of Sendai. The missionaries of the Baptist Missionary Woman's Joint Committee, a subdivision of the Reference Committee in Japan, said they would not invite her back to Japan after her furlough. To avoid unnecessary talk and rumors, they recommended that,

---

63. Ando, "Heikin Hitori Ichinichi San sen San Rin no Funpatsu" ("Efforts to Raise Three Sen Three Rin per Person"), *Mutsumi no Kusari* 26 (1935) 7–8.

64. Chiba, interview with the author, 28 March 1996.

65. Zukan Asahi Hen, *Nedan no Meiji*, 135–45.
Between 1935 and 1941, green tea sold for thirty-three *sen* for one hundred grams, approximately one hundred cups, while one cup of coffee sold for fifteen *sen*.

while on furlough in the United States, she quietly resign.[66] The committee had undoubtedly received complaints from missionaries in the past that Newbury's strong personality made it difficult for others to get along with her.[67] Margaret (Peggy) Cuddeback who came to Shokei from Mead Christian Center in Osaka had not been in Sendai more than a month when Newbury, tired of all the troubles with foreigners, tendered her resignation and bought a little house in the Kita San Banchou area just north of the school. There, with a Japanese friend, and her little dog, Nifty, she planned to live and continue serving the students and graduates at Shokei.[68] Although the news of Newbury's resignation was known among alumnae before this date, she wrote a letter on May 28th, 1935, informing the WABFMS Board of Managers of her resignation to be effective after summer activities were completed. She continued by listing her specific reasons for resigning:

> The Japan Baptist Mission is a political machine. It is organized in a very strange way, without any real head but with committees within committees. The very democracy of the mission is its greatest weakness. I find myself lost in this political machine. I do not know how to work with it; the political web has caught me; I cannot please those who are on the committees; my personality does not suit nor fit with their idea of mission work. . . . My relationship with the Japanese is most happy, and it is my firm intention to remain in Japan, if at all possible, and work for and with them.[69]

Having heard that Newbury was being asked to resign, some of the alumnae and students became very upset. They sent a letter to the American Board expressing their disappointment and anger at such a decision, and praised the work Newbury was doing.[70] Another followed this letter from her closest colleague, friend, and Shokei alumnus, Yo Suzuki. Her consternation and criticism of the Women's Committee is reflected in the following letter:

> As one of the few who know the truth of the things which have happened around here in Sendai, I feel it is a part of my duty to tell

66. Acock to Humphreys, 18 July 1935, BIM Correspondence File.

67. Ibid.

68. Kato, interview with the author, 13 June 1992.

69. Newbury to WABFMS Board of Managers, 28 May 1935, BIM Correspondence File.

70. Alumnae to Constituency, April 1935, BIM Correspondence File of Georgia Newbury.

you the truth which you Ladies over the sea would never know. Students, graduates, the new principal and the Japanese members of Trustees, all Japanese want Miss Newbury to stay in school longer, but for some reason the American members of [the] Trustees do not agree with them. Why does the Woman's Committee pigeon-hole the petitions about Miss Newbury? There are two or three woman missionaries who do not like Miss Newbury because of her characteristic personality and other personal reasons . . .

Why can't American missionaries work with her when the Japanese can work with her so nicely? . . . Didn't she come for us Japanese after all, not to serve the American missionaries in Japan? If the students ever get hold of the truth there will be a riot in the school.[71]

The Board did answer the alumnae's letter, but made no reference to the things that were troubling the graduates.[72] Perhaps they knew that not all Japanese wanted Newbury to stay! Alumnae from this era are quick to agree!

Nothing changed in the decision they had made. Afterward, some lengthy discussions continued by letter regarding what the amount of Newbury's retirement grant should be since, against the advice of the Board and the Women's committee, she had chosen to stay in Sendai after resigning. By the end of September 1935, Newbury had accepted a position as a teacher with the Canadian Presbyterian Mission in Tansui, Formosa.[73] In this way, she sadly ended a period of fruitful service spanning twelve years in Sendai and a total of fourteen years with the Woman's American Baptist Foreign Mission Society in Japan. Although it did not end happily for Newbury, her influence is still felt by Japanese colleagues and graduates even to this day. One wonders if her fruitful career might have been saved had there been a telephone available for consultation overseas!

Death of Annie Buzzell. Even though there were many memorable events during this period after Kensuke Ando became principal, one that stands out is the passing of first principal Annie Buzzell. She had moved to Sendai from Tono to reside in a house built for her by her devoted students

71. Yo Suzuki to Ladies of the Baptist Board of America, May 1935, BIM Correspondence File of Georgia Newbury.

72. Humphreys to Members of the Alumnae, 22 August 1935, BIM Correspondence File of Georgia Newbury.

73. Humphreys to Newbury, 5 December 1935, BIM Correspondence File of Georgia Newbury.

and friends just a year and a half before. On a cold day in early February 1936, she lost her battle against pneumonia, while her beloved friends surrounded her bed. People from all over Japan had already started to gather as they heard the news the previous day that her end was near. Over six hundred people came from as far away as Formosa and Manchuria and from all walks of life to attend the funeral at Shokei School and burial ceremony at the Christian section of the cemetery at Rinnoji Temple. Those who came to pay tribute to her life and the Christian legacy she left demonstrated Buzzell's impact on this small island of Japan. Missionaries Margaret Cuddeback and Goldie Nicholson were present at that time.

NEW MISSIONARY RECRUITS ASSIST IN THE ANDO ERA

The next three missionaries at Shokei all came with high recommendations. Margaret Cuddeback came from Mead Christian Center in June of 1935, two months before Newbury left Shokei, and stayed until her furlough one year later. After spending two years at Hinomoto Girls' School in Himeji, Goldie Nicholson began work at Shokei in September 1935 and stayed two years. Lora Patten arrived in November 1936, studying the language part-time while teaching, waiting for the return of Mary Jesse. Patten served until her furlough in the fall of 1940.

Margaret (Peggy) Cuddeback. Cuddeback, who came from Eugene, Oregon, felt called by God to service in Japan while at the Baptist Mission Training School in Chicago. She was only twenty-three years old at the time of application. The WABFMS rules allowed women from age twenty-four to become missionaries. However, the interview committee was so impressed with her that they hardly hesitated before approving the application of this energetic young woman who was too young. One of the members on the committee interviewing Cuddeback pointed out that "She will grow out of this handicap!"[74] With that comment and with one accord, Cuddeback was approved for a short term of three years to work at Mead Christian Center. Just before her furlough, she came to help with teaching English at Shokei for one year. Peggy Cuddeback is especially noted for the short history of the life of Annie Buzzell that she wrote upon Buzzell's death in February 1936.[75] She wrote little about her own time at Shokei because it

74. Cuddeback, interview with the author, 28 June 1996, Claremont, CA.

75. Cuddeback, "Beginnings of Work in Sendai Japan," May 1936, BIM Correspondence File.

was so short.[76] However, she did write tongue-in-cheek about how much she would be missed when she left Shokei:

> But life around the school will be much calmer when I do leave. For example, the other night we had guests and at the last minute I thought of the flowers that I was going to buy and had forgotten. You can't have a party without flowers so I thought of the grand flowers we had in the chapel that morning. School being about ten steps away from the house I walked over and borrowed them [from the high school chapel]. The next morning I went to the college chapel and after it was over, Goldie [Nicholson] came over from the high school and said that the chapel looked bare without any flowers that morning! I took them back and the teacher that is in charge of the chapel saw them the [following] morning, and in a surprised way said, "But where were they? The last time I looked they were gone.[77]

Goldie Nicholson. Nicholson was appointed to Sendai in 1932, but was reassigned to Hinomoto first, where she studied Japanese. When it was known that Newbury was leaving, the Baptist Woman's Committee asked her to help in Sendai. The graduates were informed about her coming in the letter written in response to their protest of the departure of Newbury. Nicholson helped Cuddeback to write Anne Buzzell's noted obituary. She always showed her appreciation of the work done by Kensuke Ando. In one of her joint reports with Cuddeback, she tells of the service of Mrs. Ando as well. It was her practice to write Bible verses, she wrote, in beautiful handwriting on a bulletin board out on the gateway in front of the school. "Large numbers of students and soldiers constantly walk by the school and during term examinations, students passing on their way to a near-by [sic] government school found a personal, helpful message in one of these verses."[78] She pointed out that this was just another of many personal touches this couple brought to Shokei that the missionaries thought noteworthy.

She records the surprise and excitement elicited because of Principal Ando's fast work in getting approval and funds for a new building. His justification for the need of the building during hard times and for receiving

---

76. Cuddeback, "Report," 28 January 1944, BIM Correspondence File. She wrote an extensive account of her experience during house arrest in Shanghai during World War II.

77. Cuddeback to Humphreys, 5 March 1936, BIM Correspondence File.

78. WABFMS, "Sendai," Sixty-Fifth Annual Report of the Woman's American Baptist Foreign Mission Society (1935–1936) 110.

a loan were invincible, she thought. More students were needed to generate revenue if the school was to become financially independent; the government would not approve of an increase in enrollment without a new building; no money was on hand for a new building; therefore, a loan from the WABFMS was their only solution. The loan was approved! This simple but clever reasoning secured the loan despite the school's indebtedness to the WABFMS. Nicholson and the new arrival, Lora Patten, watched the building of this new Kitakousha ("North building") that provided six new classrooms and two science labs. There was rejoicing that same month of January when forty-two students confessed their faith in Christ after three days of evangelistic meetings led by Rev. Yasumura of Mead Christian Center in Osaka. In the spring of 1937, a large class of one hundred seventy four new students created new challenges for the teachers due to a shortage of space and teachers. The total number of first and second year *honka* classes were more than twice the number of the other three classes combined.[79]

Lora Patten. Lora Patten was heartily welcomed by Goldie Nicholson and the Shokei faculty in November 1936. Patten's descriptions of the school and the times also make good reading. In one of her first letters she carefully notes cultural differences.

> One of the most striking things I notice on the train is the way in which many of the women sit. They stand at the seat, step out of the clogs they wear, calmly stand up straight on the seat, wrap their kimonos about them, drop with knees together, feet under them, and toes crossed in the rear. They usually have to drop sideways, for their big "bow" in the back, interferes with the process. If there is a baby on the back, it is still more complicated.
>
> One of the women in the seat with me took a long-stemmed pipe that looked like my school paint-brush, only there was a tiny bowl at the end, instead of the camel's hair. Several of the women smoke cigarettes on the train. One of the ways to tell a Christian here is that they seldom smoke . . .
>
> Did you know that the Japanese seldom have a horizontal fold in the eyelid as most of us have? They think that it is a very lucky sign if a child happens to be born with one.[80]

Even though she was a newcomer, she was soon given a large responsibility. Goldie Nicholson went on furlough only seven months after Patten's arrival. Until December 1937, Patten taught as many classes as she

79. Goldie M. Nicholson, "New!", *Japan Baptist Annual* (1937) 11.

80. Lora Patten to Constituency, 2 December 1936, BIM Correspondence File.

could, using a language helper two or three hours a day. Her hobby was stamp collecting. Believing that it would be a helpful project to earn money for the endowment fund, she engaged many of the students in this task. She encouraged the students as well as people in America to send all stamps to her for processing. After the stamps had been prepared, she would sell them to collectors for five yen per ten thousand stamps. More than the stamp collecting itself, she enjoyed spending many hours with the students involved in the project.[81]

Mary Jesse, whose term of teaching in the south in Shikoku had expired, was expected back in the fall, but her arrival was delayed because of her aging mother. Before the winter break, it was determined that Patten needed help with the classes, so Elizabeth Ray helped teach in January and February of 1938. With another large incoming class, and Jesse still absent, Thomasine Allen came down temporarily for three weeks from remote Kuji where she had started a new work. By the time Jesse arrived in May, Lora Patten relates, "the students could at least stand, sit, open their books when told [to in English]."[82]

Death of Kentsuke Ando. In April of 1937, Principal Ando was hospitalized. Nicholson's correspondence relates that his illness was not serious and that, because he had little pain, he could still conduct the affairs of the school from his hospital bed. He had a kind of breaking out on his arms, hands, and body that would not heal.[83] Sometimes when he was allowed out of the hospital, he came to school with bandages wrapped all over his face so that only his eyes, nose and mouth showed. Despite this condition, he continued to come and advise the teachers. November 8th, 1937, was truly a sad day for Lora Patten (the only remaining missionary), and for the faculty and students of Shokei Girls' School, because on that day Kentsuke Ando passed away. An autopsy revealed that a very rare disease of the internal organs caused his death.[84] With the help of a good economy, this man, who brought so much light, accomplished enough for a decade in only two and a half years. His accomplishments endured: confidence in Shokei within the Sendai community; increased enrollment of the student body to six hundred; government approval for several new courses in the *senkoubu* (upper division); a building that predecessors said would be impossible to

---

81. Patten to Constituency, 1 June 1937, BIM Correspondence File.
82. Patten to Constituency, July 1938, BIM Correspondence File.
83. Nicholson, "Report," June 1937, BIM Correspondence File.
84. Chiba, interview with the author, 28 March 1996.

build;" 'Society of Friends and Supporters" working for endowment; and the dream instilled in students and faculty that Shokei Jo Gakkou could be a leading Christian institution after all with God's help.

Georgia Newbery (1924–1935) (courtesy of Shokei Gakuin)

Alice Bixby (1931–1934), (1939–1941) (courtesy of Shokei Gakuin)

6

Clouds on the Horizon (1938–1941)

Mary Jesse (1938)
(courtesy of American Baptist Historical Society)

May God in his goodness guide!
The day will certainly dawn when Japan will emerge
from the dark cloud that at present envelopes her,
and make her contribution to the realization of world peace.

—TOYOHIKO KAGAWA[1]

1. Kagawa, *Christ and Japan*, 61.

T his chapter covers the years when the occupation of China by Japan had escalated into war. Privation became increasingly felt as people were asked to make more and more sacrifices to help advance the war. Principal Shigeto Takahashi was installed at Shokei, and Jesse returned to Shokei for her fourth term after a lengthy absence of six years. Basic supplies became hard to get. The attitude of the Japanese was changing, and interest in Christianity was on the decline. Then, Alice Bixby was welcomed back to Shokei just before Mary Jesse returned to the United States for her last furlough.

A NEW START WITH A NEW LEADER

A new principal has always stimulated new hope, which in turn stimulated growth. The news of the arrival of Principal Takahashi and Missionary Mary D. Jesse were especially welcomed.

Shigeto Takahashi Steps In. In April of 1938, Mr. Shigeto Takahashi became the next principal of Shokei Girls' School at age forty. He already had been assistant dean and head of the English department at the Second Middle School in Sendai. He became a Christian after reading the New Testament and works by Kanzo Uchimura, founder of the Non-church Movement (*mukyoukai*). He also was influenced by personal contact with American Baptist missionary Dr. Harry Baxter Benninghoff of Waseda Hoshien. He was baptized in 1920. For some years before becoming principal of Shokei, he served as a deacon of North Star Baptist Church near the school, and was a trustee at the school.[2] He served as Principal during some of Shokei's most trying times (1938–1949). Although he was a Christian, it took some time for him to get used to the programs and traditions of a Christian school. Although these were financially tough times, alumnae contributed three thousand yen[3] for him to spend on needs that he saw. They also gave money toward remodeling two rooms to teach etiquette. The Ella O. Patrick building was slightly remodeled to create dormitory space for the *senkoubu* (upper division, post-graduate diploma course) girls. Parents also gave seven hundred yen[4] for the completion of an athletic

2. Wynd, *Seventy Years*, 233.

3. According to Dr Mochizuki, the yen/dollar value in 2009 for donations by alumnae is 2,007,000 yen, or $21,444 (see chapter 3, footnote 7).

4. According to Dr Mochizuki, the yen/dollar value in 2009 for donations by parents

field that was the largest in the prefecture. Shokei had never been strong in sports, but in this particular year, they entered the "Girls Olympics" in Sendai and gained third place.[5] There was a small store at the school managed by alumnae where the girls could buy basic school supplies and snacks. Another change for this year included revising the system for the school store. Part of the dormitory was used for the store and a local private businessman took charge of the store, paying six hundred fifty yen[6] a year to the Graduates' Association from its profits.[7]

Enrollment continued to increase, with a total of two hundred twenty-five entering in 1938, and two hundred thirteen entering in 1939.[8] Therefore by the close of 1940, there were nearly nine hundred students.[9] Shokei was again scrambling to find more classroom space while other schools in town faced a crisis in decreased enrollment.

Jesse on the Move. Looking back for a moment, Mary Jesse had left the United States for the Southern-Baptist-related school in Kokura (presently, Seinan Gakuin) on the island of Shikoku in the summer of 1934, where she taught English as a three-year contract teacher. In the winter of 1936, just a year before her contract expired, Mabel Humphreys, the new foreign secretary of ABFMS, sent a letter asking Jesse if she would return to the Sendai field in the summer of 1937.[10] She replied in the affirmative that she felt ready, but hesitated because she said she lacked clear guidance from God about a decision. Her mother's health was still uncertain. Subsequently, she made a trip to Sendai and left some of her luggage there to assure the people at Shokei that she intended to return when God's guidance became clear.

The next letter on record is from the ship which took her back to America in July 1937 to care for her feeble mother.[11] After several months of care and rest, her mother insisted that she return to her work in Japan.

---

is 408,300 yen, or $5003 (see chapter 3, footnote 7).

5. WABFMS, "Japan," *Sixty-Eighth Annual Report of the Board—Along Kingdom's Highways* (1938–1939) 44.

6. According to Dr Mochizuki, the yen/dollar value in 2009 for yearly donation to the Graduates' Association was 4349 yen, or forty-six dollars (see chapter 3 note 7).

7. Report of the Board of Trustees, 1 May 1938 and 30 April 1939. Shokei Gakuin Archival Collection.

8. WABFMS, "Japan," *Sixty-Eighth Annual Report of the Board* (1938–1939) 44.

9. WABFMS, "Sendai" *Seventieth Annual Report of the Board* (1940–1941) 103–104.

10. Jesse to Humphreys, 10 January 1937, BIM Correspondence File.

11. Jesse to Humphreys, 25 July 1937, BIM Correspondence File.

Ten months later, in May of 1938, once again Jesse sailed the Pacific Ocean for Japan.[12]

Just as she was returning to Shokei, the war in China was escalating. Even on the ship, Chichibu Maru, she became more acutely aware of what she would find upon arrival. From her letter onboard ship she wrote:

> It wasn't easy leaving home. In fact it was the hardest thing I ever did. Mother was wonderfully brave, dressing and going to the train with me. She wanted me to go back to my work.
>
> I had a wonderful visit of five days with the Rosses in Los Angeles and saw lots of old friends who saw me off. Then we had two days in Frisco [San Francisco] and are due at Honolulu Sat. A.M., leaving that night. I am most anxious to get there [Japan]. I don't know what I will find. I do know that it will be the same Japan I left last summer. I know though that there will be many new opportunities, many sad hearts to cheer and comfort and I am glad that I can be there at this time of special need.
>
> As I listened to a group of [Japanese] men talking last night I realized as never before the tension, the strain all must live under. One had a son-in-law in the lines [China], several had suddenly been called home for work there, men who had been years in the US and who have more or less the American point of view. I wonder what attitude they will take there [in Japan]. They seem to think that the end of the war is near, that this big battle would be the last big engagement . . . Dr. & Mrs. [David B.] Schneder of Sendai are in first class . . . going back to Sendai to retire there . . . I hear that soap is scarce in Japan. Schneders are taking 200 cakes and lots of groceries, canned goods, etc. I hear that coal which was ¥14 a tin is now ¥30, wools [sic], meal, . . . are scarce. I like this boat very much.[13]

Pulling Things Together Again. Rampant inflation and many hardships awaited her, but she became fully engaged and delved whole-heartedly into her work at her beloved Shokei Girls' School.[14] The school had a whole program planned for her to engage in. With a large entering class, and almost no religious program, Mary Jesse began teaching twenty-four periods a week of studying English using the Bible, foreign cooking, and English.

---

12. Jesse to Minnie Sears, 5 May 1938, BIM Correspondence File.

13. Ibid. Coal rose from fourteen yen to thirty yen; according to Dr Mochizuki, the yen/dollar value in 2009 was ninety-four yen to one dollar, or two hundred yen to $2.41 (see chapter 3, note 7).

14. Ibid.

She helped with the religious program and called in homes of older graduates. In addition, she taught five classes outside of school. Some of these were a Bible class at First Baptist Church (currently Hosanna Church in Sendai), a class for graduates, and the meeting for nurses at Tohoku University Hospital that Georgia Newbury had so painstakingly developed. More classes for the training of Sunday school teachers were being planned. Having learned to refuse when overworked, she turned down a request to be the Sunday school superintendent several times.[15] Throwing herself fully into the work was not unusual for Jesse, but being held to a set schedule and having no time for creativity because of lack of staff and money was surely difficult for her. But it is easy to imagine that, after this long absence, it did feel good to return.

However, that first winter back seemed bitterly cold. By December 10th, there were still no heaters going at school. Since coal was scarce, lighting the heaters was delayed until later, and students were allowed to wear their coats inside, contrary to Japanese custom. Little did they know that this was just practice for harder years ahead. As Shokei geared up for Christmas of 1938, everyone was encouraged to dwell on the spiritual elements of Christmas rather than the commercial side of gift-giving. While foreign items were scarce, most other necessities for daily living could be found as before, because the people in the north were used to living with little. Nevertheless, Jesse noted, despite the cold, people were still wearing their old thin clothes and buying very little.[16]

FLUCTUATIONS IN RELIGIOUS SENTIMENT

Religious Apathy. Jesse had only been back one year, but felt that there was a big difference between the Shokei she had left in 1931 and Shokei in 1939. On the positive side, there were nearly double the number of students, which made it possible for the first time to operate in the black.[17] However, the number of missionaries was fewer than half the number eight years earlier. Principal Takahashi, while helping the school to move forward, was not trained in religious work as Dr. Kawaguchi had been. Very few of the teachers were active in Christian service, and there was neither a school-church nor a Sunday school. Therefore, it was hard to get students to attend local

15. Jesse to Sears, 10 December 1938, BIM Correspondence File.

16. Ibid.

17. Jesse to Sears, 12 March 1939, BIM Correspondence File.

churches. In addition, there were no Bible teachers and no Bible teacher assistants on the faculty. Some of the Christian faculty tried to cover some of the hours of the Bible teachers, but Jesse felt that was inadequate. The school was in desperate need of Bible classes and religious work. She was feeling anxious again, but this time it was for a different reason than years before—"Unless we push the religious work [ahead] now we are in danger of losing our distinctive character as a Christian school, and of graduating from our school girls who know very little of Christianity."[18] "Distinctive Christian Character" was a phrase that Jesse often repeated in the future as she made great efforts to help the school hold on to the eternal values.

In September 1939, Lora Patten left for language school, leaving all the missionary work and English teaching to Jesse. A part-time assistant had been hired in the spring for helping with duties at Shokei and helping with calling on graduates. When Patten left, the assistant stopped calling in homes of graduates to spend more time helping with religious work at school. Her help was invaluable. But Jesse still felt that she was losing her grip on the situation at school. Then things were made worse when, at the Annual Japan Missionary Meeting of 1939, when all the ABFMS missionaries in Japan gathered together, they decided that the part-time religious "helper" at Shokei should be reclassified as a "personal-helper." Then, the category of "worker" was cut out of the budget. These were budget-cutting measures. Up until now, a personal-worker had been assigned to each missionary to help in language study, translation, and evangelism engaged in by the missionary. She was a Bible Woman in earlier days and her salary was paid for partly by the woman's board and partly by the missionary herself from her own salary if the Board's contribution seemed too little. An assistant was different from a personal-helper, Jesse pleaded with them. Only ten dollars a month was needed for the assistant religious worker's part-time salary. Consequently, that was all that would be needed for her to help with the YWCA work at school, to teach several Bible classes, including the nurses' classes at the University Hospital, and to lead chapel services at school and call in graduates' homes two days a week. She also could continue to help with the school accounts done in English.[19] But most of all, her contribution would help in bringing Shokei out of the spiritual doldrums. This request was left unmet.

18. Jesse to Sears, 23 May 1939, BIM Correspondence File.
19. Ibid.

News from Tokyo. How was the north affected by the war in Asia? What was the Christian community learning about the war, and how were they reacting to that information? In a letter in early spring of 1939, Jesse commented that she couldn't find much to write about. But from an historical perspective, the information she gives is quite interesting. Aside from sending and receiving soldiers going to and from war, very little was being felt, she said. Food was plentiful, perhaps a little more expensive than usual. People seemed enthusiastic about building a new order in East Asia and could not see why the United States and England did not understand and cooperate with Japan's efforts of "bringing prosperity to Asia."[20] Undoubtedly these kinds of discussions were taking place among faculty at Shokei, where Jesse might have heard about it. But the story of what was really happening had not been half-told.

A pastor from Tokyo came as the speaker for special evangelism meetings at Shokei in late February. He spoke many times to the teachers, to small groups, and to the whole school during chapel time. From these meetings, ten students decided to follow Christ in baptism and another ten were studying in special classes to become Christians. This type of class continued for several years. And by 1941, the class of ten seekers had expanded to four study groups with forty in each class.[21]

Since there was little information heard in the north about the war effort, the teachers were especially interested in what the speaker had to say to them about life in Tokyo. They were, indeed, encouraged by what they heard. The following is how Jesse described it in her report to the Baptist Board in America:

> Perhaps you would be interested most in some of the things the guest speaker said to the teachers. I think it best to use no names. It seems that the department of the Army responsible for reconstruction in China, called a meeting of pastors in Tokyo, and the heads of that department spoke to them, urging them to push forward with their work, pointing out that the Christian religion had the elements, the spirit necessary to bind the three countries, Japan, Manchuria and China, into one.[22]

This reference is to the "New Order in East Asia" (*Toua Shinchitsu jou*), a program promoting unification of Japan, China, and Manchuria,

20. Jesse to Sears, 12 March 1939, BIM Correspondence File.

21. Jesse to Sears, 23 June 1941, BIM Correspondence File.

22. Jesse to Sears, 12 February 1939, BIM Correspondence File.

and later, other Asian countries. This program was ultimately unsuccessful. Jesse continues:

> He, the head of the reconstruction in China, said that Buddhism was not respected in China, but that Christianity because of its good works, institutions, schools, hospitals, etc. had won the confidence of the people. That Shinto was national and they could not expect China to embrace that as a religion, . . . They must look to Christianity to unite the three countries etc. Spoke of the work the 7000 missionaries had done in China and urged the pastors to greater effort.
>
> He spoke then of the Christian Christmas celebration in Hibiya park in Tokyo, at the request of the City Authorities [mayor] for the comfort of soldiers' families. The Buddhist [sic] had some such program but it was not a success. The Christian program was most successful, was attended by 3000 people and the Christian firms like Gideons and Morinaga gave money for gifts to each person. The authorities were most pleased.
>
> Now they want to ask that Christian churches in each ward of the city to [sic] take the responsibility for all widows and soldiers living in their ward, and comfort them, look after them, advise them in the use of their government pension, and in regard to their business affairs. All this shows the high opinion the Army leaders have of Christianity and the opportunity before the church. After all we may be facing the biggest opportunity we have ever had. Are we ready? The church . . . needs to send out its missionaries, as soon as things settle down a bit. A Christian Japan could be a mighty force. I don't think American Christians need have any fears as to their opportunities [for evangelism in Asia] should this country win.[23]

Even as the army officer had been speaking, Japan's army was committing atrocities, forcing the people of Manchuria, China, and Korea, etc., to use only the Japanese language and worship the emperor. It would still be some years before the church in Japan and the rest of the world would understand how absurd the words of the authorities in Tokyo were. Shokei was built on values of the Bible; do to others what you would want them to do to you; love God and love humanity through service. So, hearing the news of the values "recognition" of the church's desire to serve was welcomed by churches and schools alike. They had hardly been given credit for their service and great humanitarian efforts until now. But now Christians

23. Ibid.

were being asked to do what they are best at doing! However good this may have seemed, it was the first step in these institutions coming under government control. The extent to which churches lacked the conscience to protest and just gave in, has always been a deep regret of the post-war Christian church. As we will see, Shokei also tread on a slippery slope, as they delighted in serving.

PLEASURE AND PAIN

Along with the drudgery of 1940, there were also its enjoyable moments. Personal evangelism work with the students was one, and the anticipation and welcoming of Alice Bixby was the other.

Daily Living in the Winter of 1940. Upon her return, Bixby was to be assigned to live in the house built for Annie Buzzell, called the Buzzell Kan. It was such a cold winter that Jesse did not wish Bixby to experience it. Since the Ella O. Patrick building had been modified for dorm and classroom space, Jesse herself had moved into the Buzzell house, so she could imagine how hard it would be in cold weather for Bixby to go to school early in the morning and come back late because of choir practice. It was about two miles distant from the campus. The pipes froze every day, so it took great effort all day to keep them from freezing. She found it so difficult to walk such a distance on the roads. She was also worried about Principal Takahashi's family, who had moved into the large, spacious Ross house on the corner of the main campus. The house could not be heated without using a great amount of fuel, which was very hard to come by. Mrs. Takahashi had health problems and would benefit greatly from living in a "small cozy Japanese house."[24] Jesse proposed that the Ross house be torn down and the wood be used to build a house for both the Takahashi family and the missionaries on campus land.

The scarcity of fuel was the source of more complaints than the lack of any other commodity. She commented that people in Tokyo were crying for charcoal, but it was piled high at the stations along the railroad in Sendai, and therefore there must be a distribution problem.[25]

Pressing for Ministry Time. By July, Jesse was trying to convince the Baptist Mission Board to prepare some new missionaries for work at Shokei, who would be allowed to exclusively study the Japanese language

24. Jesse to Sears, 11 February 1940, BIM Correspondence File.

25. Ibid.

without having to teach classes at school. She also knew that she could be called back to the United States at any moment because of her mother's health condition. She wanted a missionary to be ready to come to Shokei in such a case. But her underlying reason for hoping for another missionary was so that she could ultimately be released from teaching English. She had made it very clear before returning to Shokei that she was returning for building up the religious education program; however, the reality was that teaching English had consumed nearly all her time for the last three years. Her patience was running out. At age fifty-seven and with her experience, she felt she deserved some consideration in the matter by the Board. Younger teachers should be teaching English full-time, and she should be directing the religious program. She had been introduced to the new students in the spring as the person in charge of the religious work; but in fact, there was almost none going on.

It was difficult for Jesse to be on campus all the time and conduct outside classes in the Buzzell house, where she lived, because it was so far from campus. She still awaited the permit to move the house to the campus and funds for the project. This never happened. However, the number of hours she taught had dropped to eighteen, and included both English language and foreign cooking classes. The *senkoubu*, numbering about one hundred girls, had a one-year and a two-year domestic science course, and a two-year kindergarten teacher training course was added.[26] She had an inquirers class on Saturday afternoon, and one Bible class for young men in the evening. She continued calling in homes of graduates and had small meetings in her own home.[27] At the end of June 1940, she managed to fit forty students and teachers into the Buzzell house, which was built for occupancy by just one person. The retreat was a significant one, however, with a lecture on the theme "Victorious Christ" being front and center. It was followed by a session in which the girls divided into five discussion groups, each with a student leader. Questions about the topic were discussed and recorded by each group. On Sunday, they all went to church together and then returned for lunch. After lunch, the teachers answered the girls' questions. Lastly, they shared what each group had learned through its discussion.[28] Jesse believed that activities such as these were what a missionary's work should consist of—being in close contact with small groups of people,

26. Alice Bixby to Constituency, 25 November 1940, BIM Correspondence File.
27. Jesse to Hazel F. Shank, 4 December 1940, BIM Correspondence File.
28. Jesse to Shank, 6 July 1940, BIM Correspondence File.

teaching about Jesus. No matter how busy she was, it was these kinds of contacts with people that made her the happiest.

Alice Bixby Returns. Bixby was expected to return from the United States to work in Sendai in the spring of 1940, but for some reason she had unexpectedly run into complications causing her delay. As Jesse anticipated her arrival, she expressed her admiration of Bixby, as a "saint" of sorts, who "shows a beautiful spirit."[29] Bixby did finally return to Japan on September 14th.[30] Before long, music was again ringing in the halls of Shokei. Bixby also keenly felt the difference between Shokei in 1934 and in 1941.[31] Foreign teachers no longer led chapel or taught Bible. Chapel was held once a week, she reported, rather than every day and was always preceded by a required patriotic ceremony.[32] Since she arrived mid-year and did not have classes assigned to her, her duties consisted of occasionally substituting in English classes, conducting singing classes in the *senkoubu*, and teaching two piano students.[33]

Stormy Surface—Calm Down Deep. As Japan marched closer to broadening its influence overseas, it began to tighten regulations at home. Shokei was prepared for these changes with careful planning by leaders who were sensitive to the leading of God throughout its history. One of the first regulations imposed by the government was that all schools become financially independent of any foreign money. Shokei had worried about this for years, but in the end, they achieved this independence two years earlier than planned. The gracious gift from the Woman's Board made it possible for Shokei to rid itself of financial dependence and add to the endowment fund for the formation of its own property holding body (*zaidan houjin*). Secondly, the Department of Education required all schools to put Japanese leadership into all parts of the schools. Beginning with the appointment of its first Japanese principal in 1926, Shokei had already complied with this regulation and had in addition put all departments under Japanese leadership. The new regulation did not affect Shokei as much as it did other

---

29. Jesse to Sears, 11 February 1940.

30. Missionary Register Card, Bixby, BIM, Archival Collections of ABHS.

31. See more details of the atmosphere of 1940 and 1941 in chapter 7.

32. This required patriotic ceremony was instituted at the request of government officials. It involved bowing to the Japanese flag draped at the back of the stage and singing the national anthem called *"Kimigayo."* Other mission schools in town resisted this ceremony until they were forced by law to have it, whereas the principal of Shokei instituted it before it was required by law to avoid trouble.

33. Bixby to Constituency, 25 November 1940, BIM Correspondence File.

Christian schools in town that were not prepared. Thirdly, the schools was asked to expand further to make higher education possible for a larger number of girls who had graduated from primarily government schools. A large new building was completed in the spring of 1941 with new laboratories. This, along with the good athletic facilities, had come to the attention of the Department of Education as the best in the north. Shokei was the only school in Sendai with enough land for expansion. Foresight in buying more land than was needed many years before had paid off.[34]

The celebration in November 1940 had a triple meaning. It was the Forty-Eighth Anniversary of the school; it was a celebration for becoming financially independent from the Woman's American Baptist Foreign Mission Society; and it was a time of recognition of the publication of Annie Buzzell's life story in Japanese, entitled *Buzzell Den*, a biography by Professor Motoi Kurihara. Kurihara gave the special address to the students and the officers of the graduates, the trustees, teachers, and friends of the school. Jesse reported that in Kurihara's speech he referred to the difficult times Shokei and Japan were facing, "that in spite of storm and tempest, that down deep the ocean was still calm, quiet, peaceful, and warm. The surface storm would pass and [he] asked us to be patient. Down deep there was no change."[35]

Tearing Apart. Because of the political situation and impending Pacific war, the time had come for all missionaries in Japan to begin to think about whether they should go back to their own country or stay on with their Japanese Christian friends The optimism of special evangelism week of 1939 did not match reality. Society was fast turning against the Christian church and against anything that had foreign influence. Government regulations held a vise-like grip on society. Jesse's furlough was approaching. She needed to decide whether she should leave in the spring of 1941, when many other missionaries were leaving in response to the United States government's advisory, or to delay until summer. She favored staying on until the beginning of the summer if the situation at home and in Japan permitted. It would give her an even number of thirty years of service in Japan. But more than that, she wanted to show support, stand by the alumnae, Christian teachers, and friends, and support them. From a practical point of view, she wanted to give the expected two hundred new high school entrants in April a good start in English. She felt that this was

34. Jesse, "Semi-Annual Report," 14 June 1941, BIM Correspondence File.
35. Jesse, "Semi-Annual Report," 4 December 1940, BIM Correspondence File.

not the time to leave Japan. Leaving earlier than her furlough, scheduled to begin in July 1941, would have a negative impact on her Japanese friends, she thought, and it might seem that she was afraid and running away from the situation in Japan. It seemed that if the school ever needed her, it was now, to help hold to the ideals and share in the problems.[36] This is what was necessary, despite the disappointments, discouragement, and heartaches. With a feeling of foreboding she wrote:

> I feel that we have a responsibility to those we have led. They need us now and if there is suffering ahead for the church here, I want to share with our Christians. I feel that the Christians in our two countries should stand together in one fellowship. There is no other bond across national and race lines . . . As for the political situation and the reasons for our governments advising return I am completely ignorant but I trust these people and I trust God. I am not afraid of the future. Of course, I should like to be with my family at home now in this time of sorrow but I hardly see what help I could be to them to justify me in leaving my work now.[37]

Jesse oversaw the construction of yet another building that was a result of the foresight of Principal Ando's promotion of the endowment fund. Then for reasons unspecified, Jesse did leave on April 6th, 1941 for furlough, instead of extending her stay to the summer as she had hoped. This time she was gone for a period of six years.

It is difficult to know her thoughts as she left. News of the war in China was restricted to the glorious stories of victory that her Japanese friends also heard. Letters which passed over the Pacific Ocean were often inspected. So, no one felt comfortable writing what he or she thought. Writing about the real situation would have put others in danger. All she could safely write about was shortages of such commodities as food and fuel, and bemoan the lack of religious spirit at school. Several years later in her annual report for 1947 she wrote more specifically about the situation: "How difficult things were when I left. So little interest in anything but war work. So few [people] with time or thought for Christianity, for Bible, for music, except military songs."[38] We know that she must have left with a heavy heart, because after she arrived home she wrote the following: "I fear that the sweeping changes

36. Ibid.

37. Ibid.

38. Jesse, "Shokei Gakuin Report for 1947," 7 January 1948. Shokei Gakuin Archival Collection.

now taking place in Japan are causing discouragement and heartache to many of our noble women who through the years have so sacrificially supported our school at Sendai."[39] Whether "noble women" refers to American church women or Shokei alumnae is not clear. Nevertheless, either way, as always, she was thinking of others' feelings and not just her own.

Finding Job Satisfaction—Poston Japanese-American Concentration Camp. After returning to the United States, Jesse was free to do as she pleased. Her mother had passed away the previous fall in 1940. Even though her mother was gone, she chose to reside in Ashland, Virginia, her mother's birthplace, where her mother and some of her siblings had lived for several years. Her younger brother was residing in the Epping Forest house. In the fall of 1941, she began to search for a teaching position, but it took another eighteen months. She updated her credentials for teaching English and history in American elementary schools, and social science for the high school level in the State of Virginia. Despite having this promising start by updating her credentials, she could not find work. It seemed that her work as a missionary in Japan counted against her. She commented, "I am beginning to feel discouraged about getting a teaching position around here. I feel that I am generally thought of as being very pro-Japanese. I admit that I am, and I can't change my convictions or be disloyal to my friends [in order] to secure a job. I'm still hoping to get some work with Japanese."[40]

Very soon after this letter was written, in February 1943, she accepted a position to work as a teacher at a Japanese-American relocation center in Parker, Arizona.[41] As a result of President Roosevelt's Executive Order 9066, Poston Concentration Camp[42] for Japanese-Americans was one of ten relocation centers designed to remove people of Japanese descent from the paranoia and hysteria of the west coast. The Colorado River Relocation Center was made up of three camps with a total of nearly eighteen thousand people. There were first generation Japanese (*issei*) speaking mostly Japanese, second-generation (*nisei*) children speaking almost no Japanese, and people who were born in the United States but educated in Japan, called *kibei*, speaking both languages, all living together. Mary Jesse found

39. Jesse to Hazel Shank, 23 June 1941, BIM Correspondence File.

40. Jesse to Shank, 29 January 1943, BIM Correspondence File.

41. Jesse to Shank, 30 January 1943, BIM Correspondence File.

42. The terminology "internment camp" is used by the government and populous, but Japanese-Americans of late use the term "concentration camp" to express the true situation in the camps surrounded with barbwire and soldiers with machine guns pointed inward.

herself in this barren place with no trees and temperatures that could get up to one hundred twenty degrees Fahrenheit in the summer. But at least she felt comfortable surrounded by Japanese faces once again.

In a book written about Poston, called *Dusty Exile*, according to a description of one of the teachers perfectly matching Jesse but with masked identity, she is described as facing her first class of twelfth grade *nisei* nonspeakers of Japanese. Instinctively she addressed them in Japanese! When her words were met with blank stares and muffled laughs, she snapped back to reality and addressed the class in English. She was remembered for being able to convey her deep love of Japanese culture, sharing with her students the beauty of Japanese characters and intriguing stories from old Japan. She could communicate well with the *issei* parents, so she often helped to solve problems between school and family.[43]

As early as January 1943, Poston and other concentration camps began allowing children to go off to college or join the armed forces. Then in 1944, relocation into mainstream society began, with Poston closing its doors by the end of November 1945 after Executive Order 9066 was rescinded and declared unconstitutional.

The details of Jesse's next move are unclear. It appears that she may have taken a job with the Yuma County Union High School in Parker. This was the address used by Hazel Shank of the WABFMS in a letter addressed to Jesse in June 1946 saying she had been cleared to return to Japan.[44] Jesse immediately returned to Ashland, Virginia. She hurriedly tried to complete the necessary paperwork, medical and dental checkups, and shopping for winter clothes to replace the clothes she gave away for post-European Relief while in the sweltering desert. All this was to no avail, because the September 23rd ship left without her.[45] But she would have another chance in December of 1946.

43. Harris, *Dusty Exile*, 50.
44. Shank to Jesse, 13 June 1946, BIM Correspondence File.
45. Jesse to Sears, 6 September 1946, BIM Correspondence File.

Principal Kensuke Ando (1935–1937)
(courtesy of Shokei Gakuin)

Goldie Nicholson and Margaret
Cuddeback (1936)
(courtesy of Shokei Gakuin)

Ms Jesse & Faculty (about 1941)/L to R: Takeshi Nakase, Shin Chiba, Misao Sato, Mary Jesse, Mitsuko Tamazawa, Shigeto Takahashi, Saburo Toshima.

7

Engulfed in the Storm (1941–1947)

Volunteer Work for Country in Agriculture (March 1944)
(courtesy of Shokei Gakuin)

In a case where she [Japan] feels that justice and honor are at stake
Japan will never yield, even though she sacrifices half of her people.
Nay, not even though it should mean utter annihilation.

—Toyohiko Kagawa[1]

The time period of this chapter overlaps part of the last chapter showing the effect the Japan-China war and the Pacific war (World War II) had
on Shokei while Jesse was still at Shokei and after she left. After reviewing

1. Kagawa, *Christ and Japan*, 67

the stance historically taken by the missionaries and the school toward the State of Japan, a chronological view of the posture taken by the school from 1937 to 1941 while Jesse was still in Japan, and from 1942 to 1947 while she was in the United States, will be presented. Included in this chapter is a first-hand description of what took place at Shokei on December 8th, 1941 and the following months. In the last section I will present the whereabouts of Shokei missionaries during the war who served at Shokei.

LOOKING BACKWARD AND FORWARD AT SHOKEI IN SOCIETY[2]

The war took its toll on both Shokei and the missionaries who had contributed so much to the school. However, the relationship between the school and the Mission Board had changed. Shokei was no longer just a beneficiary. She was now approaching independence and adulthood. As Jesse noted in a June 23rd, 1941 letter from the United States, Shokei "must no longer look to the missionary and board but must lead out by itself. The Japanese leaders are feeling their responsibility, their obligation to conserve the spirit, the ideals of the past and to keep the institution truly Christian."[3] But like a young woman growing into adulthood, Shokei at times had capitulated to the ideals taught her by teachers and missionaries of the past, but she never totally forgot them. Thus, the school personnel out of a grateful heart were especially concerned for the welfare of missionaries during the war years. She could not remain still tied to her benefactor's apron strings. But neither communication nor opportunities of consultation were possible during this period. However painful it was to be her own "person," without consultation, it was probably what Shokei needed to cut the apron strings and grow up.

2. This first Sino-Japanese war was fought during 1894–1895. But for the current conflict if we rely only on reports of the missionaries, we would not have a complete picture of what life at Shokei was like, because they were either not present or were afraid to write about the situation in letters that could be intercepted. Material written in Japanese clarified the events that took place. Material from the missionaries and the board provides information on the welfare of some of the missionaries who once served at Shokei. Information for the following section was largely taken from the book *Shokei Jogakuin Nanajuu Nen Shi* (*The Seventy-Year History of Shokei Jogakuin*) 205–296, and from personal interviews with people who experienced this period of history.

3. Jesse to Shank, 23 June 1941, BIM Correspondence File.

The previous chapter contained minimal material of what life in Japanese society and the school was like during Jesse's service from 1937–1941 because she was afraid to write about any situations and feelings. The reader should imagine Jesse in the middle of the following section to understand her feelings of futility as she tried to bring a sense of spirituality back to the school.

A Chronological View. Life did not suddenly change at Shokei. Changes appeared gradually, largely due to influences outside the school. Shokei was always known to be loyal to any national cause. The missionaries made sure of that. They respected the people of the country and admired the Emperor as head of the State (not as head of the Shinto Religion). Shokei students did all they could for the soldiers returning from the Russo-Japanese war (1904–1905). At the memorial service given for Emperor Meiji in 1912, no one seemed to give a second thought to bowing towards Tokyo (the seat of the imperial family). The missionaries did not indicate any feelings that this attention to national causes was improper for a Christian institution. Neither did they associate their behavior with the national imperial religion. They felt honored when the emperor's representative visited Shokei in 1925. Therefore, when soldiers were sent off to the war in China in 1932, it was only natural for the school to participate in the send-off, which was now encouraged by authorities more than ever to demonstrate patriotism. Likewise, in the same year, when the bodies of fallen soldiers were returned to Sendai, a contingent from Shokei was there to meet the train. In the same year Shokei participated in the "*iresai*," a national ceremony for souls of the soldiers who had fallen in war. No one wanted to show disrespect for heroes of their country in what they were told was a "holy war," even though the ceremony was distinctively Shinto. Or, was the school thinking that the ceremony was just "the Japanese way," and not in conflict with Christian values? Tighter regulations began to appear one after another almost without being noticed, as a fascist, ultra-religious state began to develop. For Shokei, it felt as if they were being slowly cut off from their roots.

1937. In 1937, Shokei's *senkoubu* Kindergarten Teacher Training course and English Literature department students began voluntarily to provide nursery-care for forty local children whose fathers had gone to war. The people-movement, called the National Spirit Mobilization Movement (*kokumin-seishin-soudouin*), encouraged deeds like this. Shokei students and staff had always volunteered their services to God and humanity, but gradually the meaning of service came to include working on behalf of the country only. It was a movement to rally the nation for an all-out effort for victory in the war against China. It advertised with slogans such as "Battle Also in the Homeland," "United Our Country Stands," etc. They encouraged loyalty and sacrifice of oneself for work for the country, strong family morale, and disciplined personal conduct. In the same year, the students packed bags with goodies and letters for the men going off to the war in China. In October, Shokei participated in a week designated for service to their country. They wrote letters of encouragement to families whose fathers were away in the war, visited their families, and practiced evacuation procedures. Beginning in November, for thirty minutes before worship, all students participated in calisthenics broadcast over the radio. Radio calisthenics was a centrally guided exercise program broadcast all over Japan, the purpose of which was to keep citizens fit and to provide a unifying start for each day. Although shorter in length, this broadcast is still heard over the radio at 6:30 AM every weekday. In this way, censorship, propaganda, and the state-controlled school system helped spread the spiritual mobilization efforts everywhere. Shokei Girls' School could hardly avoid it.

1938. Joining the armed forces was not yet mandatory, but in 1938 one male physical education teacher, Mr. Nisaku Hirai, later to become principal of Shokei, marched off to war with a big send-off by the students as nationalistic spirit ran high among them. They escorted him to the school gate, sang the National Anthem and a war march song. The much-debated National Mobilization Law (*kokka soudouin hou*), with pressure from the military, was finally passed by the Seventy-Third Diet (Parliament) in March. This law put controls on civilian organizations, labor, individual and consumer commodities, corporations, contracts, prices, and the news media. In addition, it empowered the government to subsidize war production and manufacturers who suffered losses caused by the mobilization, specifying penalties for infractions.[4] Of course, it affected all citizens in some way, but the full impact did not come for a few more years. In June, the Education Ministry informed all schools that students were to work during their summer vacation (*kaki shūdan kinro*). And in November, the Ministry of Education again declared a week of National Spirit (*kokumin seishin sakko*) where service for one's country was emphasized in the form of beautifying the school and surrounding grounds. This was a program of the National Spirit Mobilization Movement, which reached the masses

4. "National Mobilization Law," 1060.

through public rallies, radio programs and printed information, through neighborhood associations,[5] and in this case through schools, too. Other things that happened included the banning of hair perms and the institution of pantaloons (*mompe*) as the preferred dress for all women.

1939. The remains of fallen soldiers being returned to Sendai increased significantly. The school was asked to cancel nearly a week of classes in July to help rebuild a War Memorial Shinto Shrine for the dead into a magnificent structure. The shrine was located on Mount Aoba Yama, about a thirty–minute walk from Shokei. Students made bags of cotton material, filled them with rocks and sand from the Hirose River, and hauled them up the steep path on their shoulders to the top of Aoba Yama. Each student made three or four trips a day. This year, another teacher from Shokei, Nobuo Monma (Suzuki) marched off to war.

The *hinomaru bento*, a lunch which consisted of rice with a red sour plum placed in the middle to represent the Japanese flag, was encouraged as a sign of self-enforced poverty for the sake of the country. At the elementary school level, those who brought such a lunch were praised. Many poor children who could only afford such a lunch even in prosperous times could now proudly display their rice and sour plum lunch and not be made fun of. At Shokei, they decided that all students would bring such a lunch at least once a month.

World War II began in September in Europe, causing Japan to take special notice of world events instead of just being concerned about themselves.

1940. This year was significant in many ways. According to Japanese mythological tradition, it was the Two Thousand Six Hundredth Anniversary of the creation of the Japanese Islands. This called for a big celebration in November, and was used to justify an increase of national spirit activities. The vise-like grip held by the military on the Japanese common people and their institutions increased rapidly. Nationalistic propaganda accelerated. The emperor was no longer spoken of as "our father" but as "our God." Another significant event in this year was the government formulation of the Imperial Rule Assistance Association (*taisei yokusan kai*) to promote goals of the New Order Movement. This was a union of all civilian organizations.[6] Shokei felt many changes, too. For example, prefectural

---

5. "National Spirit Mobilization Movement," 1063.

6. This movement was created to muzzle the State's political and war opponents and encourage fascist ideology.

authorities called a meeting of the heads of all Christian schools in Sendai. Pictures of the emperor and empress were passed out to each school with instructions to put it in a prominent place. In April, Shokei constructed a box that framed the picture. It had a door on it that could be opened and closed. Since the school had no Shinto shrine inside the school grounds, they knew they had better comply with the instructions by setting the box in the principal's office. Students were required to bow in the direction of the picture (toward the principal's office) as they entered the school gate. The doors of the box that held the emperor's picture remained closed always, except at the entrance ceremony and graduation. At those times the box was taken up on the stage of the chapel, and the doors were opened by the principal wearing white gloves. It was thought irreverent for anyone to gaze at the face of the emperor, whether in person or portrayed in a picture, or to touch the picture. So the students bowed their heads as the door was opened.

In August 1940, a list of three demands from the prefectural government was passed down to the schools:

1. Before worship or other gatherings, all people present should acknowledge the flag (hung behind the podium on the stage of the chapel), sing the national anthem and bow toward the Emperor's palace in Tokyo.

2. All schools that had not hung the picture yet were to do so under the penalty of law.

3. The Bible could be taught but not as a subject.

In this same year, all middle school students in Japan were required to wear the same uniform. A class on national morals (*shushin*) was implemented by government ruling, which consisted of teaching new values held by the country.[7]

In September, at a gathering of sixty-six principals from the National Association of Christian Schools (*Kirisutokyo Kyouiku Domei*) held at Aoyama Gakuin in Tokyo, the central government passed down a list of regulations to be followed:

7. *Shushin* was established in 1892 by Emperor Meiji to inculcate in his subjects moral principles based on Confucian principles. Literally translated, this expression meant "establish or conduct oneself." Mission schools, as is presently the case, were also allowed by the government to substitute the (moral) teachings of the Bible for the *shushin* class. In 1940, this policy was changed yet another time.

1. The Director of the Board of Trustees and all other heads of departments must be Japanese.

2. Half or more of the Board of Trustees must be Japanese.

3. Schools which had not become incorporated (*zaidan houjin*) should declare a Japanese national judicial person as the founder of the school and become a property-holding body as soon as possible.

4. The school must become independent from all foreign church support.

Shokei had already been prepared to meet at least three of the new regulations. Regarding numbers one and two, Shokei had established Japanese leadership nearly fifteen years earlier, and by now both the director of the Board and more than half of the members were Japanese. Regarding number four, it was exactly in September of this particular year that Shokei was able to become financially independent. The third area, regarding becoming an official property holding body (*zaidan houjin*), had not yet been achieved.[8]

1941. In April, the government moved to consolidate education by nationalizing all elementary schools into National People's Schools (*kokumin gakkou*). This did not affect Shokei directly, but it would affect the mindset of students entering Shokei for the next few years.

In that same month the forty-seventh new class of students, the class of 1945, entered Shokei. They were as typical as any girls their age, having been raised on the current philosophy of education since elementary school, to be loyal to the emperor and be willing to sacrifice themselves for their country. Little did they know that in the next four years their actual classroom attendance would barely be more than eighteen months due to service for their country. To many of them, the government-prompted changes that would be occurring at Shokei would seem to be a natural progression toward their country's unification of spirit. This class of students was destined to be part of the many unsung heroes of Japan's Pacific War. They marched into their entrance ceremony and sang the Shokei School song for the first and last time.

---

8. Shokei became a legal holding body in July 1942 as Jesse had hoped, and became *Sendai Shokei Jogakkou*. The next year, 1943, their name and status changed again as they became *Shokei Koutou Jogakkou*, and were recognized as an official high school.

THE PACIFIC WAR YEARS AND SHOKEI SCHOOL

Mary Jesse left Shokei in April after the entrance ceremony of the class of 1945, but Shokei ploughed on. School trips were still allowed, so in May, Shokei third-year students took their school trip as usual. However, new rules had been imposed regarding how to spend their time on these trips. Consequently, the government required that the school include service to the country as part of the plans. The students helped clean the emperor's palace garden as their service. Afterwards they were free to tour Tokyo, Kamakura, and Eno Shima Island.

In June, the government abolished all student body organizations. In place of it, a nationally connected organization called National Appreciation Student Service Group (*houkokudan*) was formed. The student council leaders now took orders from the government regarding their activities. The purpose of this new group was laid out as following the principles of the empire, working hard as a group for the country, building a strong spirit through discipline and continuing the work of the Father, the emperor. At the same time, several other sections of the student organization received new names and purposes. For example, the religious committee (*shūkyoubu*) became Cultural Cultivation (of the mind), or Self-Improvement Committee (*shūyoubu*). The athletic department became the drill department (*tannen-bu*).

The situation of the churches also affected Christian schools. Since 1938, churches had been expected to follow guidelines set up by the government which regulated their civil behavior. Because of these duties, church attendance fell off sharply. Apart from some individuals, most Christians joined the national effort.[9] Christian churches and other religious groups were trying to assimilate over three hundred regulations issued by the government. Now in addition, a law went into effect that virtually wiped out all semblance of church life as it was before. There were three attractive features; churches were given legal security, tax benefits, and exclusion from local police periodic inspection. However, the negative side was that the leaders and their congregations were put under near-complete government control, requiring all denominations to register. Churches and their leaders found themselves busy studying the law so they would know how to fit in and not be put under the microscope. In his book *A Century of Protestant Christianity in Japan*, Charles W. Iglehart notes: "As negotiations [with the

9. Iglehart, *Protestant Christianity*, 223.

government] went on, the government set a lower limit of fifty churches and 5,000 members for any denomination to qualify for registration."[10] In other words, registration was a condition for continued existence. Five or six denominations qualified, but small denominations had to join larger denominations to survive.

For several years, the various denominations in Japan had hoped to somehow forget their small differences and unite in one cooperative group. Missionaries had, of course, debated this subject for some time. After all, they wagered, isn't unity better than divisive denominations? Now, in such perilous times, moving on together seemed to make more sense than ever. And as we have seen, the government was the impetus to make it happen. All churches were ordered to join the United Church of Christ (UCC) in Japan (*Kirisuto Kyoudan*). On the one hand, there was much rejoicing at being "forced" together, but on the other hand, some groups saw their identity and beliefs being neutralized. Groups such as the Holiness Church registered reluctantly, but continued as before. The consequence of this was that later the government persecuted and imprisoned their pastors, even leading to the death of some of them when they took a strong stand for Christ. The mainline denominations that joined the UCC decided to look at the national situation as positively as they could. In 1941 and 1942, when policies and philosophies were being formed in the UCC, combined with lack of knowledge about what was really happening with the war overseas, they publicly pledged to give all they had toward the war effort. They declared that if they prayed fervently, Japan would win.

Japan's military and economy were feeling the pressure from the embargo of oil and scrap iron from abroad and therefore needed to protect itself as it attempted to implement its Greater East Asia Co-Prosperity Sphere (*daitoua kyoueiken*) plan for economic stability. From Japan's viewpoint, it seemed incongruous for America and England to expand their influence while prohibiting Japan from doing the same. Its biggest and closest enemy of their plan was America. Taking advantage of America being entangled in the war in Europe, they made their decisive blow at Pearl Harbor on December 7th, 1941 (US time). Thus, the Pacific War began.

Alice Bixby was the only missionary left at Shokei on this fateful day of December 8th (Japan time). She gives insight into what it was like at the school from the viewpoint of the new "enemy."

10. Ibid, 231–32.

The morning of December 8th, while I was eating breakfast, my cook's brother burst into the dining room in great agitation, saying that news had just come over the radio of war between Japan and America. Though for some time I had been mentally prepared for such news, still I could not believe it. When I arrived at school at 7:20 am . . . I heard nothing about war so hoped it was a false report. However, after [our weekly] prayer meeting was over one of the teachers told us definitely that war had been declared by Japan. Few of the teachers said anything. It apparently was a great surprise to them and they went about their tasks with rather dazed faces. At 8 o'clock when I asked the Principal if I should attend chapel services . . . he said, "Yes, but perhaps it would be better not to preside at the piano; someone might think it strange." The next hour I also attended chapel exercises in the Higher Department and then during the day taught several English classes as usual. Rather early in the forenoon all the students and teachers were again assembled in the auditorium to hear the formal declaration of war broadcast by the government, and during the day there were other broadcasts which everyone had to hear. I did not leave the classroom and each time the students returned I went on with the lesson. All the girls seemed very quiet and looked at me with sympathetic eyes. I saw no change in their attitude which had been very friendly ever since my return from America the year before. At noon I ate my lunch with the teachers as usual. After the day's work was over I asked the Principal whether I should return the next day. He said, "Yes, but don't go far from home this evening as some unruly fellow might be rude."

A few days previous I had invited about six of the teachers to my home for a dinner party that evening—a farewell to one of the teachers who was soon to be married. . . When I asked them if under the circumstances they would prefer not to come, they replied that they wished to come as planned. At dinner and during the games which followed, though our hearts were heavy . . . we did not mention the awful news of the day until I was called to the door to meet one of the men teachers who brought a message from the Principal that I was not to attend school [the] next day. Then I knew that the break in our relationship had come. Returning to the room I told the teachers that anything might happen and pointed out certain things I wished them to have in case I should be taken away suddenly. I think I realized better than they the changes that would come. They said little but I knew that there was, and would be no change in our friendship. We prayed together very earnestly, then talked quietly until they had to leave. I was not allowed to see them again.

Early Tuesday morning the pastor of the church . . . called and offered to do anything he could to help me. "If you need anything at any time let me know quickly," he said. While he was still there the local policeman came—a pleasant chap who had often dropped in to talk with me. He said that he thought I would not be molested in any way. When I asked if I would be sent away he replied, "Oh no, there will be nothing like that. You will be quite safe here. I will look out for you." At about ten o'clock six plain clothes men appeared at my home "to help me pack." When I asked for details they told me it would be necessary "for your protection" to go to some other place "for three or four days." I was to take some food and canned goods, plenty of warm clothing, a mattress and bedding, and toilet articles. While the others were looking around the house, with the oversight of one of the men I packed the things most necessary for an indefinite stay. I was permitted to take three or four books "as you have been in the country a long time." I was not unkindly treated.

In less than an hour a taxi was called and I was taken to the compound of the Catholic Bishop, near the center of the city.[11]

1942. By this time, English had become a non-required subject and it was strongly recommended that the school not have worship nor teach the Bible. "Freedom of Religion Law" made it impossible to force cessation of these. Shokei still had morning worship during this year after a patriotic ceremony. However, Shokei's principal chose to follow the recommendation the following year rather than be subject to scrutiny by the government. This action and attitude would eventually cost him his job. On the other hand, if the school had not followed this edict, the government would have used other methods, skirting the law, to force them to stop anyway. With such a huge war now in progress on two fronts, pressure on institutions and society became intense. Japan exerted its power and influence through all Southeast Asia by forcing subjection to the emperor. They moved to block the encroachment of troops in Asia from the European theater, and of course keep American troops from getting in the way of what Japan considered progress. The all-important oil from Southeast Asia was needed to mobilize industry at home.

Schools were called into action, too. Work assignments issued by the government began for some Shokei students in the fall of 1942. They

11. Bixby to Constituency, 16 September 1942, BIM Correspondence File.

worked in rice and potato production in Ayashi Village until 1945. Each morning they walked from school to Ayashi, which is presently an eight-kilometer distance by car. Other students visited the air force base in Natori and encouraged troops with homemade cards and by singing. An inspection took place at school, forcing the removal of Christian-related pictures from the walls. Jesse had brought most of these from the United States. They were replaced with flowers or pictures of scenery. This was very upsetting to many students and teachers.

In this year, the schools were forced to take a more powerful teaching stance in the morals class (shushin). Two things were emphasized: 1) Everyone should be helpful to the country; and 2) Japan was an imperial country whose supreme ruler will also rule the world. In addition, all teaching of democracy was forbidden and replaced with the teaching of nationalism. Teachers were in fact asked to suspend normal education and work on becoming one in spirit and thought. They needed to make the *houkokudan* ("Student Service Group") active and were supposed to fill their time with service projects.

1943. There were no more morning worship services, and only one hour of English each week when the students were not working. By this time, all men age twenty and up were required to serve in the armed forces. Shokei students again participated in the "*iresai*." This time it was closer to the heart. It was for those who had fallen in the battle of Guadalcanal in the Solomon Islands, the site of the first Allied invasion. Over seventeen thousand men from various battalions had perished. The battalions on this island were largely from Sendai. The ceremony was a solemn one indeed when the remains of the soldiers were brought back to town for burial.

Wartime work of the church increased in intensity. Reeducation classes were held for pastors so that they could teach their congregations Japanese culture of the past and present ideology.[12] They did hospital visitation, helped raise money for airplanes and joined in patriotic ceremonies. The government sent church representatives overseas to help in pacification of nationals under Japanese rule.[13] Churches felt an uncomfortable acceptance with the praise and encouragement of the government for their help in this "holy war," as it was called.

---

12. Iglehart, *Protestant Christianity*, 244.

13. Ibid., 245–46.

1944–1945. With America now showing its power in the Marianas and Japan's position weakening, more and more Japanese men and boys marched off to war.

On the home front, Shokei continued each year to accept students who passed their entrance exam in March. Thirteen-year old Akiko Suzuki decided to take the entrance exam to get into Shokei. But a lot was different this year than what she had heard from her friends. The exam was not given at school, as usual, but at the prefectural office, along with students trying to get into other schools in Sendai. They all took the same exam, monitored by the teachers from the target school who had gathered at the site. When the results were posted, she found that she had passed! She was excited but cautious. There were instructions advising that no skirts were allowed. Akiko was unprepared for this, but her grandfather came to the rescue, giving her a pair of his own pants. After elastic bands were sewn into the pant-leg cuff cinching them like a drawstring, she was all set.

The first day she arrived at school, she found another change. There was no morning worship. Instead, the principal read the Imperial Rescript on Education. This continued to the end of the war. But now, along with her first-year classmates, education in the classroom was rare. Instead, as the upper-class students departed to factories, she and her classmates stayed behind and began the arduous task of repairing army hats by meticulously removing the red strips with dull pairs of scissors. Later in the year, they were assigned to serve at an agricultural school in Ayashi (eight kilometers from Shokei) to thin out the new plants. They were told to keep the plants they pulled up to take home and mix with their rice. Occasionally they received rations of sweet red *azuki* beans and sugar from the military. How she would have loved to take this precious commodity home, but it was more noble and unselfish to give her share away as her classmates were doing, giving to the upper-level classmates working hard in factories.[14]

Losing the men to the war effort left the countryside, the heart of the economy, without workers. Since the first three weeks of May were the critical days for planting, all ninety-five students from Shokei's kindergarten and home economics departments (*senkoubu*) were sent all across the prefecture to do child care and tend the prefecture's kindergartens so that all women could work fulltime in agriculture. In August, some students from the fourth year of the high school went to receive training as flaggers on

14. Akiko Suzuki, interviewed by Mari Sato, 9 June 2017, Japanese transcript with author.

boats in Matsushima Bay. In September, all students at this grade level were required to receive basic training in marching, beginning in the evening. This included thirty-kilometer (eight-hour) marches to the seaside town of Shiogama.

By November of 1944, the army was discovering Shokei's nearly unused buildings, and it took up several floors for offices in the nutrition department. Meanwhile, there was also an acute shortage of workers for the war factories. The naval yards were just outside of the city in Tagajo town, where there were war factories. While some students went there to work, others, like the *senkoubu*'s home economics students and third- and fourth-year *jogakubu* (formerly *honka*) students were required to go to work in other local war factories. The *jogakubu* third-year students were sent to two factories in the town of Nagamachi south of Sendai. They were a machine parts factory (*kayaba seisaku sho*) and an electric parts company (*denki kojou*). Those from the *senkoubu* went to work in two different rubber factories in Nagamachi also. This left kindergarten *senkoubu* course students and first and second year *jogakubu* students at school to continue their classes. The kindergarten *senkoubu* course students under the label of "practice teaching" were occasionally sent away in limited numbers by the government to local kindergartens in Sendai. The schedules were decided at the prefectural level for Shokei, and it was rumored that the especially hard jobs were assigned to students in Christian schools. With little choice, teachers escorted and stayed with each of the groups at their assigned work area.

Whether at the behest of military officers around campus or not, in their spare time, the teachers began painting camouflage markings on the buildings. According to Suzuki the teachers began digging crude bunkers underneath the school. After completion in the spring, the students had drill after drill, donning their protective cotton batten hats and rushing into the dirty, dark caverns holding each others hands for dear life. They would later emerge covered in soil and water that dripped from the ceiling of the bunker. The bunker was large enough to hold all five classes of three hundred students.[15]

Vignette of the Class of 1945. Shokei's forty-seventh entering class, now fourth-year students, were split into three groups. Those students with health concerns were assigned to the school to sew gloves and do finishing work on soldier's uniforms. One hundred eighty-nine students of this

15. Ibid.

class were assigned to work in Tokyo Keiki Company, one hundred forty-six going to the central Kamata Honsha factory in Kamata-Ku Tokyo, and forty-six to its Yokohama branch in Chigasaki. This factory manufactured measuring instruments, such as meters for airplanes.

The students were very excited about this new venture. By now, these fifteen- and sixteen-year-olds were veterans at service for their country. Harvesting soy beans, rice, digging up *konyaku* roots, working in the weapons factory, training as flagmen, night marches—they thought of nothing but working for the stability of their nation. Infused with patriotic spirit, they gathered at Sendai Station with students from all the area schools who were joining the country's student mobilization (*gakusei dōin*), and headed for the awesome city of Tokyo. The parents sent them off with mixed feelings of fear and pride.

The next day, the hopes of the students in Tokyo soared when they saw their first main meal, a full bowl of rice and two sweet potatoes. It was a rare sight indeed for these students who had been on skimpy rations at home. But suddenly, reality struck. The air raid warnings began to wail. There were no air raid shelters, so the girls ran for cover among wood building materials. They grabbed what they could and ran for cover. One student recalls dropping a big sweet potato in the rush. It rolled down and wedged itself in a crack. There was no time to retrieve it. For years, she's never forgotten staring at that sweet potato and then at the face of Vice-Principal Nakase, whose face reflected his feelings of utter helplessness and misery knowing how valuable that potato was to this innocent student.[16] It was the students' first view of a B-29 American bomber. No bombs were dropped, but it brought both terror and renewed determination to their hearts. This was going to be their battle as well!

Life settled down into somewhat of a pattern of waking up early, getting in formation, marching to the factory while gustily singing patriotic songs, eating a less-than-adequate breakfast, working a full day, and returning to the dorm. There were some diversions during this month, as the girls were determined to live life as fully as possible. One alumna recalled them sneaking into a movie theater on the way back from dinner after they made

16. Fifteen members of the Forty-Seventh Graduating Class of Shokei Girls' School, interview by author, 27 August 2002 at Shokei High School. Experience of Reiko Hiura Horie.

sure that a "look-out" kept her post to spot any teachers who might pass by.[17]

Since the bombings were increasing in Tokyo, the students there were moved to the Chigasaki branch south of Yokohama after their first month of orientation was concluded. There on a nearby beach, with Mount Fuji towering in the distance and the beauty of the deep blue sea on the other side, the students welcomed in the new year with the disappointing news that they would not be allowed to return to Sendai for a short New Year's break as had been promised.

One day melted into the next. Rice all but disappeared, and was replaced by rice porridge, a *miso*-based soup with leafy vegetables. The meals were immediately satisfying, but never lasted until the next meal. One student's aunt who lived several hours distance in Shibuya district of Tokyo, worked for a cafeteria. One day she managed to save two bucketsful of porridge and carried them all the way to Chigasaki by train.[18]

In March, two graduation ceremonies were held for the Forty-Seventh Graduating Class, one was held at Shokei in Sendai and one at the Chigasaki factory. For the latter ceremony, Vice-Principal Nakase brought the certificates in his backpack. It was so hard to hear with the noise and clatter of the factory that students stood, sat, bowed, and walked up front with visual cues. The special meal afterwards was supplemented by boxes of *miso* paste and *udon* noodles sent by anxious parents.[19] Students who had been accepted for higher education and those who had jobs left one hundred and four other students to continue working at the plant.

Meanwhile, entrance exams continued all over the country as usual. But this time the government required all schools to put a test problem on the exam. It read something like, "What is the most disgraceful way for a person to die?" The answer they were looking for was "dying for a reason other than service to one's country." However, in March of 1945, after entrance exam results were known, all private schools from junior high and above were declared closed for working toward one final drive to win the war. Without this young labor force from educational institutions, life would have come to a standstill. After Shokei was closed, the students continued to be assigned to work.

17. Ibid., experience of Teiko Kudo Oshima.
18. Ibid.
19. Ibid., experience of Yoko Oshima.

The students at Chigasaki still took time out for some fun, like traveling short distances to some scenic spots, and sneaking out for forbidden conversations with the boys from the factory. But in the final few months of the war, the nation was heading toward near starvation. Everything was being rationed. The girls at Chigasaki used their little spending money in search of "bargains." Some girls found "curry rice" made with wheat instead of rice, but it left one student with a case of diphtheria. A *mikan* ("mandarin orange") here, a potato there, seeds of any kind were sought after to supplement their meager diet. Students left at Shokei heard of the shortage of food, and gathered and sent rice to their classmates in Chigasaki through no little sacrifice of their own. The night-shift workers were so hungry that they could not keep up the same pace of work, and talked about striking. The accompanying teachers got wind of the talk and solved the problems with the company. Conditions improved slightly. The girls were needing a break, so one by one they were allowed to return to Sendai for a few days, taking with them a handful of letters for some very worried parents. One of those letters preserved by a family gives us a look at how a sixteen-year-old was dealing with the present circumstances:

Dear Mother,

How longingly you waited June 2nd thinking I'd return. I haven't words to describe how sorry I am. All I have are feelings of home sickness. In this war situation, they can't so easily send us back . . . My turn will come soon, I'm sure. I'm waiting longingly for that day. The thought of wanting to return is always on my mind.

It seems that Sendai is hot. Can you get enough sweet potatoes yet? It must be difficult to get vegetables, also. In Chigasaki at meal-time, we have onions, cabbage, Chinese cabbage, dried burdock and taro [*sato imo*]. Today we had the first crop of cucumbers. They were delicious. Mackerel is in season but as usual we have very little rice. Dinner tonight was porridge. We work very hard every day, so this porridge is not enough food. It's best to perspire in the heat and then eat, but we immediately feel hungry instead. If we had rice we could make it in our rooms when necessary but it's not possible. Even if we go out to the local fields to buy potatoes, they can't sell anything to us because of the government rations. Three days ago, on the way back we found a place that gave us 4 kilos of very tiny mountain potatoes. When we got back my room-mates and I boiled them. We didn't have soy sauce but got some salt. The next day we were indescribably content. They were tiny potatoes and very good. Everyone said that they got the prize! I felt so hungry that I bought some pumpkin seeds. I bought 2 go for 3 yen[20] at a seed store. I gobbled them down without pealing [sic] them, so my chest began to hurt and I had diarrhea. I learned my lesson and will never do such a contemptible thing again. When I have my turn to return I hope to carry some rice back. I've come to heartily appreciate the taste of rice. I heard that even the supply of beans in Sendai has been exhausted. It's the same everywhere.

Every evening there is a lookout for the enemy . . . We can't let down our vigilance.

I'm really busy but work just stacks up. It seems as though we are boiling in our own perspiration. . . . I heard that there was new water in the bath but it was just tepid so I returned feeling quite uncomfortable. I haven't taken a bath in several days. I just wash by dipping a towel in cold water. I've got to do washing but I used up all the soap distributed last week, so there's nothing more I can do. We're all having a hard time. All we can do is to rinse our dirty handkerchiefs out. Please send some soap back with Mitsue. Also, please send my summer school uniform and the rayon underwear that I made before coming here . . .

Some parents are complaining that the principal could not get us released from the factory. But the factory refused saying they'd be in great difficulty without us. The principal tried his very best but no arrangements could be made on such short notice. We were all disappointed and didn't want to do anything. On the other hand, we felt so sorry for the soldiers in Okinawa who are dying with honor, that we received courage and swore to continue to give our best to a noble finish!

. . . There aren't any fleas at home, right? In the dorm we have mosquitoes and fleas. It's really uncomfortable. Even while writing this letter I picked off five. They jump onto the bed. I can't rest well. It's almost 11 pm. I can hear the sound of the waves. It's getting late so I'll close. Forgive me for writing such a confusing letter. Say hello to the neighborhood association.

Kazuko, July 2, 1945[21]

Kazuko had her wish and she headed home for a break with a few other students to a "safer" place on July 9th. As soon as she and a few of her

20. According to Dr Mochizuki, the yen/dollar value in 2009 for the "2 go" measurement of seeds (three hundred sixty milliliters or one and a half American cups) was eleven yen, or eleven cents (see chapter 3 note 7).

21. Kazuko Sato Kikuchi to Mother, 2 July 1945, letters in Students' File. Shokei Gakuin Archival Collection.

friends arrived in Sendai about 11 PM, the air raid warnings began. After eating a welcome-back meal at home and beginning to relax, the bombings of Sendai began. Her first thought was that of thanksgiving; God had allowed her to return so that she could die with her family. The bombing continued into the early morning hours with devastating results.[22] But she had survived with her family, and so had the other students who had accompanied her back to Sendai. The rest of the students in Chigasaki continued working with great unease, not knowing the condition of their families, but gradually all returned safely to nostalgic Sendai.

Meanwhile, Akiko Suzuki was a second-year student on that infamous day. She heard the rumors from her classmates about the pamphlets floating down from the sky. "Sendai, a paper country in July and August, a city of ashes!" Rushing home with the rumor on the tip of her tongue, Akiko and her aunt buried themselves in the bedding closet with a music box, adjusting the music volume low enough so no one except them could hear. They listened to song after song as if they might not ever be able to listen to music again. Suddenly the sirens began to wail and then abruptly stopped. Relaxing, they drifted off. The sirens again instantly woke them up, just as a roaring firebomb incinerated a tree in their garden. They couldn't find the suitcase they had prepared, so they grabbed the box with Akiko's father's ashes and headed out blindly in the direction of the edge of town, calling to the family members in the total blackness. As if by design, they all gathered at a relative's house. Ten days later, Akiko and her mother left the back-country for their house in Sendai. In the middle of the destruction, in front of their house, there stood their tall garlic plants with blackened heads that had grown four inches taller than when they had left. Surprised at the strength of the heat, Akiko just absent-mindedly yanked them out of the ground. Around where the kitchen should have been, she lifted the roof tiles one by one and found a flattened pan they heated milk in. She found a round stone and pounded it until the shape had somewhat returned. She then found an iron kettle and its lid and, in the closet, they found the clay pot they were making *miso* bean paste in. But now it had tiny bubbles and was fully fermented! The glassware in the cupboard had melted into little droplets that looked like clear candy.

---

22. For further reading, see Bradley, F. J. "Contribution of Major Fire Raids Toward Ending WWII." In *No Strategic Targets Left*. Nashville: Turner, 1999. ISBN 1–56311–483–6.

The Akiko's family moved seven times before winning a government sponsored lottery in 1948, from which they received a house.[23]

Shokei dormitory was destroyed in that raid. It had been a "store place for [military] provisions and so became a target."[24] Since the students were disbursed for work, none of them were living in the dorm, and there was no loss of life. Other events followed quickly with the dropping of the atomic bomb on Hiroshima on August 6th, on Nagasaki on August 9th, and the surrender of Japan on August 15th, 1945. Even though Japan lost the war, the dedication, loyalty, sheer determination, and fiery love of country made these girls at Chigasaki and elsewhere winners, and they should be numbered among the heroines of World War II in Japan.

MISSIONARY WHEREABOUTS DURING THE WAR

Where were they? What were their experiences? Even though the records are not complete, there is some information about missionaries who served at Shokei. Excerpts from a letter written by an I. J. Fisher in May 1942 assumed that many of the women missionaries still left in Japan to date would be "safe because they were pro-Japanese." Most of them were "safe" but in internment camps.[25] Many stories too long to retell here are stories of endurance, some of heroism. But a thread that runs through all the stories is not one of hatred and bitterness toward Japanese, but one of confidence and faith in the basic character of the Japanese people. Their attitude was typical of the attitude taken by the son of ABFMS missionaries to Japan who were beheaded by the Japanese Imperial army in the Philippines: "We weren't angry at the Japanese people for this horrible crime. It wasn't they who committed the crime but the Japanese military machine. There is a big difference."[26] In the order of their service at Shokei, a part of the stories of those who were still in active service during World War II, both long and brief, are summarized below.

Thomasine Allen (Shokei: 1918–1927): "Tommy" was in Kuji, Iwate Prefecture, at the outbreak of the war. She had just established a Kuji kindergarten. From December 9th, 1941 for nearly two years, she was interned

23. Suzuki, interview; Sato, recording.

24. Jesse to Sears, 7 February 1947, BIM Correspondence File.

25. I. J. Fisher, excerpts from a letter to Miss Kelsey, 19 May 1942, The War Years Collection, Japan.

26. Alice Covell Bender to author, January 1997.

in four different locations: in Morioka, two places in Sendai, one in Tokyo. In Morioka, a large town in northeast Japan, Iwate Prefecture, she was interned with Cornelia Schroer, German Reformed Church missionary, and her two daughters. (Husband Gilbert Schroer had been jailed as a suspected spy. He was released with no charges just prior to their departure to America.) Added to that number were French Canadian Dominican priests and Belgian Dominican nuns. The mental torture of not knowing if she would be imprisoned because she was thought to be a spy was more difficult for Allen than the lack of heat and food. She remarked often of the kind gestures made by the guards, as "a candle of kindness."[27] The foreign internees were only allowed to use Japanese language with each other. Meals were not provided by the police, but were prepared and delivered by the missionaries' own servants. In March of 1942, she was transferred to Sendai where she was interned for six weeks in a missionary's residence, then transferred to Motoderakoji, the Catholic Church compound where she met Bixby. More than thirty Roman Catholic priests and other Protestant missionaries were also interned there. Worship services were allowed, and through them "Tommy" received the spiritual nourishment she needed, even though physical nourishment was lacking. An incident such as the following also helped to uplift her spirit:

> One time in Sendai [internment] several girls came with flowers which they wanted to give us. They were girls from the Christian schools, Miyagi and Shokei. They wanted to show us that they sympathized with us and they loved us in spite of the war. The guard turned them away, but they came back several times. Finally, seeing that they couldn't get in, some of them came to a house near the one in which we were interned, they spent one whole evening singing and playing the little organ that they had moved outdoors so we could hear it. I think that evening of music was one of the most touching things that had happened during the whole time.[28]

In September, Allen was again moved, this time to an internment camp in Tokyo. There she was reunited with many other missionaries from Tokyo who had been free to go wherever they wanted during the first year of the war. She had been envious of them but now she realized that she had had it better than they. As one woman from Tokyo described it to her, "the tension of loyalty and friendship for the two warring nations was almost

27. Hemphill, *A Treasure to Share*, 78.
28. Ibid., 78–79.

unbearable. 'It was like having a chronic headache; if you turn to the right, one side ached, and if you turned to the left the other side started. When we were interned, it was a great relief to us.'"[29] Her decision to leave Japan was influenced by the report of the lack of food, even in the countryside, from where the internment camp had been receiving its food. She did not want to be a burden on anyone any longer. Finally, in September of 1943, Allen boarded the last prisoner exchange ship, the Teia Maru, for the Portuguese island of Goa. From there, she and others were transferred to the SS Gripsholm.

After returning to the United States, she had some difficulty adjusting to the fact that she was now in a free country. But as time passed and she could begin to share her experiences with American church members she began to relax. In Japan, she had been thought of as a spy by the Japanese government, and now in America, as a long-term resident in Japan, she was again suspected as being a collaborator with the Japanese. Even though the FBI followed her and listened to her speeches wherever she went, they did not interfere, and healing did take place. She became aware of another need. In the spring of 1944, she decided to apply for a job as a translator with the War Relocation Authority. She was assigned to work in Tule Lake, California, where hearings were taking place. Some of the Japanese-Americans in the camp had given up their American citizenship, but now they wanted their American citizenship back. Others were afraid to leave the concentration camp, and a third group of hard-core Japanese sympathizers remained. Allen helped as an interpreter during these hearings until her reassignment to Japan in March 1947, when she was again able to help in shining the light of Jesus toward her beloved Japanese.[30]

Ruth Ward (Shokei: 1921–1926): Ward was teaching at Soshin Girls' School at the time of the outbreak of the war. She had resigned from the Mission Board in 1934, but now taught under private contract with Soshin school. The police put many foreigners in the Tokyo/Yokohama area under scrutiny for some months before they were interned. Some in Yokohama were never interned. News of Ward came from information received by Bixby in Yokohama as she left for repatriation. According to Bixby's source, Ward continued to teach at Soshin until May 1942, and was considering repatriation at the time Bixby heard the news.[31]

29. Ibid., 79.
30. Ibid., 84–90.
31. Bixby to Constituency, 16 September 1942, BIM Correspondence File.

Winifred Acock (Shokei: 1924–1926): Acock taught at Soshin Girls' School along with Ruth Ward. They could live on campus until July 1942 but not teach. From that time Acock stayed with ABFMS missionaries Dr. and Mrs. William Axling in Tokyo. When the authorities came to remove the Axlings, strangely enough, they did not require Acock to leave. Japanese were so overly kind by bringing her their food rations, depriving themselves, that she thought it was necessary to move again. She moved in with other missionaries in Tokyo until the police came to escort her to the repatriation ship, Teia Maru in September 1943.[32]

Emma Brodbeck (Shokei: 1927–1928): She had served in West China, beginning in 1918, but taught at Shokei for only one year. After she left Shokei she returned to China, continuing to serve there until 1939. After a year of furlough in the United States, she returned to China in 1940. But since all entry from the east into China was blocked by Japan, her ship sailed on to Rangoon, Burma. From Rangoon, via the Burma Road, she entered West China "through the back door" to the town of Ipin in Szechuan Province. There she spent the war years under Japanese occupation. She suffered with her Chinese friends during the bombing-raids and other difficulties of the Japanese period of occupation, but the earlier, short missionary experience in Sendai enabled her to be sympathetic toward the Japanese people in her "homeland" in China.[33] In 1947 she was transferred to the remote town of Loshan, West China. She had formerly worked in education, but now she worked directly with the church, teaching English conversation classes, a children's story hour, directing girls' clubs, entertaining both Chinese and foreign travelers who passed through her town. All these activities ceased when the Communists took over. She experienced house arrest and was imprisoned several times. Her house and possessions were confiscated before she left for the United States in September 1951.[34]

Georgia Newbury (Shokei: 1924–1935): Newbury taught in Taiwan after resigning from the Woman's American Baptist Foreign Mission Society. For a short time, she worked for the English language newspaper, called the *Japan Times* in Tokyo. After the war began, the Japanese government took control of that newspaper, as well as an American newspaper in Japan called the *Japan Advertiser*. She moved to that office to work along with Mr.

---

32. Acock to Constituency, 10 December 1943, BIM Correspondence File; Missionary Register Card, Acock, BIM, Archival Collections of ABHS.

33. Brodbeck, Book Cover, *China Farewell*, n.p.

34. Ibid., 82.

I. J. Fisher, who stated in a letter to the Woman's Board that he thought she would be safe during the war because she was pro-Japanese.[35] It is not clear whether she returned to the United States or not during the war.

Agnes Meline (Shokei: 1926–1928): Meline resigned from the Woman's American Baptist Foreign Mission Society some time after July 1932. Later she returned to Japan and worked in non-mission schools.[36] Allen met Meline in the Tokyo internment camp in December 1942. Her repatriation date is unknown.

Margaret Cuddeback (Shokei: 1935–1938): After returning to America and studying for two years at Columbia University, she returned to Japan as acting director of Mead Christian Center. In the summer of 1941, she went to the Philippines. However, from the Philippines, she went on to Shanghai to visit friends. She stayed on there because she found a teaching position. She was interned in what she called "a Japanese concentration camp" on February 23rd, 1942 with over one thousand other foreigners. She sailed from Shanghai on September 19th, 1943 to join the same ship on which Thomasine Allen returned.

Alice Bixby (Shokei: 1930–1934; 1939–1941):[37] When she was interned at the compound of the Catholic Bishop of Sendai in Motoderakoji in December 1941, there were other Americans and British subjects of Sendai, Protestants and Catholics, missionaries and non-missionaries. By the end of December 1941, there were a total of fifty-six Protestant and Catholic missionaries, and one couple who taught at the local Imperial University. The following is a summary of Alice Bixby's letter describing what life was like in the internment camp: When life settled down, the internees began to organize themselves. Wood was brought from their own homes for heat as well as canned goods, dishes, tables, chairs, and other necessities. Responsibilities were divided up into food preparation, cooking, cleanup, and cleaning the buildings. Police brought in butter from Hokkaido, bread, and occasionally meat, fish, and vegetables. Since the convents had good gardens, Chinese cabbage, carrots, and other vegetables were grown there. But occasionally, Japanese helpers who had worked for foreigners before incarceration brought in vegetables, eggs, and milk. When that supply ran

35. I. J. Fisher, excerpts from a letter to Kelsey, 19 May 1942.

36. Ibid.

37. The following section is a summary and some quotes from Alice Bixby's letter written to her constituency on September 16, 1943, after she returned to the United States.

out, a limited supply of milk from a Japanese dairy was brought in. These items were not available to the Japanese at that time.

Since there were no washing facilities, servants of the missionaries came on an appointed day to receive laundry. Satsuki Kobayashi, a long-time helper of missionaries, faithfully washed and returned Bixby's clothes to the police guard at the gate.

For the first two months, daily running expenses for things such as supplies, food, etc., were paid for by the internees themselves. But in February of 1942, the government took over the expenses, and money used by the internees was refunded. This was welcomed, since some people had no money and most had difficulty getting money from their bank accounts.

In February, mail being held by the censor since the foreigners had been interned, was delivered. Mail that they had sent from November until the day of internment was returned to them, unsent. A newspaper from Tokyo was delivered for the first time in some months, and only occasionally after that.

All contact with the outside was censored, aside from an occasional newspaper. Only under rare circumstances was a visitor allowed. The police carefully inspected all bundles of clothing sent in and out. Flowers and gifts were refused on the basis that "individuals could not receive special treatment." At New Year's, the neighborhood outside sent in a gift of mandarin oranges (*mikan*) to all in the camp. Three times Shokei teachers came to visit Bixby, but were not admitted, and once the pastor came and was refused entry. During the allotted period of exercise in the garden, passers-by often stopped to look in through the iron gate. The police waved them on saying "This is not an exhibit. People should not stop to look in." All communication, even the waving of hands, was prohibited. The punishment for non-compliance was elimination of the exercise period for the whole group. No one passing by was rude. Eventually, a high board fence was built between the gate and the house, allowing for more privacy. From that time on, the internees could go out into the garden at any time during the day.

Just before Bixby was interned, she received two Christmas boxes from her home church in United States. These were the only two boxes that the police allowed anyone to bring into internment other than personal possessions. The police cataloged the contents of the boxes and kept the boxes until Christmas. Then they gave permission for the contents of the boxes to be opened and the sweets inside were divided into sixty portions by the internees, rewrapped with the wrapping paper found in the box, and distributed to all who were interned. It provided a moment of joy during a gloomy, difficult time. From the adjoining church kindergarten, a small organ was brought in for an unrehearsed Christmas program of songs in English and French by the internees. Even the guards seemed to enjoy the time.

The police allowed Mass and Protestant services, and anyone could use the Catholic Church when Japanese were not using it. One of the Catholic priests played for the services and asked Bixby to play for him when he sang a solo. The police gave him permission to give a concert one evening where Bixby was the accompanist. On Sunday, services were held separately, organized by the Protestant and Catholic internees in the rooms where they slept, since Japanese citizens used the church. In the spring, the Protestants began holding morning prayer services daily.

Once a month everyone joined in a social program that was often humorous. The internees laughed and joked together to keep up their morale, but the police felt that they should maintain their dignity by not showing that they enjoyed the program. The internees didn't find it easy to be suspected and watched all the time, and to accept irritating experiences calmly, so this program provided the needed emotional release.

One morning a serious fire across the street from the Catholic compound destroyed eight homes. The residents with their furniture occupied the compound garden for some time. In late March, Allen was moved to Sendai from Morioka. But because of the overcrowding at the Catholic Compound, she soon moved to another location. Bixby did not see her until three weeks before she left Japan.

In early April, a representative from the Swiss legation came to meet American citizens. They accepted applications for leaving the country in case an evacuation boat arrived. For the first time, Bixby discovered that her name was not on the list of Americans living in and around Sendai. Since her name was not on the list, they decided that she had better sign an application to leave, even though she desired to stay on. Some foreigners in Tokyo could still move about freely, but her hope of that happening in Sendai had vanished. They heard nothing more until late May, when the Swiss legation came with a list of those who would be repatriated. Some who had requested repatriation were not on the list to leave, and some who had not requested to leave were on the list. Bixby was on the list, but Thomasine Allen was not.

Bixby was taken by police to her house (Buzzell Kan), and then on to Yokohama with other missionaries. Ten days later, on June 17th, they boarded the *Asama Maru*. The ship stayed in the harbor for another week until June 25th before it set sail for the big prisoner exchange in Goa. Before Goa, there were stops in Hong Kong, Saigon, and Singapore. The solemn prisoner exchange occurred in Lourenco Marques, Goa. There they boarded the Swedish ship SS *Gripsolm* and traveled to Rio de Janeiro before docking in New York harbor. After eighteen thousand miles and four continents, Alice Bixby saw the welcoming figure of the Statue of Liberty at last.[38]

A month or so after her arrival, and upon much reflection, she wrote of her experience in the Japanese internment camp:

> We were not mistreated in any way and were wonderfully protected from sickness . . . It certainly is true that no matter what happened, very little complaint was heard, and though there was constantly in our hearts a great desire to know what was going on outside, a great anxiety for the schools and churches, for our friends in Japan and also in America from whom we had not heard in so many months, God gave strength, endurance and good cheer.[39]

First Day of Factory Work at Naval Yards in Tagajo (1944)
(courtesy of Shokei Gakuin)

38. Ibid.
39. Ibid.

Fire Drills at Shokei
(courtesy of Shokei Gakuin)

Principal Shigeto Takahashi (1937–1949)
(courtesy of Shokei Gakuin)

8

Welcoming Free And Brighter Days
(1947–1950)

Great occasions do not make heroes or cowards;
they simply unveil them to the eyes of men.
Silently and imperceptibly, as we wake or sleep,
we grow strong or weak and at last some crisis
shows what we have become.

—BROOKE FOSS WESTCOTT[1]

*O*ut of the Ashes is the title of a booklet telling the post-war Japan story of churches, social and educational institutions published by the Japan Missionary Fellowship. The title aptly expresses exactly what happened in Japan after the shock of defeat subsided. The resiliency of the Japanese people was soon evident. The Japanese Christians took the first step by writing to their American Christian friends, urging them to return. Missionaries were then mobilized to return to Japan—among them, Mary Jesse. In the meantime, Shokei began functioning as best as could be expected. With the return of Jesse, the school spent two years in the recovery phase. Conflict over the resignation of the principal and its effect on the construction of the gymnasium cast a shadow over the school for a period of time.

1. Westcott, BrainyQuote.com. https://www.brainyquote.com/quotes/quotes/b/brookefoss194199.html.

REBUILDING TRUST

The recovery process required that both sides, Japan and America, extend the hand of friendship. The strength of the bonds of friendship developed in the years before the war became clear when the Japanese Christians extended the invitation for missionaries to return.

Moves Toward Reconciliation. In addition to being concerned about the general uprooting and devastation experienced by nearly every Japanese, American Baptists, then called the Northern Baptist Convention, were also concerned with the wreckage of seventy-five years of mission work caused by United States B-29 bombers and the resulting fires. Nearly four hundred thirty-five buildings of the one thousand eight hundred Protestant congregations related to the United Church of Christ in Japan, of which Baptists were members, were destroyed or declared unstable.[2] Fifty of those were Baptist churches. But, bombers and fires could not destroy the gracious spirit of the Christians. "Christian work has been disturbed not a little," wrote Dr. Yugoro Chiba:

> Christian workers and believers are scattered all over the country. It is a serious question how to rebuild these buildings and the work. We are at a loss, but not dismayed, for we believe [that] Almighty God [is] with us and feel strong in the Lord; and are ready to continue to fight the good fight of faith.[3]
> . . . By [the] wonderful providence of God, the old Japan was destroyed and thrown away, and the new Japan was started on the 15th of August. Since then phenomenal changes are taking place in all spheres of national life . . . Among these, three most outstanding, penetrating utterances are heard everywhere. One is the cry for democracy, another is international friendship, and the third is the cry for bread. We had long been suffering from militarism and despotism and now we are very glad to welcome free and brighter days approaching on the eastern horizon.[4]

Every family and institution had to deal with its own pain. The pain of recovery was great no matter what degree the damage was. Shokei Girls' School fully realized that its situation, although difficult, did not compare to that of their sister schools. Soshin Girls' School and Kanto Gakuin schools were destroyed.

2. Elmer Fridell, "Japan," 14 November 1947, The War Years Collection, Japan.
3. Yugoro Chiba to A. F. Ufford and Hazel F. Shank, 10 November 1945.
4. Ibid.

Organizing for a New Start. Immediately after the armistice, victorious allied forces in Sendai began looking for places to live and operate. Shokei was among several schools commandeered for their use. Staff and students were asked to move from their school campus into two separate elementary schools, Hachiman Kokumin School to the north, and a private school for girls located to the west.[5] It was only a short walk from the campus, but in three days' time the staff and students carried necessary equipment and supplies to the two locations. The school was split up and had to share the facilities with elementary students, making the educational process less than comfortable and efficient. All grade levels studied together in the same large auditorium with only a curtain dividing them. Not much actual teaching took place under these conditions, but for the first time, many students were exposed to hymns of the Christian faith. During the last few years of the war, worship had been de-emphasized or abandoned. Shokei students who were sent out to work in factories, fields, and in nursery schools had little or no exposure to Christian hymns and teaching, and the Christian spirit of the school which was nearly lost had to be rediscovered.

This difficult arrangement did not last long. Through the efforts of occupation forces chaplains, Shokei regained its buildings within three weeks. Classes resumed on campus on October 10th, 1945. By the time Jesse returned to Sendai in late January 1947, a new spirit was permeating the school. Students were hungry to learn about Christianity. The occupation forces chaplains were also helpful in leading chapel services. While classes continued, they awaited the new educational system to be established by the MacArthur government.

Return of Missionaries to Japan. As far back as 1943, the American Baptist Foreign Mission Society began to envision what post-war Japan might look like. Records reveal the belief that they thought United States would win the war. In discussing the probable feelings of "a conquered" people toward returning missionaries of the "victor" country, it was noted that the Japanese Christians

> will be the first to grasp our hands in fellowship. But we cannot approach them as representatives of victor nations nor as would-be benefactors offering to rebuild what the war has destroyed. We

---

5. The private elementary girls school was on the corner of the grounds of what is now known as First Girls High School (*Ichi Joukou*).

shall have to engage first and foremost in a ministry of reconciliation . . .

With a decisive defeat of Japan, the church leaders could very easily be embarrassed at reestablishing any relationship at all with the American church. But it is also possible that . . . it would incline towards accepting assistance in its work even from Christians of former enemy countries.[6]

These estimations were not too far off. Thanks to efforts of former Japan missionaries who were part of the Occupation staff, contact was made with Japanese Christians shortly after the war.[7] As early as November 1945, letters from Japanese Christian leaders began to pour in to the various mission boards in the United States and Canada asking for missionaries to return. Mission boards of North America joined hands to reestablish contact with churches in Japan. A committee called the "Japan Committee" was formed with representatives from almost all the Protestant mission boards, which coordinated all actions related to Japan. This included sending missionaries and raising funds for relief of pastors and churches. A commission of six people was appointed from the "Japan Committee" to act as the official liaison to the Supreme Command Allied Powers (SCAP) in Japan. Since non-military personnel were forbidden entry into Japan by SCAP, it took some months before this committee could enter Japan. Douglas MacArthur wanted missionaries to return, but SCAP policy prohibited any religious favoritism. Finally, a special regulation was made to allow the committee as visitors into the country. It was based on the requirement of the Potsdam Declaration to rebuild normal society to resume world relationships.[8] On April 15th, 1946, the first two people of the "Commission of Six" arrived in Japan. One person was to coordinate relief from overseas and the other to be the contact person for SCAP in opening the way for missionaries to return and coordinating the needs of Japanese churches. They surveyed the extent of damage and assessed the food and housing situation for missionaries who would eventually return. They made recommendations to the Japan Committee who in turn made efforts to fill the need for missionaries in education and rural evangelism.[9] Four more mem-

6. "Preliminary Considerations for Post War Study on Japan," 20 March 1945, War Years Collection.

7. Iglehart, *Protestant Christianity*, 273.

8. Ibid., 282.

9. Foreign Missions Conference of North America, "The First Postwar Year," January 1947, The War Years Collection.

bers of the Commission of Six arrived by June. They in turn were assigned responsibility for contacting Japanese churchwomen, Japanese churches, and Christian schools to reconnect them to churches in the West.[10] The Commission of Six continued their work for another year.[11] Baptists, in the meantime, were doing their own assessment of damage. In the next year and a half, Dr. Elmer Fridell, the ABFMS foreign secretary for the Orient, made two trips to Japan, and visited all the areas where ABFMS work was located to examine the needs.[12]

From lists received from all Protestant denominations, the Japan Committee compiled a priority list of thirty-eight missionaries who would be the first to return to serve in Japan. This list was then sent to the Commission of Six. The commission investigated each missionary's situation and work destination to assure SCAP that housing and food would be available. Then military clearance was granted. The Woman's American Baptist Foreign Mission Society's priority list submitted to the Japan Committee included Thomasine Allen and Alice Bixby as top priority, with other veteran missionaries following. The actual list of thirty-eight approved missionaries from the Supreme High Command in Japan included Mary D. Jesse and Alice Bixby, but not Thomasine Allen. It seemed that missionaries working in middle and higher education received first consideration.[13]

Because Jesse's appointment was unexpected, she did not have time to prepare for the planned departure. In addition to needing dental work and winter clothes, she needed to retrieve some of her belongings that she had stored at the house of former Sendai missionaries, Charles and Sadie Ross in southern California, and could not reach the ship before the September 23rd sailing date. She had to forfeit her place on the ship.[14]

Shipping Woes. Nowadays, we can hardly imagine what it was like to travel by ship for reasons other than pleasure. But from 1814 until the early 1960s, missionaries traveled back and forth by ship. Many letters are on file from missionaries who had finally settled in to "enjoy" the trip across the ocean. Preparations for the trip abroad for a full term of service are always complicated but, in 1946, when no one knew what to expect in a war-torn country, all the things needed to live comfortably for five years were packed

10. Iglehart, *Protestant Christianity*, 282–83.

11. Ibid., 292.

12. Fridell and Sears, "Japan Statement," 14 November 1947.

13. Shank to Jesse, 13 June 1946. BIM Correspondence File of Mary D. Jesse.

14. Jesse to Shank, 6 September 1946, BIM Correspondence File.

and shipped. Jesse found preparation for this trip particularly exhausting. Once she boarded, she wrote an informal letter with travel advice for Thomasine Allen and Margaret Cuddeback who would follow later.

When all bags were ready, they weighed in at fifteen hundred pounds (six hundred seventy-five kilograms). It was the largest amount she had ever taken, because she had to ship food. She compared herself to ten Methodist missionaries whose shipments topped three thousand pounds each at a cost of five thousand dollars per person. An important part of their shipment was sugar. How to find sugar that could be exported was a problem for everyone. Even the shipping company had to apply for a special license just to carry it. Some stores sold it for export exclusively in twenty-five pound allotments. Jesse took twenty-five pounds, but the Methodist women somehow got fifty pounds of sugar each. Jesse passed along an address for buying sugar with the comment that she was not sure whether it was a black-market company or not.[15]

Some people used crates especially built for shipping; others used steel barrels, which added more weight, while others just used cardboard cartons. She could not find a company to transport her crates to Seattle without going through a broker. She was required to be at the port four or five days before the sailing date because it took two or three days just for inspection and loading of baggage. Baggage limits were imposed, but inspectors seemed to realize that people going overseas this time needed more supplies than usual. Two pieces of her baggage were temporarily lost. They were found and loaded on the ship at the last minute, since she had processed the paperwork on them already. Paperwork consisted of listing all items no matter what the size and the cost of each item. A day after the second- and third-class passengers boarded, the first-class passengers came on board. The ship finally left port the following day, December 23rd, 1946.

Jesse's letter continues: Her accommodations were more adequate than she expected, she wrote. Until then, most ships provided small rooms sleeping two to six people. This time the accommodations were more communal with one large room sleeping twenty-four people. Bunks were narrow, two deep in rows with walking space between. There were a few chairs in the room. One deck below there was a large lounge with tables and chairs, "no style of course," but there was little room for exercising. The meal served while the ship was in port was "good but not dainty." It included soup, steak,

15. Jesse to Sears, 23 December 1946, BIM Correspondence File.

vegetables, salad, and ice cream. It was not a bad menu for missionaries who would spend the next few years on tight rations![16]

Miserable Arrival. Back in Japan. On January 7th, 1947, sixty-four-year-old Jesse stepped off the ship and began her last five-year term of service. She wondered if at this age, she could really be of service. Her first concern was her health. While on the dock at Yokohama trying to find her luggage, she caught a horrendous cold. Although she planned to go to Sendai within a day or so of her arrival, she was so sick that she did not actually reach Sendai until January 23th, 1947.

In her first letter after arriving in Yokohama, she shared her first impressions. The destruction was terrible, she observed, but the Japanese do smile, are cheerful and seem hopeful; there seemed to be no feelings of resentment and they showed the same kindness and courtesy as before. She did not expect to find this attitude. She observed that the Japanese people seemed determined to build a free Japan. This explained their new interest in English and the Christian religion; they were pushing on, attending extra classes and clubs, seeking information everywhere with surprising energy.

She related several stories of people facing harsh conditions. One pastor and his family lost everything, but arranged to live in a hospital room where dead bodies were kept until relatives came to identify them. She wondered how that pastor could stand up before his congregation week after week and preach an inspiring sermon. Another pastor she talked to had also lost everything. Then his wife died, and he was without a salary for a year and a half. Two US army chaplains helped him get materials to build the walls and roof of a church. There were no windows or doors yet, but at least thirteen people had been baptized in the first two weeks of January.[17]

Other things occupied her mind, too, while she recovered from her cold. Where and how would she live after returning to Sendai? Mr. Takahashi offered her a room in his house for a while until she could move into the Ella O. Patrick building again. She worried about taking up space that was needed for students now that there was no dormitory. The Buzzell House, where she lived with Bixby before the war, was being used by Sendai Baptist Church. Pastor Yamada and his wife lost their lives protecting their young daughter when the church was hit in an air raid. Jesse had also been advised to have a helper since it was so difficult to procure goods.

16. Ibid.

17. Jesse, "Shokei Report for 1947," 7 January 1948, Shokei Gakuin Archival Collection.

Although she was too sick to attend a Christian teachers' conference in Tokyo, she received enough of a report to cause her to begin planning necessary changes that needed to be made. She anticipated some of the problems that Shokei would face because of the reorganization of the government and its institutions by the MacArthur administration. Probable requirements for co-education and hiring more specialists concerned her. At government request, Christian schools that were intact and had buildings were asked to take over the education of all junior high school students until government schools recovered. Aid would be given to schools that consented but religion could not be taught. Jesse was burdened by the thought of receiving government aid that would benefit teachers greatly, "but at the expense of not being able to teach Christianity?" She closed her report by saying "Everything seems so different and strange here."[18]

Arrival in Sendai Without Fanfare. Jesse was the first missionary to arrive back in Sendai after the war. Reservations on regular trains were hard to get, but she found an army train going north and rode without a ticket. Although a hundred or so friends and students had gathered at Sendai station to welcome her back, they were disappointed. The train was delayed for six hours because of heavy snow, and she arrived in Sendai at two in the morning rather than early evening. A few friends were there to greet her, but there were no taxis either. An American military policeman called for a jeep for her and Mrs. Takahashi, her traveling companion. According to the private memoirs of Principal Takahashi, Jesse and his wife took the jeep ride to the campus, arriving at about 3:00 AM. But according to a teacher and Hosanna Baptist Church minister, Rev. Koumoto, there was indeed another story. Some students at that time agreed with this story. When offered a ride in the jeep, Jesse said, "I'm not related to the military," and walked back to school.[19] Whichever story is true, anyone would agree that her return was less than triumphant!

She found the destruction in Sendai so complete that she had a hard time locating streets and finding her way around, especially in the central part of the city. The people were badly in need of clothing of all kinds. In fact, it was the appearance of the people rather than the physical destruction that most shocked and disturbed her. However, she wrote that they loved and honored General MacArthur and were deeply thankful for the kind help, protection, and guidance he and the United States were giving

18. Ibid.
19. Takao Kaoumoto, "Jesshii no Tsuioku," *Mutsumi no Kusari* 4 (1968) 32.

to the defeated "enemy" country.[20] Most important, when the people saw Jesse's smile, they felt happy and deep nostalgia.[21]

"A ROLLING STONE GATHERS NO MOSS"

Shokei had experienced a time of little forward movement. Compliance with wartime ideology for years and the eternal problem of lack of funds had taken their toll, causing Shokei to become like a stone gathering moss. Jesse felt that she had not been able to fulfill her own goals while she waited for the war to end. Now everyone was filled with excitement. The heavy cumbersome stone began to move, shedding moss as it rolled.

From Stationary to Animate. Principal Shigeto Takahashi was surely glad to have Jesse back. He made every effort to help her settle in. There was much work to do before the new school year began in April. The dormitory had to be rebuilt and nearly everything needed repairing. Although Shokei now worked hard on a financial plan, everyone knew that even if money became available, materials probably would not. But Shokei had buildings in which to conduct school, while some other schools had no buildings at all. Jesse observed that without some repairs to the campus, passersby might wonder whether they were open for business or not.[22] A three-year plan for repairs was sent to the Woman's ABFMS Board, requesting the most urgent repairs for 1947. She didn't know if the plan would even be considered, since Shokei had become financially independent several years before, but she thought she would inquire anyway. In response to a request for more specific costs of the repairs, Jesse wrote a letter giving some interesting insights into Shokei's post-war physical situation.

> Dear Mrs. Sears,
>
> At our Shokei Trustee meeting Saturday we took up the request per your last letter. You perhaps have the cable we asked Mr. Foote to send but thought perhaps I should write some further details . . . The request we sent was based on the estimates we are working on from June 1st. We need $6,000 for urgent repairs on present buildings at present prices and costs but we feel that prices are increasing all the time. Then there is the dormitory to be rebuilt which

20. Jesse, "Shokei Report for 1947," Shokei Gakuin Archival Collection.

21. Masako Numazawa, interview by Mari Sato, 9 June 2017, Japanese transcript of recording with author.

22. Jesse, "Shokei Report for 1947," Shokei Gakuin Archival Collection.

we think will cost ¥700,000 and we are thinking that we can raise ¥200,000 leaving ¥500,000. If you can help us with this it would be of the greatest encouragement and help to us and to the work. You may wonder at the larger request for repairs. I might give you some items of the estimate. All the buildings need repairs.

- ¥20,000   for glass (current value: /$695)
- ¥16,000   electricity (current value: $556)
- ¥51,000   playground (Hachiman) (current value: $1771)
- ¥30,000   repairs, painting on inside of college building (current value: $1042)
- ¥70,000   repairs on outside of college building (current value: $2431)
- ¥50,000   repairs on High school buildings (current value: $1736)
- ¥30,000   repairs on Foreign Houses (current value: $1042)
- ¥30,000   stone wall, permanent gate (current value: $1042)

We are at work now on No. 2, 5, 6. You may wonder about No. 3 but for safety [during the war], holes and tunnels were dug, caves to hide in. These must be filled up and too, bombs made holes. The wreckage of the dormitory must be cleared away and an athletic field laid out again. The college building has to be repainted on the outside. For safety it was smeared and colored with black and yellow streaks. The last finish was never put on the outside. It is a sight now.

Gates were stolen or removed, walls broken down, grounds need much attention.

We estimate the total cost to be about ¥337,000.[23] We are raising as much as we can so we are requesting the $6,000.[24]

In 1947, some money to begin repairs on six buildings was found.[25] They seemed to be experiencing forward movement even though they only had a small percentage of what they needed.

---

23. According to Dr Mochizuki, the yen/dollar value in 2009 for the total of the repairs would be 1,095,250 yen, or $11,704, in 1947 (see chapter 3, note 7).

24. Jesse to Sears, 2 June 1947, BIM Correspondence File.

25. Jesse, "Shokei Report for 1947," Shokei Gakuin Archival Collection.

Getting By Without a Dormitory. With the destruction of the Stafford Memorial Dormitory came years of waiting for a new one to be built. It had been the center of spiritual development. For several years after the war, no facility could be set aside for such use. Each out-of-town student had to find her own housing. But in 1953, Principal Takahashi's former residence (the Ross's old house) on the southeast corner of the main campus was remodeled so that twenty-nine of the students from distant places could be accommodated at last.[26]

Later, in 1955, part of the Ella O. Patrick missionary residence was remodeled to house more out-of-town students. Finally, in 1963, after a wait of seventeen years, a new dormitory was built across the street from the Hachiman (Nakajima-cho) grounds.

Fertile Fields White Unto Harvest. A question that most concerned all missionaries as they returned to their places of service was what the spiritual climate would be. This would indicate just how effective their years of labor had been. Jesse writes about what she found at Shokei in her 1947 annual report:

> As to the religious life of the school, I think it gave me one of the biggest surprises of my life. How difficult things were when I left! So little interest in anything but war work, so few with time or thought for Christianity, for Bible, for music except military songs. I can never forget the thrill of my first chapel. Our big auditorium packed, and the way they sang and listened to the message! I could hardly speak, so great was my joy and gratitude. I was not expecting anything like that. And the surprises continue—the calls, the opportunities, the interest in Bible classes, the new spirit of appreciation and earnestness, the interest in everything American.

Since it was outside of the policy guidelines of the United Church of Christ in Japan, Shokei did not immediately begin a school-church on the campus. Instead of forming their own churches on campus, Christian schools were encouraged to send their students to local churches in the community. As the students became Christians, they were to be baptized into the fellowship of a local church. However, there were impractical implications in this policy. After the war, pastors of local churches in Sendai were so busy trying to rebuild their own lives, their congregations, and church buildings that they had little time to help at Shokei. The general

---

26. Matsumura, "Report of Shokei Jogakuin," c. 1953, Shokei Gakuin Archival Collection.

population was experiencing such revival that the small church buildings could not even hold the crowds trying to attend. Therefore, the pastors felt that they could not properly care for an additional influx of students into their churches. As it was, North Star Baptist Church baptized fifty of their own during the year, while First Baptist Church, whose building had been destroyed, struggled to survive by holding services first in the Buzzell House and later in a new parsonage built on the property of their destroyed church. Their first Christmas service in 1946 had only twenty in attendance, but over three hundred fifty came to the same service in 1947, making it necessary to borrow the *senkoubu* chapel in the Indiana Building at Shokei. That year they had sixteen baptisms.

Everyone said that the Christmas celebration at the school was one of the best ever. While there was not much in the way of gifts, the true spirit of Christmas seemed to permeate the programs. Luxuries such as candy were all but absent in post–war Japan. When Jesse received a box from an American friend, she counted out one piece of untarnished hard candy for each of the newer students. The older students were delighted to receive a recycled Christmas card also provided by American friends. Jesse remarked, "Yes, they were cold and hungry but happy in spite of it all and very thankful for the gift of the Savior."[27]

Dizzying Schedule. Throughout her letters in 1947, Mary Jesse recalls the overwhelming number of opportunities she had for speaking and teaching outside of the school. In a February 1947 letter, she tells about the difficulties of travel and her class in Shiogama:

> This term I teach 15 hours in school. Two hours of Bible. I have promised to teach a Bible class at Shiogama beginning next Sunday. The church is crowded. They have 450 in the Sunday School and they have to hold two sessions, one after the other, for lack of space. I am told that they have 70 in the Bible Class waiting for me. I start at 8:00 and get there by 10:15 for the service. We have lunch together and then Bible Class at 2:00 and a two hour trip home will about fill my day. Travel is so slow and uncertain here now, and such crowds.[28]

Then, in May, she adds to the description of her schedule:

27. Jesse, "Shokei Gakuin Report for 1947," 7 January 1948, Shokei Gakuin Archival Collection.

28. Jesse to Sears, 7 February 1947, BIM Correspondence File.

Last weekend I was in Kesennuma and the one before that, in Kurihara gun. I felt most encouraged at the attendance at the meetings
and the response of our graduates. On Sunday in Kesennuma, in
spite of the pouring rain, so many gathered. I spoke at the morning
service at church, then came lunch and a meeting with graduates
till 3:00 when I went to a school to speak to a large crowd of teachers, parents, students gathered there, till about 5:30 when I went
to the home of a graduate for supper, and back to church where I
spoke again. This was followed by a question period which lasted
till late, 10:30 or later. The trip back on Mon. was most difficult,
almost 12 hours, and such crowds.

School till Sat. noon and in the afternoon a Bible Class here for
graduates from 2:00–4:00, and that night at 7:30 I was due to teach
a Bible lesson at a club for University boys, largely, but I could not
get there. Yesterday, (Sun.) worship service here at 9:00 and then
Bible class over at Buzzell Kan [building] at 11:30. From there over
to the Odatsume home, near the station for lunch and graduates
meeting. It was a meeting of the older graduates. The youngest one
present was 50 and the oldest was 64. We spoke of the school and
its plans, and of our evangelistic opportunities today.[29]

In addition, Jesse taught nurses at the University Hospital, spoke at the
chapel of the Army hospital, at a hospital for tuberculosis patients, and at
meetings of the parent-teacher association for public schools.

Distribution of Clothing. By the summer of 1947, clothing from
American Baptist women began to arrive. In August, Jesse wrote to Minnie
Sears about distributing clothing to twenty very needy students and included a thank-you letter from the father of one of the students. The twenty
girls chosen were either from repatriated families from Manchuria or families whose homes had been burned down in the bombings. Each member
of the chosen families was given something. She could not imagine how
these families would survive the next winter with what little food, fuel, and
clothing they had. She wrote, "I feel that I am failing to convey to you folks
the gratitude, the thanks of these people."[30] She pleaded with women of
American churches to send any used clothing they could spare; even scraps
of cloth could be used for *zori* or *geta* string. "If the people at home could
see how much the clothes mean I am sure they would gladly share."[31] The
translated letter from the grateful father follows:

29. Jesse to Sears, 26 May 1947, BIM Correspondence File.
30. Jesse to Sears, 12 August 1947, BIM Correspondence File.
31. Ibid.

Dear Miss Jesse,

Thank you for your kindness to Yoshiko. Recently Yoshiko came joyously home from school with a big furoshiki. When we opened it we found it contained many dresses. We have been so troubled, so anxious about clothes. The reason is we are about the same as naked, not having clothes. So we were very, very glad.

When the American soldiers took over Japan, we all thought they would be cruel and brutal to us, but they did not hate us at all, but with a big heart they control Japan. For this our gratitude is very great.

Now at this time, besides all this, your country's people with great sympathy have sent these things. We can find no words to express our gratitude.

By your country's leadership our Japan must become a democratic country. Our country is gradually changing in that way, and so we are very fortunate.

At present we have not enough food nor have we clothing. We are in a sad condition but we are working with all our might to overcome this suffering state, and to make Japan a heaven-like country. Then all of us Japanese may be able to show in some way, our appreciation to great America for these many blessings.

This is not the thought of me alone but that of the 70 million Japanese. Every Japanese, I believe, without any untruth, feels this same way, has the same spirit. Truly, I thank you, thank you very much. Excuse my thanking you by letter.[32]

Gardening, a Hobby for Health. Although the economy in Japan was beginning to recover, there was a shortage of many commodities. Feeling the need for better nutrition, Jesse began putting a lot of work into a home garden. Not only was it a relaxing hobby, it also provided healthy exercise. One graduate came by to visit her after a twenty-year interval and found her working in her garden. The graduate wrote a thank-you letter and noted the following:

Dear Miss Jesse,

How happy I was to see you back in Shokei again. I was surprised to see you tilling the field, but felt relieved for you looked healthy. Can you believe it is twenty years since I was studying in Shokei? You do not look a bit altered from what you were 20 years ago.[33]

32. Father of student to Jesse, 12 August 1947, BIM Correspondence File of Mary D. Jesse.

33. Tai Iikawa Kusakabe to Jesse, 12 May 1948, *Jesse sensei he no tegami* ("Letters to

The following month, Jesse wrote that she could harvest and give away peas, beets, potatoes, greens, turnips, lettuce, cucumbers, and cabbage.[34]

THREE STEPS FORWARD, TWO STEPS BACK

Progress is all too often accompanied by setbacks. While Shokei was modernizing its educational system, crippling internal problems occurred which almost brought the school to a standstill. But most people saw the conclusion of the problem as a step forward in the unity of the school.

School System Revisions. Of utmost concern to the school itself was aligning its program and curriculum with the guidelines issued by the MacArthur administration, known as Civil Information and Education (CI&E). It involved raising the school standards, and to some extent, re-organization. During this year of 1947, preparation was made for a new school year to begin in April 1948. It followed the new CI&E guidelines for a new grade level system, six years of elementary, three years of junior high, three years of high school and two years of junior college. This would replace the current four-year *koutou jogakubu* and three-year *senkoubu* (higher department) education.[35] However, fourth year students (1947) who should have graduated had their education extended one additional year to comply with the new system.

The transition from the old educational system to the new system went moderately well as far as the junior high and senior high were concerned.[36] In January of 1948, Shokei's Board of Trustees decided to apply for junior college status, too. After surveying the needs of the Tohoku area and receiving many requests, the Board decided that three departments would make up the new junior college. They would be English literature, domestic science (food preparation and sewing), and physical education. There were hopes that a third year of junior college could be added in the future.[37] The transition from the *senkoubu* to junior college status did not go as smoothly. These problems are addressed later.

Mounting Collision Course. These big plans for the near future re-sulted in a troubled 1948 and 1949. To meet the requirements and demands

Jesse—Teacher File"), Shokei Gakuin Archival Collection.

34. Jesse to Sears, 10 June 1948, BIM Correspondence File.

35. Jesse, "Shokei Jo Gakuin Report for 1947," Shokei Gakuin Archival Collection.

36. Ibid.

37. Shokei Jogakuin, "Annual Report," 1947, The War Years Collection.

for the future, two seemingly unrelated things were needed. The first was a gymnasium. All high schools were now required to have one. Shokei had been using the basement of the chapel that had been built in 1917. Since Sendai winters were so harsh, physical education classes could not be conducted outside, and the chapel basement was inadequate. In addition, the gymnasium would be needed for the physical education department training for recreation and gymnastic teachers that was being proposed for the new junior college. The need was especially acute. The second need was for a leader with a vision for the future. These two needs crossed paths and collided.

Although a gymnasium was an absolute necessity, there were almost no funds for such a structure. Details of the gymnasium problem and financial worries were described in several personal letters exchanged between Mary Jesse and Jesse R. Wilson, then-treasurer of ABFMS and formerly a missionary in Sendai. Jesse wrote that at last the PTA decided to fund the construction on the site of the Stafford dormitory destroyed in the war, and to give it to the school as a gift.[38] Construction began in September 1948. Materials were purchased, the foundation was dug, timbers were cut, and the foundation ditches were filled with rocks when suddenly construction came to a grinding halt.[39] The reasons for the construction halt are not entirely clear, but the results were clear.

In October, a certain contingent of alumnae petitioned the trustees with a request to find a new principal for a new era. The PTA was asked for their opinion, but they found no reason for dismissing Takahashi. Rumors that the principal would be forced to quit caused great distress and divided opinions in the PTA. Faculty and alumnae were also divided. The gymnasium project was completely abandoned and the PTA organization broke up. The trustees did not receive the request from the alumnae with great surprise because they also had been discussing Takahashi's tenure for some time. They had been disturbed by the fact that the principal so easily capitulated to the Japanese authorities during the war. They had wanted him to take responsibility somehow. In November, they asked him to resign, while parents asked him to stay on. But it was not until January 1949 that Takahashi finally sent in his letter of resignation. Because of feeling responsible for turmoil leading up to the resignation, the trustees wrote an open letter the day of, announcing the "principal's decision" and apologizing for

38. Jesse to Jesse R. Wilson, 30 May 1949, BIM Correspondence File.
39. Jesse to Sears, 6 March 1949, BIM Correspondence File.

the confusion. In the same letter, they announced that Mary Jesse, who was endorsed by Takahashi, would be his successor. At the same time, she was named president of the school.[40] This came as a shock to students and staff who were not privy to the content of the numerous meetings. According to Masako Numazawa, a former student and an accountant in the Shokei office at the time, Principal Takahashi was always so kind to the students and always returned to Shokei office after his evening meal to be present until Masako finally finished the books at 9:00 PM each evening. She wondered why he was forced to resign.[41]

The announcement of Jesse's appointment caught her by surprise. She felt the tremendous weight of responsibility again upon her shoulders. When Jesse took the position of principal, the trustees agreed that she would not have to have responsibility for the building of the gymnasium.[42] Therefore she purposely tried to stay out of problems surrounding the principal and the gymnasium. In retrospect, one missionary found fault with Jesse's silence and thought that she could have more openly supported Takahashi.[43] But as we shall see, Jesse had her own reasons firmly in mind.

By the spring of 1949, the materials for the gymnasium had been left untouched for more than six months, except by the thieves who had begun carrying some of them off. The wood was becoming weathered, and cement was spilling from the bags.[44] Although the trustees had taken over the responsibility for the building, nothing had happened. Jesse tried to explain to the American Board's treasurer why the building materials had not been properly stored:

> The matter was not as simple as that. There was a disagreement as to who was responsible and as to who really owned the material. In claiming that it was not ours, the PTA was doing the building, not the school, so it was up to the contractor and the PTA, not a school affair. If we had taken over the material and cared for it we would have weakened our side in the agreement . . .
>
> . . . The Trustees recently decided to assume responsibility but not till that matter of ownership of material was settled. The division over the problem of the principal broke up the PTA and the

40. Minutes of Board of Trustees, 25 January 1949, Shokei Gakuin Archival Collection.

41. Numazawa, interview; Sato, recording.

42. Jesse to Sears, 1 July 1949, BIM Correspondence File.

43. Gertrude McCulloch to Sears, 28 January 1952, BIM Correspondence File.

44. Jesse to Sears, 6 March 1949, BIM Correspondence File.

school Board has had to take over the task of building, but we here have to do the work. I do wish our Board [ABFMS] could help us. It may look as though I were trying to force the hand of the New York Board, in this project, but that is not the case. This responsibility was forced on me.[45]

When the full Board of Trustees decided to take over the building project, they estimated that they needed six million yen[46] to complete it. With the help of the alumnae, they would try to raise three million yen.[47] They planned to ask the WABFMS Board for a special grant for the remaining three million. As had happened so often in the past, the alumnae came to the rescue of their ailing school and worked very hard, organizing fund-raising events such as bazaars. Individuals also contributed money by taking on extra jobs. One woman went to the hills and carried many loads of wood back to Sendai to sell and earn money to give. She skinned her back doing it, but could contribute two thousand five hundred yen.[48] Another woman did other people's laundry at home and contributed the money so she could do her part.[49]

Shokei trustees applied through the Shinsei Shadan organization (Japanese property-holding body of the American Baptist Foreign Mission Society) for half of the money needed. When they found that it would be impossible, several trustees went to Tokyo to ask the Shadan representatives directly for a loan, because the alumnae and PTA fundraising effort was not going well. In September, the Shadan replied that it could not help with a loan.[50]

"The Principal Is Responsible." The decision of the trustees to take over the gymnasium project was made with the understanding that Jesse would not be held responsible. However, after that decision, almost nothing was done on the building until summer. While she implored the Woman's Board for the 3.5 million yen, Jesse's efforts were also needed to bring the

45. Jesse to Wilson, 30 May 1949, BIM Correspondence File.

46. According to Dr Mochizuki, the yen/dollar value in 2009 for the gymnasium project was 11,400,000 yen, or $121,800 (see chapter 3, note 7).

47. According to Dr Mochizuki, the yen/dollar value in 2009 for the amount shouldered by alumnae was 5,700,000 yen, or $60,904 (see chapter 3, note 7).

48. According to Dr Mochizuki, the yen/dollar value in 2009 for the donation was 4750 yen, or fifty-one dollars (see chapter 3, note 7).

49. McCulloch to Constituency, 12 June 1949, BIM Correspondence File.

50. Minutes of Board of Trustees, February–September 1949, Shokei Gakuin Archival Collection.

two sides together, satisfy students, parents, alumnae, and to placate the public at large. She was being pulled in many different directions all at once. She was in constant demand as a speaker outside of school as well, to help the Japanese understand democracy, to promote the school, and do evangelism. Of course, she had a teaching schedule at school and numerous Bible studies continuing from the previous year. It was difficult for her to let go of these numerous small duties in preference to school management, as it would have been for any other missionary suddenly thrust into such a position. Her call from God was to go to a foreign country to tell individuals about salvation through Jesus Christ, not settle disputes. It became more and more difficult for her to attend meetings and manage crises in lieu of opportunities for personal contact and personal evangelism. She held on tenaciously to her personal small groups, even at the risk of her physical and emotional health.

Even so, she felt that she could no longer insist that the gymnasium problem was not her responsibility while human relationships among the groups deteriorated. Working for peace is also a part of bringing the gospel of salvation. She realized, too, that Japanese custom dictated that nothing would happen in a school without the principal's leadership. The materials were deteriorating; parents who had contributed money toward the building were complaining that their daughters were graduating without having used the building; other parents were demanding, "Build or give back our money." The public was being asked to help financially but they saw no progress on the building.

In trying to deal with these pressures, Jesse often had to cancel her school classes and her extracurricular Bible classes. When people came to her house for counseling, she had to turn them away because she could not give them any of her time. She was the only one available to give training to those students who wanted to be baptized, but where was she to find the time for such an important thing?

In her letters, Jesse was sending out another SOS signal of desperation that was reminiscent of her situation back in 1927–1928, at a time when her responsibilities had seemed overwhelming. But this time she was in the right position to do something. She could also rely on her years of experience. It came down to the fact that she had only two options: to resign and return to America, or give the go-ahead to start building without any money in sight. She chose the more courageous option, reminding herself that "it is better to fail trying than to give up and do nothing."[51] After all, "the principal is responsible to the parents and to the public," she wrote to Jesse Wilson. The Japanese expected no less.[52]

Mending Relationships. The breakthrough came at the end of June. The PTA was reorganized with good leaders in place. They were unanimous in the feeling that they must go forward with the building at once. A building committee was elected, which then met with the trustees to study the situation and decide on how to raise money. They resolved to do their best to raise money for the next of three installments. They would leave it up to Jesse to get the rest of the money. Jesse's assessment of her position after that meeting was recorded in a letter to Minnie Sears, Foreign Vice President of WABFMS:[53]

> You can see from this that my responsibility is greater than I dreamed when I took over this job, and if I don't get this money and this building, more than my reputation is at stake. It would be disastrous for the school, and some think that a second failure to finish this building would ruin the school, because they would have still more money sunk in it than now, and nothing to give in return either in money or service.[54]

The building committee and trustees were, rightly or wrongly, confident that "if they do their best, surely their friends in America will come to their aid and finish what they cannot do."[55] It would not be that easy, as they would find out. According to a July 15th, 1949 letter from Wilson, not only could the ABFMS not help, they knew that the WABFMS had no additional funds, either. However, Wilson encouraged Jesse to "patiently, persistently and with understanding keep coming back to Sears until the need was met."

The next two letters from Sears, not on file but referred to in later letters, repeated the fact that there was no money to be had for a gymnasium. Jesse did not have the heart to share the content of the letters with the PTA. She did not want to add to their discouragement. The building contractor asked for the first payment in July, thus making it necessary for Shokei to take out a bank loan.[56] But the school was now experiencing a fine sense

51. Jesse to Wilson, 2 July 1949, BIM Correspondence File.
52. Ibid.
53. Formerly Minnie Sandburg.
54. Ibid.
55. Ibid.
56. Minutes of the Board of Trustees, 22 July 1949, Shokei Gakuin Archival Collection.

of unity. Parents were getting acquainted with each other. The split that existed between Christian parents and non-Christian parents, "which we deplored deeply," Jesse said, seemed to have disappeared. The cornerstone was laid for the gymnasium on July 17th, 1949.[57]

Untimely Missionary Residence. Since before the end of World War II, the school needed a new residence for the missionaries. All housing was needed for the students who had lived in the dormitory. But the school continued to allow missionaries to use room space for residence. Money for a new residence had been put in the WABFMS budget and building was to begin in the spring of 1949. These arrangements were being made by the property committee of the Committee on Relations (COR, formerly known as the Reference Committee) in Tokyo. The Thurber Company of the United States, which had constructed buildings in Japan before, issued its estimate of the costs for building. It was far above the budget limits. Instead, a Japanese company and Japanese contractor were hired by the COR because of the good yen/dollar exchange rate (three hundred sixty yen/one dollar).[58] The building permit was long in coming, but construction across from the gymnasium site began in August 1949. Although Jesse was happy about the thought of finally having a residence for missionaries, she felt uneasy about its being completed and paid for when the gymnasium still lacked two-thirds of its funds. The COR submitted a request to delay the building of the missionary residence, and on behalf of Shokei's Board of Trustees (not the missionaries), to borrow one thousand five hundred dollars from the mission residence money and one thousand dollars from the fund called "The Carpenter Fund." All of this was to be repaid within a year. This request was not granted either. The American Board wanted the long-awaited mission house to be completed without delay to ease the living situation of their missionaries.

The American Board misinterpreted the request for the delay from the COR; it was not because the school trustees thought the mission residence was unnecessary. Nor, on the other hand, was this request to be interpreted as a criticism of the American Board for finally building the mission residence instead of the school gymnasium. On the Japanese side, "insiders" as Jesse called them, understood the American system of itemized budgeting. However, since the financial system of the mission was not open to the public, people were asking why a mission house was being built when the

57. Jesse to Sears, 12 August 1949, BIM Correspondence File.
58. Jesse to Sears, 4 May 1949, BIM Correspondence File.

school could not pay for the gymnasium? It appeared to the public that the principal, Mary Jesse, was using the school money for building a house for the missionaries, while there was no money to finish the gymnasium for the students.[59]

Grants, Loans, Gifts. Word that three thousand five hundred dollars of the money requested of the American Board would be granted to Shokei came just as the dedication ceremony for the gymnasium was taking place.[60] Everyone expected that the money would arrive soon, but it did not come. Another payment had to be made in early November. Both the alumnae association and the PTA had exhausted their resources. The trustees decided that their only choice was to borrow again from a local bank. The Shadan tried again to negotiate with the American Board, but to no avail. Money was again promised, but it did not arrive. All the people involved were wishing that they were rid of this debt. The year 1950 was a good year financially for Shokei, so in May 1951 the trustees decided to put the extra money toward the debts incurred.

How and when the money promised by the Woman's Board finally arrived is not clear. However, in a January 1952 letter to Sears, Jesse gave a full accounting of the gymnasium financing. The item that closed the books was a grant of two thousand dollars which came from the Yotsuya kindergarten property sale in Tokyo. Per Jesse's report, the total cost of the gymnasium was over four million yen ($11,240). Less than half came from the American Board; the graduates contributed five hundred thousand yen; Board of Trustees, two hundred eighty-two thousand yen; parents, one hundred sixteen thousand yen; and teachers', general public's, and missionaries' combined gifts came to two hundred ninety-six thousand yen.

Celebration for the Gymnasium and for Shokei. Although October 9th, 1949, was a celebration of the completion of just one building, it held deeper meaning for all who participated. The school had once again been brought through a major crisis by the grace of God. Although the financial part remained unsolved, broken relationships were mended and the school could now move on into a progressive phase of growth. Everyone was keenly aware that, if this crisis had not been met, a brighter future for the school would have been jeopardized. In a sense, then, it was also a celebration of the healing of relationships.

59. Jesse to Sears, 10 September 1949, BIM Correspondence File.
60. Jesse to Sears, 19 October 1949, BIM Correspondence File.

The dedication was held in the school chapel with parents, graduates, friends, and two hundred students attending. The students insisted on having a praise and thanksgiving service of their own on the unvarnished, unfurnished floor of the gymnasium. Later, the alumnae gathered there to have their own worship service. These various worship services are evidence that perhaps all of those involved had the feeling that the completion of the gymnasium was recognition that Shokei had experienced divine guidance once again in a very tangible way. At the time of celebration, no one knew that it would be another year and a half before all the bills were paid. Sometimes it is better not to have a glimpse into the future!

Controversial Gymnasium (Completed in 1949) (courtesy of Shokei Gakuin)

**New Missionary House for American Baptist Missionaries in Sendai (1949–1979)
(courtesy of Shokei Gakuin)**

9

Destinations and New Beginnings
(1950–1952)

Mary Jesse Bids Farewell at Sendai Station (July 1952) (courtesy of Shokei Gakuin)

God is the hub of the wheel of life.
The closer we come to God the closer we come to each other.
The basis of community is not primarily our ideas, feelings and emotions
about each other but our common search for God.
When we keep our minds and hearts directed toward God,
we will come more fully together.

—HENRI J. M. NOUWEN[1]

1. Nouwen, *The Genesee Diary*, 212–13.

This chapter focuses in on several major processes that finally found completion. Mary D. Jesse's last major contribution to Shokei was to guide the school on the road leading to junior college status for their *senkoubu* department. After seeing this process completed, we look back at the daily life of the school once again, including the re-establishment of their school-church because of the revival taking place in Japan. Finding new leadership was an agonizing and disappointing process. This long road led to a suitable destination. Finally, we look at Jesse's journey to retirement and what she has left us as a legacy.

ROAD TO THE JUNIOR COLLEGE

Looking back at the thirty-year history of the *senkoubu* department (postgraduate diploma course), and forward to the process leading to junior college status, is helpful in sensing that the timing was right for the school and thus, in a sense, foreordained by God. It was a fitting time to reestablish the purpose and spirit of education at Shokei Girls' School.

Looking Back. Although the transition to the new educational system had gone fairly smoothly for the *koutou jogakubu* (later called Shokei Jogakuin or Shokei Gakuin Junior and Senior High School), it was not such a smooth road for the transition from the *senkoubu* to a junior college. The recent history of higher education at Shokei revealed that the domestic science course of study gave stability to the *senkoubu*. The English course, on the other hand, had its ups and downs. For its success, Shokei was constantly dependent on the number of foreign missionaries and the popularity of the subject in Japan. In 1936, the *koutouka* (upper department) changed its name to the *senkoubu* and students had a choice of a two or three-year course. But by 1940 English had become a very unpopular subject due to its association with the United States. There were only a few English course students and only one foreign missionary teacher left. The domestic science course continued, while the English course was closed.

Looking Forward. In 1946, under the old system following the war, the English course was reopened with an enrollment of sixty students. The school still strongly believed that it had a great opportunity and role to play in building Christian character in the women of northern Japan. Subsequently in 1949, there was a flurry of planning and activity to prepare the facilities for junior college status. As previously mentioned, Shokei applied to the government for recognition of a college with three departments: home economics, English literature, and physical education. The library in the *senkoubu* was separated from the library in the high school and moved by the students to the second floor of the Ella O. Patrick building. The students worked hard to prepare the biology lab and the home economics lab for inspection in November. The gymnasium that was just been completed still had no equipment. While these preparations were being made, the school administration found it difficult to find teachers qualified to teach in a junior college, since this concept was new in Japan. They asked Tohoku University's English department and home economics department for help in finding teachers. Miyagi Prefecture's physical education and health department also gave much help in finding physical education teachers.

After the government inspection was conducted, the Department of Education approved a two-year course in English and home economics. Jesse reported that the first notice of the recognition by the government came by telegram from the National Christian Educational Association (Kirisutokyuo Kyouiku Doumei) congratulating the school; a few days later, newspapers carried the report. The government announced that it would grant teaching licenses to many Shokei graduates from former years. Shokei was one of one hundred eighty-one schools around Japan given junior college status. Eighty percent of these were schools for women. Two other schools in Sendai also were given junior college status, but Shokei was the only one in town with English and home economics day-courses. There were three disappointing results. The physical education department was not approved, the process for acquiring a teacher's license was put on hold, and graduation certificates for current students would only be granted to those who began as first-year junior college students.[2]

This latter point truly caused the most pain and disappointment among the students. In 1948, anticipating the opening of the junior college in 1950, the school had promised Shokei's fifth-year *honka* students seats as second-year junior college students if they entered Shokei's *senkoubu* department's first-year class. Now that this promise could not be fulfilled because of the new regulations, it threw the students into much confusion. They would have to choose to repeat their first-year, quit without a higher education graduation certificate, or find a four-year university that would accept transfer credits. Despite these challenges, in April, nineteen English

2. Jesse to Minnie Sears, 20 March 1950, BIM Correspondence File.

department students and twenty-nine home economics department students entered as the first-year class of Shokei Women's Junior College.

Dedication of the New Junior College. The dedication and celebration of the new junior college was held the following November coupled with Culture Week, Founder's Day, and a school athletic meet. The student organization, PTA, and alumnae all united together in planning the program. On one occasion, one hundred thirty alumnae, some from as far away as Tokyo, came to help plan. November 11th was a day full of special events. The central program carried greetings from dignitaries, a short concert, a play, and two lectures. Mary Jesse, as president of the college and one of the dignitaries, gave greetings too. Normally these speeches were ten to fifteen minutes long, but with Bunya Odatsume's on-the-spot translation, her speech took a full hour. The speech carried such significant thoughts for the knitting together of Shokei's past and future that a substantial part should be quoted here:

> Now something as to our aims and ideals and the kind of education we seek to carry on here. May I say quite frankly that Shokei is a Christian school based upon Christian principles and ideals. We believe in education based on these principles, but that does not mean that we do not believe in high educational standards of scholarship.
>
> We strongly feel though that something more than intellectual training is needed, something besides book knowledge, as important as that is. A trained intellect does not necessarily make a noble personality. Knowledge must be carried on into conduct and so the emotional nature, the feeling aspects too, must be trained, heart as well as head if we are to have, instead of automobiles or machines, warm-hearted, cooperative, self-less, optimistic personalities with love as a motive and will to serve. . . For the development of better human relations, we must go back to the home. Concern for home and family life is one of the main interests of modern education. The great need the world round is for better homes, better family relationships, for relationships out in the world are not too different from those we have in the family circle and a good family member can easily adapt to the relationships in the world outside of home. . . .
>
> In Japan, old loyalties, customs are gone, old foundations, ideals, beliefs are without influence today. Yet, life to be meaningful and worthwhile, must have a supreme dominating, sobering interest—center—That great center is God. Young people must have something outside of self, to live for, and if need be to die for, if life

is to be worthy. Else they are adrift, like a ship without a rudder on a rough stormy sea.

To me there are especially three teachings of contributions of Christianity that are especially needed in a democratic society and so as a basis for education in a Christian school. They are

1. The Christian ideal or teaching of the Fatherhood of God and the brotherhood of man. This means the value of every individual as a child of God, and love as a motive of life.

2. The Christian Ethics, the ideals found in the life and teaching of Jesus.

3. Christian fellowship, centering in the church, a fellowship which includes all races, nations and classes of people and world fellowship—no race or national boundaries.

These are the broad concepts underlying our type of education, and by teaching and emphasizing these, we believe we can best serve in this new day in Japan.[3]

NEW BEGINNINGS

In this new post-war era, nearly everything could be done in a new way and with a new attitude. Although the old ways and programs at school felt comfortable, now with new freedoms granted Japan, many things could be creatively reformed.

Missionary Staff Additions. During these short, tumultuous years, Jesse was not the only missionary present. In 1948 and 1949, two veteran missionaries were added to the staff at Shokei. Fortunately, we can learn about other aspects of life at Shokei through their letters, since Jesse was preoccupied with administrative details. Gertrude McCulloch, arriving from the Shanghai evacuation in December 1948, already had had a full career behind her when she arrived in Sendai. She served with difficulty at Shokei through September 1951. To the students, she seemed particularly shy, thus making her integration into the school difficult. Her biggest enemy at age fifty-nine was the Japanese language. Even within those limitations, the students saw her as a very active missionary. While Jesse was facing difficult times as principal, McCulloch taught English to high school students, piano to the higher department *senkouka* students, and

3. Jesse, "Building Together For a Better Shokei," 11 November 1950. Shokei Gakuin Archival Collection.

developed a choir in the school-church. Vida Post arrived in August 1949, having also already served for thirty years at Hinomoto Girls' School in Himeji, Japan. She served at Shokei until her retirement in 1961. She was skillful in Japanese and knew the ways of Japanese mission schools well. She took Jesse's place on the Board of Trustees, serving there until she left Shokei. Shortly after arriving in Sendai, the post office discovered that her name was the same as its name. Every year from then on, the post office sent flowers on July 4th in celebration of her country's founding.

Discovering Beulah M. McCoy. Jesse was ever watching and praying for a young missionary to come to Shokei before she left Japan, who would be able to make her career at Shokei. At the first post-war, new Baptist convention (Shinsei churches), consisting of all the Baptist churches in the Church of Christ in Japan in September 1947, Jesse got a good look at the newcomer to Soshin Girls School. Beulah M. McCoy had only been in Japan for a short time, but at this meeting she came face to face with the "veterans" of the WABFMS, Alice Bixby, Winifred Acock, Thomasine Allen, and Mary Jesse. McCoy's first impression of Mary Jesse was that she stood out among other missionaries as "the Southern Lady, with her erect posture, Virginia drawl, and fastidious manners. . . . She had a great sense of humor and was the 'life of the party.'"[4] During the next five years, each time McCoy met Jesse, she could tell that her whole heart and soul was in the work at Shokei. Jesse tried several times to convince McCoy to leave Soshin and come to Shokei. McCoy continued to feel called to Soshin. Finally, after McCoy's first furlough was completed, she was reassigned to Shokei in May 1952, just in time to see Jesse's departure. McCoy continued at Shokei for a long period of time, serving as teacher, principal, and president at various times until her retirement in April 1979.

Rebuilding the School-Church. The religious program at Shokei continued as well as could be expected, considering the shortage of Christian leaders. Students were responding to the gospel message, but the churches could not accommodate them. The need for a worship service was so acute that one was organized inside the school. There was such a great interest in Vacation Bible School in the summer that more neighborhood children came than could be accommodated. In September 1948, a Sunday school was started. Graduates and some older students volunteered as teachers under the leadership of Misao Sato. First- and second-year former *honka*

---

4. Beulah McCoy, "I Remember Mary D. Jesse," *Mutsumi no Kusari*, Special Edition (1968) 81.

students attended the Sunday school while the third- and fourth-year and the *senkoubu* students attended worship services held at the same time. Two hundred seventy-three Shokei students asked for baptism. But because pastors had no time for pre-baptism classes, and because the school-church was not an officially recognized church, no students were baptized in 1947 or 1948.[5]

Finally, pre-baptism classes were held, and the decision was made to begin a church within the school. On May 22nd, 1949, the first baptism service since Jesse's return was held in the Hirose River in front of the school. This also marked the beginning of Shokei Church. Missionaries Rev. John Foote and Rev. Bill Hinchman, and former principal, Dr. Ukichi Kawaguchi came from Osaka and Tokyo to help celebrate. Dr. Foote baptized thirteen people: the three male teachers were heads of departments at the school, one was a female teacher and wife of one of the male teachers, and nine were students. These thirteen people formed the nucleus of the new church.[6] It was the first time that Gertrude McCulloch had seen a river baptism. She reported that all baptized members returned to the chapel at school, where they had their first communion service together. The four adult members and the students carried out, in turn, the responsibilities of leading worship and ushering. A different Christian teacher gave the message each week. In September, Dr. Foote baptized four more students.[7] One hundred students remained on the list of inquirers for baptism. Jesse wrote that she wished that she had more time to help and lead them.[8]

McCulloch's choir grew steadily in numbers and skill. In October, on the same day as the gymnasium dedication, they had a dedication service for the choir members. McCulloch hoped that the dedication service would have an impact on students in the choir who were not Christians.[9]

Bible Story Hours. McCulloch had a vision of having Bible story hours throughout the neighborhoods of Sendai with the students taking the responsibility for finding the places and telling the stories. She realized, however, that if the girls themselves did not catch the vision for this, the

5. Woman's American Baptist Foreign Mission Society, "Reconstruction for Schools for Girls," *Seventy-Ninth Annual Report of the Board—Along Kingdom Highway* (1950) 15.

6. Jesse to Jesse R. Wilson, 30 May 1949, BIM Correspondence File.

7. McCulloch to Constituency, 29 April 1950, BIM Correspondence File.

8. Jesse to Wilson, 30 May 1949, BIM Correspondence File.

9. McCulloch to Constituency, 19 October 1949, BIM Correspondence File.

program would fail. She felt helpless to make this happen with her limitations in the language.[10] What seemed to her a handicap was perhaps an asset in getting the Japanese to "own" the program. One year later she reported that Misao Sato had greeted the idea with enthusiasm. In turn, she presented the idea to her high school girls, who also enthusiastically embraced it. In the spring of 1950, sixteen girls from the Shokei school-church began leading a Bible story hour weekly in their own homes for children living nearby. Sato gave the girls training each Thursday. Eight other Shokei high school students from other churches' Sunday schools also attended the training sessions.[11]

School Admissions. Despite the troubles surrounding the resignation of Principal Takahashi and the ensuing problems with the gymnasium, the spirit of cooperation among the students, graduates, board members and teachers continued. "Fine groups" is how McCulloch, who didn't understand the language, referred to the renewed relationships in and amongst the groups in 1949.

The student body began growing slowly in 1949 and 1950, and then there was an explosion of growth in 1951. Mission school education had become highly sought-after. The excitement was like the enthusiasm that occurred in 1921. Jesse felt that because so many students were applying for admittance, if possible, none should be turned away. According to Jesse's letter of March 30th, 1951, more than two hundred students from government junior high schools applied for fifty seats in the first-year class of the high school. The fifty seats had been pre-approved by the Prefectural Board. One hundred sixteen students were being graduated from the junior high into the high school. The total number of students expected was one hundred sixty-six to one hundred seventy students. Jesse wrote her thoughts:

> It just seemed impossible to refuse the earnest and repeated pleas of parents, Jr. High teachers and friends of the students, who just would not take no for an answer, but kept coming, phoning, writing, getting influential friends to come, bringing gifts, all in spite of our repeated statement that we just had no space.
>
> When examination day came and our chapel was almost filled. . . . I just did not know how to greet them or what to say to them, only my regrets that we could not take in even one-third, even though they passed the exam. But I did promise that I would do my best and take in every one possible. Those eager anxious

10. Ibid.

11. McCulloch to Sears, 29 April 1950, BIM Correspondence File.

faces I could not put out of my mind, so I spoke to our teachers that there must be some way, that we had a responsibility since these students had come to our door.[12]

The faculty stretched the number of the original plan from fifty students to sixty. A representative teacher took the plan to the Miyagi Prefectural office, where he asked permission to increase the number to one hundred twenty students. Shokei proposed that a special fee be assessed each student who was taken in above the sixty students to cover the cost of desks, chairs, and supplies. Jesse did not know how many could afford it but knew that it was their only chance to let others in. The plan was approved. The new entering class figures tell us that in the spring of 1951, Shokei accepted students numbering almost twice its capacity.[13] This trend continued for a few more years, bringing the student body population for all three schools, junior high school through junior college, to over one thousand two hundred students and bringing a new demand for more classroom space.

Students at Work. In 1949, the student body organization was reestablished. The following year, the first officers were elected. The new student body president kept busy leading a very active group of girls. The students found many activities needing their attention in this post-war era. For example, the previous year, faculty decided to redesign the school uniform. During the war, the government dictated what clothes students could wear to school. After the war, students wore whatever they had. Each class had a representative on the committee and, with the assistance of the teachers, a modern design for a uniform with pleats was decided on. It was Jesse's suggestion that there be only three pleats in the back and front, with a straight design on the side rather than the more typical design of pleats around the whole skirt. This plan saved on material and held down the cost of making the uniform. But, the school still could not require the students to wear uniforms because of the poor conditions of the economy. That first year only a handful of girls could wear the new uniform. But gradually, as the economy improved, more students began to have their mothers and grandmothers make the uniform for them. It was not until some years later that uniforms were ordered from a professional seamstress and later from

12. Jesse to Sears, 30 March 1951, BIM Correspondence File.

13. Gakusekibou (Student Attendance Record Book), May 1951, Shokei Gakuin High School Office, Sendai, Japan.

department stores. This box pleat design, unique to Shokei, is still being used after more than sixty years.

In addition to helping to change the uniform, a movement was launched by the students to reestablish the annual school excursion. The excursions were terminated abruptly in 1942. Again, financial considerations were uppermost in everyone's mind. For that reason, pleas of the student officers to reinstate a school trip fell on deaf ears. At last, the head teacher suggested that the student body president see Principal Jesse about the matter. The president, Keiko Yoshida Tada, recalls that she stood before President Mary Jesse with fear and trembling. The interview was not very pleasant and went as she had feared. Thinking of the welfare of all the students, President Jesse knew that there would be some girls who could not afford the proposed trip, and therefore refused to give permission. But in the end, she agreed to the plan with one condition: all students must be able to go; even if one student with financial problems could not go, then no one would go. Keiko returned to the officers with the good news that the trip had been conditionally approved. Through the diligent efforts of the student council, enough money was raised by student donations in the following months to allow all students to go. In the meantime, each student enthusiastically received a topic to research about the places and historical points they would be visiting.

On October 2nd, 1950, the third-year high school students boarded the local night train bound for Tokyo. After a night's stay in a tourist house in Ueno, they went to Nara by night train. They stayed one night in a Japanese inn in Nara, and another in Kyoto. On the return trip, they stopped in Kamakura. Keiko Tada recalls that, although taking night trains saved somewhat on expenses, all things considered, it was a rather luxurious trip for those days.[14]

Health Nurse Training. Shokei has always listened to the voice of their students. During this period of transition, many students requested training as health nurses. As an alternative to a junior college course of study and in cooperation with the local government authorities, a plan was devised. The government sent a specialist to the school to give lectures on Saturdays, then arrangements were made with elementary schools and hospitals for the girls to learn the practical side. On completion of this training, they would be able to take the examination to be licensed. In 1951, forty-two girls took this work in their free time on Saturdays and holidays. Jesse

14. Keiko Yoshida Tada, telephone interview by the author, 15 December 1998.

comments that it meant a heavy load for them, but they were sticking with it and doing well.[15]

Camping. Vida Post reintroduced camping at Shokei. Throughout her letters, she mentioned about the need for Shokei to have its own camp. This is how important she thought camping was for these students. The first post-war camp was held on the school campus. Forty-nine girls slept overnight in the classrooms. There was much enthusiastic singing, as the girls at this camp and the succeeding camp got into the "camp spirit." Rev. Ryouzo Hara, pastor of the Kita-San-Bancho Church, led an excellent Bible study.[16]

The following year, several camps were held. One camp was held for three nights and four days on Katsura Island in Matsushima Bay. The camp included numerous first-time experiences for the girls; for example, prayer meetings as the sun set, campfires, stunt night, and a decision-making service. At the latter, students were encouraged to think about how this camp had affected them personally, and some girls made decisions to become Christians and be baptized.[17] A highlight of the camp was the opportunity for students to lead activities for the village children. They organized Bible story and recreation times that were so well-received that the children were invited to the students' campfire the following evening.[18]

One of the village children used to squat in the shadows outside of the dining room and enjoy listening to the students sing grace before their meals. Forty-five years later in her baptismal testimony, she recalled listening to the Bible stories and wishing she could be a student at such an interesting school to learn more about Jesus and how to sing! She never became a student at Shokei, but eventually met Christ as her Savior through activities of Shokei students.[19]

Post's dream of a camp was fulfilled the year before she retired with the establishment of Morigo Christian Campsite in Rifu town. Rev. Hisayoshi Saito and missionary Ted Livingston developed the camp for use of Baptist churches and schools in the northeast.

15. Jesse to Sears, 4 July 1951, BIM Correspondence File.

16. McCulloch and Vida Post, dialog letter, 3 August 1950, BIM Correspondence File.

17. McCulloch to Constituency, 31 July 1951, BIM Correspondence File.

18. Post to Constituency, 21 August 1951, BIM Correspondence File.

19. Kyoko Akama, interview by author, December 2003.

NEW LEADERSHIP FOR A NEW AGE

A search for new leadership has always been a grueling task. Shokei wanted to find the right person for this time in its history. However, it did not have the luxury of choosing the best from many candidates. Instead, the school became desperate to find even one who would say "yes" and carry through with that answer.

Leadership Dilemma. It was the resignation of the principal, Shigeto Takahashi, in 1949, that stimulated the four-year search for new leadership. Jesse had never planned nor thought of taking that responsibility, but the trustees, who were anxious to have visionary leadership, threw the job into her lap. The school asked her to temporarily take Principal Takahashi's position, as well as the new position of president of the forthcoming junior college. As if it had been their clandestine plan all along, the alumnae celebrated. Jesse saw this assignment as temporary, but others did not. These two different viewpoints tended to complicate the situation. Jesse was the representative of the Woman's American Baptist Foreign Mission Society to Shokei, but the Japanese also saw her as the representative of Shokei (of the trustees, teachers, alumnae, PTA, and students). The one pressed her to retire, and the other pressed her to stay on as long as possible. The predicament was like two different sports teams sharing a player very loyal to both teams!

Before returning to Japan in 1947, she and the American Board had mutually agreed that she should not be a dominant figure at Shokei, but instead be a kind of "enabler." Jesse was already sixty-four years old when she returned to Japan. The standard retirement age for missionaries was sixty-five. She was supportive of the principal, but stayed out of the ruckus surrounding him. The school, on the other hand, although desiring to be independent of foreign assistance, wanted her direct leadership.

The Search. During 1949 and the first half of 1950, the trustees and sixty-eight-year-old Mary Jesse searched for a person among Japanese Baptists who could lead Shokei into the next half of the century. In August, they concluded that there was no qualified Baptist to take the job as president, and asked Sears in the WABFMS home office if it was permissible to look for a leader who was not Baptist.[20] Some people question why Sears had to be asked, if the school was trying to be independent. It is a difficult question in retrospect, but could perhaps be compared to a young adult consult-

---

20. Jesse to Sears, 5 August 1950, BIM Correspondence File.

ing with parents in a moment of uncertainty. Sears must have answered in the affirmative since the search continued both inside and outside Baptist circles. During the six months after the official opening of the new junior college, only one person, Professor Takaaki Aikawa of Kanto Gakuin College, was approached for the job. After he refused by letter, it seemed hopeless that anyone could be found to take Jesse's place for the new school year in April 1951. In a last-ditch attempt, in March, school officials made a special trip to Tokyo to persuade Aikawa. He agreed to reconsider, thinking that it would be possible to take the leadership in the fall. The trustees asked Jesse to continue as both the principal of the junior and senior high school and president of the junior college until October. Jesse's hopes soared as she began to think about retirement. Then, Rev. Ryouzo Hara, who had been acting principal in the high school, was denied the position under the new post-war educational system. Jesse remarks despairingly, "There seems no way out for me."[21]

The home office in New York was applying pressure on her to firm up her retirement plans. In July, she responded in a very frank way. As much as she wanted to be rid of the responsibility, she felt stuck and unable to move. She did not appreciate the Home Board implying that the Japanese would not find a replacement "as long as she stayed in Japan."[22] It was not the first time that she had been caught between a rock and a hard place. In succeeding letters, she continued to say that retirement should be well-thought-out so as not to offend those involved. But who would understand such reasoning unless they had spent their whole life among the Japanese! She reminded the American Board that her responsibility was not just to the Baptist mission, but also to trustees, parents, and the Japanese government. She wanted all groups related to the school to support the next president and know that he was her choice too.[23]

When word came that Aikawa must delay making a decision, setting no time frame, Jesse accepted the responsibility with great anxiety. She had heard a rumor that a church leader in Tokyo had advised him to refuse the job, with the reason that Shokei School didn't want him badly enough to build a special residence for him. People living in the south don't want to come north without big inducements. Perhaps he had heard that money

21. Jesse to Sears, 30 March 1951, BIM Correspondence File.
22. Jesse to Sears, 4 July 1951, BIM Correspondence File.
23. Ibid.

would not be granted for repairs by the American Board, as it would be for the other Baptist schools, she conjectured:

> I had thought that I might be relieved this fall but now with no head for the whole school, and no principal for the high school, can I just walk out? I do not want to keep on with this responsibility. But I do want to do the right thing. I believe in Divine guidance. As I look back I feel that I have been wonderfully guided, sometimes by the closed door as well as by the open one. If the door is closed in spite of all my effort, does it mean that my work is not yet completed?[24]

While experiencing these emotional ups and downs, she drew the Board's attention to a young man whom she had followed for many years. Tamotsu Yanbe was a graduate of Shokei's first kindergarten when Jesse became principal back in 1919. He had spent time as a child in the Howard and Sadie Ross mission house on Shokei campus. While working for the Allied Forces, he was active in the PTA on behalf of his younger sister, who was a Shokei student. As his English was excellent and he showed a Christian spirit, Jesse saw in him potential for leadership in education in Japan, possibly Shokei. She related the fact that, since he was headed for the United States for study, she hoped that the American Board would have a look at him and make it possible for him to speak for Shokei at local Baptist churches. As time went on, Jesse's mind kept going back to Yanbe. If he was not put under further obligations to work for a company when he returned to Japan, she thought that he would do as good a job as anyone at Shokei.[25] The Board promised to meet Yanbe.[26]

Very shortly, Rev. Takashi Nakai, then Rev. Nobuo Tokita was approached. Tokita initially accepted the job, but later, by November, had backed out. Vida Post and Bunya Odatsume were both approached about becoming president.[27] But time was ticking away and decisions needed to be made for the new school year beginning in April. Jesse stuck to her plans to relinquish her duties in April 1952. Finally, at the end of March, the Shokei Board of Trustees made their chairperson, Rev. Hisayoshi Saito, temporary president of Shokei; Rev. Ryouzo Hara was made acting director in the

---

24. Jesse to Sears, 8 August 1951, BIM Correspondence File.

25. Jesse to Sears, 4 July 1951; 1 December 1951, BIM Correspondence File

26. Sears to Jesse, 18 January 1952, BIM Correspondence File.

27. Minutes of the Board of Trustees, 11 March 1952, Shokei Gakuin Archival Collection.

president's office and assistant to the Board president; Odatsume became acting director in the junior college office. In the absence of principals, deans were also named for each school: Saito for the junior high, Nisaku Hirai for the high school, and Takeshi Nakase for the junior college.[28]

Next, Rev. Junryo Hashimoto was suggested as president. To the delight of all, he accepted the position, attended the Sixtieth Anniversary Celebration, and was introduced to the faculty and public. But before he could take the office as he promised, he reported that he would have to delay it for another year and a half.[29]

Another candidate was approached with negative results. But about the same time, Mr. Yoshitoshi Matsumura was discovered. In late 1952, Dr. Elmer A. Fridell, Baptist foreign secretary for the Orient, introduced Matsumura to the American Baptist office staff in New York. Sears wrote to Jesse, who now resided in the United States, "this man is warmly Christian, his personality is good and is an outstanding scholar of botany. . . .When I mentioned to him that teachers and administrators were needed in our Japanese schools, his face lightened considerably."[30] Matsumura, who was unknown to the school until then, returned to Japan, where he was introduced. At long last, an answer was found in Yoshitoshi Matsumura. In April 1953, he was appointed president and moved into the dormitory with his wife and daughter, with the promise of the school providing a house in the near future. At long last, the search for a leader was successfully completed and another destination was reached. However, Matsumura's term was short-lived. Unfortunately, he was more of a scientist and scholar than an administrator. A teacher's union was formed for the first time in Shokei's history, and the union effectively forced Matsumura to resign in March 1956.

THE ROAD TO RETIREMENT

Mary Jesse had been retired for almost a year before she had the satisfaction of knowing that Shokei now had adequate leadership. When she finally decided that no matter what happened, she must leave Shokei, everything looked quite bleak. But as she reiterated her life theme in her speech at the

28. Minutes of the Board of Trustees, 28 March 1952, Shokei Gakuin Archival Collection.

29. Jesse to Sears, 9 June 1952, BIM Correspondence File.

30. Jesse to Sears, 19 December 1952, BIM Correspondence File.

opening of the new junior college, "I believe in Divine guidance," she knew that she was being tested as to whether she was just mouthing words or not.

Plans for Departure. Even though no new leadership had been found, Mary Jesse found that making definite plans for her departure took her mind off the seemingly unsolvable problems at school. Her plans came together rather easily once she had decided to step down from the leadership, no matter what happened. Since returning to Japan after the war, she had been so preoccupied with Shokei that she had not kept up with what her missionary colleagues were doing in other parts of Japan. She had had little time for rallying the support for Shokei among the graduates scattered all over Japan, nor any time for doing evangelism with their help. For these reasons, she planned a three-week trip to visit all the Baptist work in Japan, and along the way hold meetings to which graduates could invite their friends to hear a gospel message. If she made such a trip as this, she reasoned, she would feel more prepared to speak about Japan to American Baptist churches when she returned. The Sixtieth Anniversary Celebration was planned for May 26th, 1952, and her departure for the United States on July 25th. With this plan before her, she handed over the reins of the school to temporary leadership without hesitation. Her trip around Japan left her with a feeling of satisfaction and a sense of completion. Now she was ready to close out forty years of service in Japan.

Decoration by the Emperor. One of the many memorable events of her last days in Japan was the Decoration of the Fourth Order of the Sacred Crown from the Imperial Household. It was an award given to her at the Sixtieth Anniversary Celebration by the vice governor of Miyagi Prefecture, and was followed by an audience with the empress. Jesse's description of how she first received word of the award and her description of the award itself lent a humorous side to this event:

> The first I heard of it was a telegram from Tokyo saying such an honor would be granted, and for some one to come for it . . . The day the telegram came I was in the beauty parlor having my hair done when the evening paper came, and it caused great excitement among guests and operators. Soon too, as I sat there it came in over the radio that I had been thus honored. On the way home people came out of their little shops to congratulate me. Of course this was all too much for me but if it helps advertise the school that is good.[31]

31. Jesse to Sears, 12 June 1952, BIM Correspondence File.

The beauty parlor mentioned here is the Sugawara Beauty Salon located in the center of Sendai. Fourth generation proprietor Kunio Sugawara recalled that Jesse was his wife's customer. When the author asked about Jesse's visits, he said that she was a weekly customer beginning after World War II, that the impression he had each time she came to have her hair done was that she had a kind of spiritual aura about her, as if she were at peace with herself and the world. When asked if she ever seemed perplexed about the difficulties at Shokei, he replied that she never seemed worried about anything. He remembered clearly the day she received notice of the award while in his beauty parlor, and recalled it as a truly exciting moment.[32]

These are Jesse's comments on the value of the award:

> It is true that I have spent the best years of my life here but it is also true that I could have done little had it not been for the splendid loyalty and cooperation of the Trustees, Graduates, the P.T.A. and the general public. The decoration, I feel is too, an appreciation of our school and of the work we are together doing here. It will mean much to the school in the future . . .
>
> I do not know much about the meaning only that the Japanese think it is something. It is the Fourth Order, whatever that may mean, but friends think it a high order. I will send you a picture taken the next day, with the medal, which by the way, is not in itself the real thing but is only the symbol signifying that I have the big diploma-like-paper, which is the real treasure, but can't be worn at ceremonies, which seems to be the chief purpose of the medal. The medal is gold with rubies and is tied with a ribbon.[33]

The Sixtieth Anniversary. The school celebrated its anniversary during the week of May 26th, 1952. Beulah McCoy, the new missionary, had arrived only two weeks earlier. She gave an account of the celebration in one of her reports: The celebration also included farewells for Jesse. Formal celebrations were held on Monday with congratulations from city, Ministry of Education, Christian school association, church, and mission officials. In the afternoon, a memorial service was held for former faculty members who had passed away. Tuesday was alumnae day with a farewell for Jesse in the morning and a luncheon meeting in the afternoon. An exhibit was held Wednesday and Thursday. Friday included practice for the annual field day by the students. On Saturday, students, teachers, and alumnae participated

32. Kunio Sugawara, interview by the author, Sendai, 1 April 1999.
33. Jesse to Sears, 19 December 1952.

in the field day. In closing, an evangelistic service was held on Sunday afternoon.[34]

Saying Good-bye. With this celebration behind her, Jesse finished her final preparations for departure. There was a constant stream of visitors for the next month as people from all over came to say their goodbyes. On June 10th, she had an audience with the empress. According to an article in the Shokei School newspaper, the interview lasted about forty minutes and included a variety of topics of conversation. One question the empress asked was why she was not returning to the United States by airplane. Jesse's answer made a deep impression on Shokei. She said that if she went by airplane, it would take less than a day and she feared that she would forget Shokei. But by going by ship, she wanted to take twelve full days to carve her impressions and memories deep in her heart. During the days prior to her departure, she was entertained by the mayor and had farewell functions with the students, teachers, and the PTA. Reporters from the Sendai Kahoku Newspaper and Tokyo newspapers also wanted some of her time.[35]

Finally, the day for her departure arrived. On July 12th, the biggest crowd since the ending of the war had gathered at Sendai station to say good-bye. The cacophony of sound, police bullhorns, the noise of the crowd, the singing of the students ("God be with you till we meet again"), and the flash from reporters' cameras left a deep impression on all. But as one writer put it, the lasting impression will not be from the farewell parties and her departure day, but will be her winning smile and spiritual lessons she has taught us all these years.[36]

As Mary Jesse chose the slow method of transportation home after forty years of service, we can imagine some of the things she recalled about Shokei girls during her voyage. And many of these remembrances are also the impressions that the reader might have:

- The students' enthusiasm and zest for life poured out of each day, whether it was a cause within their school or working their hearts out for their country during the war.

- Their reaction to hardship was a creative mindset which said "we can do this!" from the raising of funds to purchase of custodial supplies,

34. Beulah McCoy, "Report," 21 June 1952, BIM Correspondence File.

35. "Sensei Kougou Heika ni Gomenkai" ("Teacher's Interview with the Royal Family"), *Shokei Shimbun* (*Shokei Newspaper*) 19 (22 July 1952) 1.

36. Ibid., picture caption.

to helping the school move the whole library from one building to another, or assisting in support of students experiencing financial distress.

- The innocence shown when responding to the call of God on their heart, embracing the whole Gospel as they prayed for their classmates and were actively engaged in teaching others what they had learned about Jesus Christ.

Jesse surely left Japan with a smile on her face as she remembered all the "flowers in her garden!"

Jesse spent the next sixteen years in the United States in California. After a period of active retirement, which included speaking to churches on behalf of foreign missions, in 1960, she entered Atherton Baptist Retirement Home in Alhambra, California. There she joined other missionaries who had served at Shokei. Even from there, she continued to send greetings to Shokei, received guests, and kept the school foremost in her mind. In 1962, she returned briefly to Shokei for its Seventieth Anniversary Celebration. In November of 1966, Shokei students received one last letter from her. One year later she went through an operation for cancer. Before she went into surgery she wrote a note to a Japanese friend. In it she expressed her feeling of peace. "Don't worry. Everything is in God's hands, and God will make all things work out. Praise God."[37] She survived the operation and was able to hold on until the spring of 1968. On May 12th, she slipped from this world and went to be with the heavenly Father she served for so many years.

As the Apostle John wrote in the last chapter of his Gospel, "And there are also many other things which Jesus did, which if they were written in detail, I suppose that even the world itself would not contain the books which were written." (John 21:25, NASB) This could also be said of Mary Jesse. Much material was left out of this work, and for each student, teacher, and friend, there could be an additional chapter written about their remembrances and experience.

A FLOWER WITH ROOTS

What can we learn from the life of Mary D. Jesse? What kind of legacy did she leave for our world?

Faith as a Legacy. She will never get an award for being a great philosopher or theologian, and her message to others was never wordy or full

---

37. Henshū Inkai, *ECHO no Hibiki LEVOL* 20 (3 March 1969) 24.

of Christian jargon. It was always simple and to the point. Her last letter to the students was typical of her Christian message throughout her career. She urged all people to establish a standard of judgment. She believed that, to establish a true standard of judgment, one must establish values based on God as the center of life, and God as Love and Light. For her, truth, standards of judgment, and behavior are derived from Jesus' words and teachings. She seldom elaborated on these in detail in her letters and collected writings, as some missionaries did, but she always pointed people back to the Bible, which was her source for these thoughts and her faith.

Leadership Models as a Legacy. Perhaps we can summarize what she has left for us in terms of models for behavior. Several times when her life became very difficult and she did not know what she should do, she said "But . . . I believe in Divine guidance." She was a very intuitive person, and it was almost as if she felt moved by a Force outside of herself. Of course, that "Force," for her, was God. Her colleagues would soon see her back at work with the same energy and determination as before. Her actions and attitude showed that she once again felt God's presence in her life and in the life of the school. Perhaps this pattern is a reflection of her favorite Bible verse: "I can do all things through Him [Christ] who strengthens me." (Phil 4:13, NASB) She gave us a model for overcoming insurmountable obstacles, not by a person's own will, but by the will and guidance of God.

One thing that stands out very prominently in her career is her style of management. She had the ability to pull people and resources together in difficult times, but she never held on tenaciously to the power given to her. Fairness tempered her decisions, policy or behavior. Judgment superseded policy or tradition, and often erred on the side of compassion. If all the students could not participate, none could participate unless the students found a way for all to participate. She felt early on that Shokei needed a Japanese principal and needed to become financially independent. She was the paragon of diplomacy, and the ultimate negotiator when trying to find agreement on issues of importance. She was never political in the sense of taking sides, but she had her own opinions and cautiously presented the facts. After the war, she often spoke out about the necessity of democracy and people-participation. Although she often bemoaned the fact that she could not complete tasks which she started, she did her best to bring closure whenever possible. She leaves us with a model of management that is both people-oriented and task-oriented.

Jesse had deep love for Shokei and what it stood for. Where this love could best be seen is hard to say. Perhaps it was at times when she was away from Japan agonizing over its problems, or when she was working at Shokei amid turmoil after having made the decision to resign, but then she continued. It might have been seen when she was rather flustered with all the commotion caused by the decoration from the Imperial Household when she gave credit for the award to others, not herself. In many of her letters, she was quick to say, "I'm thankful for the staff and the graduates." Mary D. Jesse has given us a superb model of loyalty and humility, and always showing appreciation.

The Legacy of a Flower with Roots. In her speech at the ceremony of the opening of the junior college, Jesse shared a story she had heard which expressed the nature of the heritage she wanted to leave behind.

> Several years before the recent war, I heard an elderly "Japanese" gentleman speak and one statement he made is still fresh in my memory. In discussing the national situation then, he referred to the incoming of US civilization as a veneer, and then he turned to the Americans present, and said in English "Yes, you have given us flower without the root and it has withered in our hands." The Americans spoke afterwards about his words and felt rebuked that we, while sharing material things had not shared our best, our religion. And so the flower without the root, Christianity had withered. It may do that again. We here can serve by bringing the root and planting deeply in the hearts of our students, so that it may flower in the soil of family life, in human relations, making for a better society based on Christian principles.[38]

Mary D. Jesse, along with the twenty or more other missionaries who served at Shokei during her forty-year career, tried to give Shokei Gakuin a flower rooted in faith in God. Jesse said that Christianity is like a flower. In today's terms, she believed that in order for the flower to flourish, its roots need to grow deep in the soil of faith, with God at the center. We each have a chance to take that flower with roots into our homes, our work places, and even our churches. But if the flower is cut off at the roots and is only a decoration in a vase, it will eventually wither. The depth of faith we choose to have will produce a flower with a short-life of beauty or a flower of beauty with roots that will last.

---

38. Jesse, "Building Together For a Better Shokei," 11 November 1950, Shokei Gakuin Archival Collection.

Second Year Class of the Junior College English Department (1950) First Row:
Gertrude McCulloch, Second Row: Mary Jesse & Vida Post
(courtesy of Shokei Gakuin)

Gertrude M. McCulloch and the Choir (1948–1951)
(courtesy of Shokei Gakuin)

Beulah M. McCoy (1952–1979) (courtesy of Shokei Gakuin)

Students, Faculty, the Community Gather at Sendai Station to Say Goodbye To Mary D. Jesse After More Than Forty Years of Service (courtesy of Shokei Gakuin)

Afterword

Shokei in the Present. Since Shokei Jogakkai was founded in 1892, Shokei Gakuin has grown into a general educational institution which consists of a graduate school, university, high school, junior high school, and a kindergarten. The high school and junior high school remain in the Hirose-Hachiman area of Sendai, while the graduate school, university, and kindergarten are located in nearby Natori City.

Shokei Junior College has been providing many talented graduates for society since its establishment in 1950; graduates have been working as dieticians, kindergarten or nursery-school teachers, elementary, junior high or high school teachers, public servants, office workers, and so on, and earned a good reputation for their professional achievement. However, in response to social demands, the departments of our two-year junior college have been restructured into four-year college courses. The last department of the junior college, the Department of Child Care was abolished in 2010 and replaced with a new four-year course in the same year. Because of the environment surrounding children these days, life has become so complicated that young parents are sending up distress signals about caring for their children. Greater demands are being put on teachers to be able to counsel parents who come for consultation. Shokei has added an additional two years of training to equip graduates to give appropriate advice to parents of small children who seek help with child-raising.

A very big change in Shokei's history occurred in 2003, when co-education began at the university and again at the high school and junior high school in 2008. As of May 2016, there is an enrollment of six students in the graduate school, one thousand eight hundred eighty-eight in the university, seven hundred sixty-two in the high school, seventy-four in the junior high school and one hundred twenty-one children in the kindergarten, respectively. According to the office of Shokei Gakuin Alumnae Association, more than six hundred thousand people have graduated from Shokei Gakuin since its foundation.

Ella O. Patrick Home. Originally this home was built in 1896 as the first missionary residence and schoolhouse on the Hirose campus because of a large donation from parents of Ella O. Patrick. Since then, this schoolhouse was used extensively for education activities of Shokei Gakuin, and has been loved by many students, alumnae, and staff. Reflecting Ella's understanding of the importance of education of women in Japan in Meiji era, this building has been a symbol of the founding spirit of Shokei. This western style building of the Meiji era has been popular among citizens in Sendai, and, in 1997, was granted an award for its value as an historical and cultural heritage site of Sendai. However, the building became structurally unsound over the years and was eventually torn down in 2008.

Reconstructed Ella O. Patrick Home (courtesy of Shokei Gakuin)

The Board of Shokei Gakuin decided to restore the Ella O. Patrick Home to its original condition on the Natori campus for transmitting the founding spirit of Shokei to future generations. In the tearing-down and restoration process, many of the original parts were preserved and used;

some of these include stairs, fireplace, windows and door frames, floor-boards and doorknobs. The restoration was completed and the doors opened to alumnae on November 24th, 2010, on Founding Day. Since then, many people, including staff and students and, of course, alumnae, visited this "new" Ella O. Patrick Home. A significant course was developed for all the freshmen of the university in which they visit this new Ella O. Patrick Home to learn the history of Shokei, with the help of some alumnae who volunteer to guide them around; it is a good opportunity for different generations within Shokei to communicate with each other. Reflecting Shokei's rich history of cooperation, alumnae, together with the staff, board members, and students' parents contributed more than half of the costs for this restoration project.

The Great Disaster. A deeply indented coast line, called Rias or Sanriku, extends along the Pacific Ocean in Tohoku district. Many Shokei students have traditionally come from this area. This coastal scenery is very beautiful, so much so that it has been designated as a Quasi-National Park where many tourists visit. It is famous for its active fishing industry and marine products industry.

However, on March 11, 2011, this area was marred forever by a disastrous earthquake with a magnitude 9+. Of course, such a large earthquake itself did serious damage to people in the whole northeast area, including Shokei Gakuin. However, more disastrous and tragic was the huge tsunami which hit the Sanriku area and the coastal plains after the earthquake. Nearly twenty thousand people were killed by this so called Great Eastern Japan Earthquake and Tsunami disaster. More than two hundred fifty thousand houses were completely destroyed or seriously damaged, among which nearly ninety thousand were simply washed away by the tsunami. What further worsened the situation and made local residents more anxious, was the accident of Fukushima nuclear power plant damaged by the tsunami. Because of radiation leakage and its effects, the district within twenty kilometers from the nuclear power plant, was designated as a danger zone where people are forbidden to live and work. Nine municipalities are included in the danger zone, and more than seventy-eight thousand people were forced to leave their houses and their hometowns.

Fortunately, the school buildings and major equipment on both campuses of Shokei Gakuin were not damaged seriously; costs for repairing damaged buildings amounted to forty-two million yen (five hundred twenty-five thousand dollars), but cannot be compared to other schools hit worse in the area. We deeply regret that two of our university students were killed by the tsunami and several students and staff from Shokei Gakuin lost their families. The houses of nearly two hundred people related to Shokei Gakuin collapsed or were washed away due to the earthquake and tsunami, and some students had to leave their homes within the danger zone of the Fukushima nuclear power plant.

The Board of Shokei Gakuin decided to immediately grant emergency scholarships to the students whose economic circumstances changed abruptly due to this great disaster in order to encourage them to continue their education. A total of one hundred sixty-six students were given condolence money gifts. In addition, emergency scholarships equivalent to half-year tuition, or one hundred seventy thousand yen ($2125) was granted to each high school student and two hundred fifty thousand yen ($3125) to each university student. Shokei Gakuin initiated a fund-raising campaign in cooperation with Shokei Gakuin Alumnae Association for financially helping students at Shokei who suffered from the great disaster. The slogan for this campaign is "Joining Hands Together, All Shokei!" Eventually we hope that nearly ten million yen ($125,000) will be collected to be distributed to two hundred forty-two students, including seventy alumnae who suffered from the disaster. This action, "helping each other," is evidence showing that the flower has taken root at Shokei.

Komei Sasaki, Ph.D.
President of Shokei Gakuin University

Appendix 1

Glossary of Japanese Words

asama maru	name of a Japanese ocean liner
anata no atama wa kazari mono	Your head is just a decoration piece
azuki beans	red beans cooked with sugar added is a favorite Japanese confection
Buzzell Den	Biography of Anne Buzzell
daitoua kyoueiken	Greater East Asia Co-Prosperity Sphere program
furoshiki	four-cornered cloth used to tie bundles
futon	thin quilt-like mattress placed on a floor for sleeping
gakkou	(generic) school
gakuin	school, but often used by privately sponsored school
geta	Japanese wooden clog with toe supports.
go	a volume measurement
gokujinja	War Memorial Shinto Shine
Henshū Inkai	editorial committee
hinomaru bento	lunch with a red plum in the middle of the rice, representing the Japanese flag
honka	a term used for basic education department, beginning at age twelve; the upper age changed according to law and organization of the school
houkokudan	National Appreciation Student Service Group (formally, "student body")

iresai	a national ceremony for souls of the soldiers who had fallen in war
jinrikisha	a small two-wheeled cart-like passenger vehicle pulled by one person
kaki shūdan kinrou	Student summer group work
kakushu gakkou	unaccredited school
Kayaba seisaku sho	Company making parts for the production of meters
kirisutokyo kyoudan	United Church of Christ in Japan. A church body formed during WWII for church denominations having fewer than five thousand members each. This was a stipulation issued by the government as a requirement for existence.
kirisutokyou kyo-uiku doumei	Christian Education Union (Union of all Christian Schools in Japan)
kokka soudouin hou	National Mobilization Law
kokumin seishin sakkou	National Spirit
kokumin-seishin-soudoin	The National Spirit Mobilization Movement
konyaku	konjac; devils tongue; a root made into a gelatinous food commonly eaten to improve digestion; arum root
kokumin gakkou	government schools
koutouka	Refers to level of education beyond basic education department (*honka*); eventually, it came to mean the same as grades ten through twelve, and was used up until 1936
kunrei-dai-jūnigo, shukyou kyouiku-kitei	Education Act
kyoukai	church
kyūdousha	a person seeking to become a Christian
mikan	Japanese orange (tangerine)
miso	soy bean paste used as a soup base and for flavoring in Japanese cooking
mompe	pantaloons bound at the ankles
Mutsumi no Kusari	Shokei Jogakuin's alumnae monthly journal
noroi	sluggish

"nosoi"	a word created by Margaret Haven combining the two Japanese words *noroi* and *osoi* to describe how the students were singing lethargically
osoi	late, slow
rin	Japanese unit of money; one thousand rin = one yen
sen	Japanese unit of money; one hundred sen = one yen
senkouka	term used for higher department or post-graduate diploma course above koutouka, from age eighteen, from 1936–1950
shinseikai	An organization formed after WWII made up of Baptist churches of all denominations forced to join the United Church of Christ in Japan. Those Baptist churches which remained in the UCC met together in mutual support as they tried to maintain Baptist distinctive. Those churches which left the UCC to form their own organization, the new Japan Baptist Union and Southern Baptist (Japan Baptists) being two of them, maintained loose ties with the Baptist churches which stayed in the UCC of Japan.
shinsei shadan	a corporation set up to manage property
shūshin	morals class
shūyoubu	Cultural Cultivation-Self Improvement Club (formerly, Shūkyoubu Religious or Christian Affairs Club)
soudan	consultation
taisei yokusan kai	Imperial Rule Assistant Association
tamashi	soul
tamashin	Thomasine Allen's name in Japanese
tannen-bu	Drill Department (formerly, *taiikubu*, Athletic Department)
tatami	A thick woven straw mat used in Japanese houses as floor covering
toua shinchitsujo	New Order in East Asia
udon	thick noodles made of wheat flour
zaidan houjin	property-holding body
zori	a Japanese sandal made with straw

189

Appendix 2

Alphabetical List of Letters/Annual Reports and their Origin

The letters and reports used in this work are listed below in the third section. All have come from the personal correspondence files of the writer. The first section lists the abbreviations for groups and places listed in the Personal Letters and Unpublished Annual Reports. The second section identifies the people to whom the letters are addressed. The third section is the actual list of Personal Letters and Unpublished Annual Reports. "Source" indicates the place where the correspondence is archived.

ABBREVIATIONS USED

ABHS American Baptist Historical Society, Atlanta, GA

LMJC Letters to Mary Jesse Collection, 1948–1952, Shokei Jogakuin

SMLC Shokei Missionary Letter Collection, Shokei Jogakuin Archives, Natori, Japan

WABFMS Woman's American Baptist Foreign Mission Society

PERSONS ADDRESSED

Alumnae Alumnae of Shokei Jogakuin

Constituency   Northern Baptist Churches (written for general distribution in the denomination)

Dinsmore, Carlos   Executive Director, Indiana Baptist Convention

Humphreys, Mrs. Charles (Ethel)   Foreign Secretary, WABFMS (1935–1937)

Harris, Florence   Personal friend of Anne Buzzell. Collections of her letters are on file in the Archival Collections of Shokei Gakuin

Jesse, Mary D.   American Baptist Missionary

Maine, Grace   Acting Foreign Secretary, WABFMS (1933–1934)

Maddry, Dr. Charles   Executive Secretary of the Southern Baptist Convention

McVeigh, Mabelle Rae   Foreign Secretary, WABFMS (1922?-1926)

Newbury, Georgia   American Baptist Missionary

Sandburg, Minnie   Foreign Secretary, WABFMS (1925–1932)

Sears, Mrs. C. H.   (Formerly Minnie Sandburg) Foreign Vice President (1935–1952?)

Shank, Hazel F.   Foreign Secretary, WABFMS (1938–1942?)

Tenny, C. B.   Missionary, Corresponding Secretary for Japan Baptist Mission

Ufford, A. F.   Secretary, American Baptist Foreign Mission Society

Wilson, Jesse   Treasurer, American Baptist Foreign Mission Society

Woman's American Baptist Foreign Mission Society   Executive Board and officers

PERSONAL LETTERS, PUBLISHED AND UNPUBLISHED ANNUAL REPORTS

	TYPE	DATES	ADDRESSEE	SOURCE
Missionaries:				
Winnifred Acock	Annual Report	1923–1924	WABFMS	ABHS/ SMLC

	TYPE	DATES		ADDRESSEE	SOURCE
	Letter	18-Jul	1935	Mrs. Humphreys	ABHS/ SMLC
Alice Bixby	Letter	25-Nov	1940	Constituency	ABHS/ SMLC
	Constit- uency	16-Nov	1942	Constituency	ABHS/ SMLC
Anne Buzzell	Letter	16-Dec	1916	Florence Harris	SMLC
Emma Broadbeck	Annual Report	January	1928	WABFMS	ABHS/ SMLC
Freda Clause	Letter	August	1931	Minnie Sandburg	ABHS/ SMLC
	Letter	25-Mar	1933	Minnie Sandburg	ABHS/ SMLC
Margaret Cuddeback	Letter	5-Mar	1936	Mrs. Humphreys	ABHS/ SMLC
	Annual Report	October	1936	WABFMS	ABHS/ SMLC
	Buzzell Obituary	8-Feb	1937		ABHS/ SMLC
	Report	28-Jan	1944	Constituency	ABHS/ SMLC
Mary D. Jesse	Letter	June	1923	C.B. Tenny	Kanto Gakuin Library
	Letter	7-Sep	1925	Mabelle McVeigh	ABHS
	Annual Report	Novem- ber	1927	WABFMS	ABHS
	Letter	2-Apr	1927	Dr. Carlos Dinsmore	ABHS
	Letter	4-Sep	1927	Mabelle McVeigh	ABHS

TYPE	DATES		ADDRESSEE	SOURCE
Letter	18-Jan	1928	Mabelle McVeigh	ABHS
Annual Report	25-Mar	1929	ABFMS	ABHS
Letter	6-Apr	1933	Minnie Sandburg	ABHS
Letter	20-Apr	1933	Minnie Sandburg	ABHS
Letter	31-Apr	1933	Minnie Sandburg	ABHS
Letter	15-Jan	1934	Grace Maine	ABHS
Letter	12-May	1934	Grace Maine	ABHS
Excerps	July	1934	Grace Maine	ABHS
Letter	29-Jul	1934	Grace Maine	ABHS
Letter	28-Oct	1934	Grace Maine	ABHS
Letter	6-Apr	1933	Minnie Sandburg	ABHS
Letter	20-Apr	1933	Minnie Sandburg	ABHS
Letter	10-Jan	1937	Mrs. Humphreys	ABHS
Letter	25-Jul	1937	Mrs. Humphreys	ABHS
Letter	5-May	1938	Minnie Sears	ABHS
Letter	10-Dec	1938	Minnie Sears	ABHS
Letter	12-Feb	1939	Minnie Sears	ABHS
Letter	12-Mar	1939	Minnie Sears	ABHS
Letter	23-May	1939	Minnie Sears	ABHS
Letter	16-Feb	1940	Minnie Sears	ABHS
Letter	6-Jul	1940	Hazel Shank	ABHS
Letter	4-Dec	1940	Hazel Shank	ABHS
Semi-Annual Report	14-Jun	1941	Foreign Mission Board	ABHS
Letter	23-Jun	1941	Hazel Shank	ABHS
Letter	29-Jan	1943	Hazel Shank	ABHS
Letter	30-Jan	1943	Hazel Shank	ABHS
Letter	6-Sep	1946	Hazel Shank	ABHS

	TYPE	DATES		ADDRESSEE	SOURCE
	Letter	23-Dec	1946	Minnie Sears	ABHS
	Letter	7-Feb	1947	Minnie Sears	ABHS
	Letter	30-May	1949	Jesse R. Wilson	ABHS
	Letter	1-Jul	1949	Minnie Sears	ABHS
	Letter	2-Jul	1949	Minnie Sears	ABHS
	Letter	12-Aug	1949	Minnie Sears	ABHS
	Letter	10-Sep	1949	Minnie Sears	ABHS
	Letter	19-Oct	1949	Minnie Sears	ABHS
	Letter	20-Mar	1950	Minnie Sears	ABHS
	Letter	5-Aug	1950	Minnie Sears	ABHS
	Letter	30-Mar	1951	Minnie Sears	ABHS
	Letter	4-Jul	1951	Minnie Sears	ABHS
	Letter	8-Aug	1951	Minnie Sears	ABHS
	Letter	January	1951	Minnie Sears	ABHS
	Letter	9-Jun	1952	Minnie Sears	ABHS
	Letter	19-Dec	1952	Minnie Sears	ABHS
			1952	Minnie Sears	ABHS
Agnes Meline	Annual Report	15-Jan	1927	WABFMS	ABHS/ SMLC
	Annual Report	July	1927	WABFMS	ABHS/ SMLC
			1927	WABFMS	ABHS/ SMLC
Gertrude McCulloch	Letter	12-Jun			ABHS/ SMLC
	Letter	19-Oct	1949	Constituency	ABHS/ SMLC
	Letter	29-Apr	1950	Constituency	ABHS/ SMLC
	Letter	28-Jan	1952	Minnie Sears	ABHS/ SMLC
With Vida Post	Letter	3-Aug	1950	Constituency	ABHS/ SMLC
	Letter	31-Jul	1951	Constituency	ABHS/ SMLC
	Letter	28-Jan	1952	Minnie Sears	ABHS/ SMLC

	TYPE	DATES		ADDRESSEE	SOURCE
Georgia Newbury	Annual Report	October	1925	WABFMS	ABHS/ SMLC
	Letter	25-Apr	1928	Mabelle McVeigh	ABHS/ SMLC
	Letter	22-Jan	1931	Constituency	ABHS/ SMLC
	Letter	25-Feb	1931	Constituency	ABHS/ SMLC
	Letter	8-Apr	1932	Minnie Sandburg	ABHS/ SMLC
	Letter	8-Apr	1933	Constituency	ABHS/ SMLC
	Letter	August	1933	Constituency	ABHS/ SMLC
	Letter	7-Apr	1934	Grace Maine	ABHS/ SMLC
	Letter	7-Jun	1934	Grace Maine	ABHS/ SMLC
	Annual Report	15-Jul	1934	WABFMS	ABHS/ SMLC
	Letter	10-Aug	1934	Grace Maine	ABHS/ SMLC
	Letter	13-Feb	1935	Grace Maine	ABHS/ SMLC
Goldie Nicholson	Report	12-Jun	1937	WABFMS	ABHS/ SMLC
Lora Patten	Letter	2-Dec	1936	Constituency	ABHS/ SMLC
	Letter	1-Jun	1937	Constituency	ABHS/ SMLC
	Letter	July	1938	Constituency	ABHS/ SMLC
Vida Post	Letter	3-Aug	1950	Constituency	ABHS/ SMLC

	TYPE	DATES		ADDRESSEE	SOURCE
Sadie T. Ross	Annual Report	1923		WABFMS	ABHS/ SMLC
	Annual Report	1927		WABFMS	ABHS/ SMLC
Florence Skevington and A. Emma Brodbeck					
	Annual Report	October	1927	WABFMS	ABHS/ SMLC
Ruth E. Smith	Letter	4-Jun	1925	WABFMS	ABHS/ SMLC

Foreign Secretaries and Others

	TYPE	DATES		ADDRESSEE	SOURCE
Edith Humphreys	Letter	22-Aug	1935	Alumnae	ABHS/ SMLC
	Letter	5-Dec	1935	Georgia Newbury	ABHS/ SMLC
I. J. Fisher	"Ex- cerpts"	19-May	1942	ABFMS	ABHS/ SMLC
Charles Maddry	Letter	8-Jun	1934	Grace Maine	ABHS
Grace Maine	Letter	6-Feb	1934		ABHS
	Letter	7-Jun	1934		ABHS/ SMLC
	Letter	11-Jun	1934		ABHS/ SMLC
	Letter	3-Oct	1934		ABHS/ SMLC
Minnie Sandburg	Letter	3-Apr	1933	Georgia Newbury	ABHS/ SMLC
	Letter	4-Apr	1933	Georgia Newbury	ABHS/ SMLC

	TYPE	DATES		ADDRESSEE	SOURCE
Minnie Sandburg Sears	Letter	18-Jan	1952	Mary D. Jesse	ABHS/ SMLC
Hazel Shank	Letter	13-Jun	1946	Mary D. Jesse	ABHS
Jesse Wilson	Letter	15-Jul	1949	Mary D. Jesse	ABHS

Shokei Jo Gakuin Related:

Father of student
Translated Letter

	TYPE	DATES		ADDRESSEE	SOURCE
	Letter	12-Aug	1947	Mary D. Jesse	ABHS/ SMLC
Ukichi Kawaguchi	Letter	5-Apr	1929	WABFMS	ABHS
	Partial letter	July	1934	Mary D. Jesse	ABHS/ SMLC
	Letter	7-Jul	1934	Grace Maine	ABHS/ SMLC
Tai Kusakabe	Letter	12-Aug	1948	Mary D. Jesse	LMJC
Shokei Alumnae	Letter	April	1935	Friends in America	ABHS/ SMLC
Shokei Faculty	Letter	12-Jul	1934	WABFMS Officers	ABHS/ SMLC
Shokei Jogakuin	Report	7-Jan	1947		SMLC
Yo Suzuki	Letter	28-May	1935	WABFMS	ABHS/ SMLC

* ABHS: American Baptist Historical Society, Atlanta, Georgia
* SMLC: Shokei Missionary Letter Collection, Shokei Gakuin, Natori, Japan
* LMJC: Letters to Mary Jesse Collection (1948–1952) Post-War Special Collection
* WABFMS: Woman's American Baptist Foreign Mission Society, Board of International Ministries, Valley Forge, PA
* ABFMS: American Baptist Foreign Mission Society

Appendix 3

Personal Information					Service in Japan					
Names English	Title	Birthdate	Death	Home State	Dates: Japan	Dates: Shokei	Status	Subject	Special Notes	Other Places of Service
Acock, Amy	Miss	1877	1964	Indiana	1905–1936	1907–1909	Missionary	English	Country Evangelism	Morioka/ Himeji
Acock, Winifred	Miss	1883	1974	California	1922–1950	1924–1926	Missionary	English/ Honka		Soshin
Allen, Thomasine	Miss	1890	1976	Indiana	1915–1976	1917–1927	Missionary	English/ Honka	Country Evangelism (sixty-one years)	Morioka/ Kuji
Anderson, Ruby L.	Miss	1890	?	Nebraska	1917–1929	1920–1922	Missionary	Music/ English	Music	Soshin
Axling, Lucinda	Mrs.	1893	1901–1960	Nebraska	1901–1950		Missionary, Part-time			Morioka/ Tokyo
Axling, William	Mr.	1873	1901–1963	Nebraska	1901–1950		Missionary, Part-time			Morioka/ Tokyo
Bishop, Norma	Mrs.		2016	Colorado	1986–1988	1986–1988	Special Service Worker	English/Jr. College		

Personal Information					Service in Japan					
Names English	Title	Birthdate	Death	Home State	Dates: Japan	Dates: Shokei	Status	Subject	Special Notes	Other Places of Service
Bixby, Alice C.	Miss	1885	1973	Vermont	1914–1953	1931–1939–1941	Missionary	Music/English	Choirs	Soshin/Hinomoto
Bristol, Margaret	Mrs.	1910	1998	Massachusetts	1967–1975	1967–1975	Special Service Worker/Missionary	Eng. Conv. Sr. High/Jr. College	Became Missionary in 1972	
Brodbeck, Emma	Miss	1892	1989	Illinois	1927–1928	1927–1928	Missionary	English/Honka & Senkoubu		China
Browne, Harriet M.	Miss	1860	?	Kansas	1896–1896	1886–1889	Missionary	Pre-Shokei/Boarded girls		Fukushima/Shimonoseki
Bullen, Evelyn	Mrs.	1871	1929	Rhode Island	1904–1913	1907–1908	Missionary, Part-time	English/Honka		
Bullen, Walter B.	Mr.	1897	1947	New Hampshire	1904–1913	1905–1908	Missionary, Part-time	English/Honka		
Buzzell, Annie S.	Miss	1866	1936	Nebraska	1892–1936	1892–1919	Missionary	English/Home Ec/Bible	First Principal (twenty-six years)	Tono
Calvin, Edith	Miss	1913	2002	New York	1971–1978	1971–1978	Special Service Worker	English/Jr. College		

Personal Information					Service in Japan					
Names English	Title	Birthdate	Death	Home State	Dates: Japan	Dates: Shokei	Status	Subject	Special Notes	Other Places of Service
Carl, Margret	Miss	1917	2011	New York	1981–1984	1981–1984	Special Service Worker	English/Jr. College		Equador/ Marshall Islands
Carlson, Margaret	Mrs.	1924	?	Idaho	1984–1987	1984–1987	Special Service Worker	English/Jr. College		
Clause, Freda J.	Miss	1897	?	Ohio	1930–1933	1930–1933	Missionary	English/ Honka	Library work	
Cuddeback, Margaret E. (Clarke)	Miss	1909	?	Oregon	1931–1953	1935–1936	Short Term/ Missionary	English/ Honka	Author, Interned in Shanghai	China
Evans, Maggie	Miss	?								
Fife, Nellie E.	Miss	1857	?		1887–1905	1887–1891	Missionary	PreShokei/ Boarded girls		Odawara
Gifford, Ella May	Miss	1887	?	New York	1920–1925	1924–1925	Missionary	Honka		Morioka
Gilson, Ruth (Fox)	Miss			Pennsylvania	1980–1982	1980–1982	Special Service Worker	English/Jr. College		
Grace, Dorothy	Mrs.	1913	2010	California	1982–1984	1982–1984	Special Service Worker	English/Jr. College		

Personal Information					Service in Japan					
Names English	Title	Birthdate	Death	Home State	Dates: Japan	Dates: Shokei	Status	Subject	Special Notes	Other Places of Service
Haven, F. Marguerite (Somerton)	Mrs.	1885	?	New York	1916–1930	1924–1930	Missionary	Music/ Honka/ Koutouka		
Holland, Robin Harvey	Mrs.			Pennsylvania	1982–1991	1983–1991	Missionary	English/Jr. College		
Hughes, Grace Anne (Mills)	Miss	1872	?	Nebraska	1900–1912	1910–1912	Missionary	English/ Honka	Acting Principal	Osaka
Jenkins, Louise F.	Miss	1888	1970	Connecticut	1920–1932	1928–1930	Missionary	English/ Honka		
Jesse, Mary D.	Miss	1881	1968	Virginia	1911– 1931,1938– 1952	1911–1931, 1938–1952	Missionary	English/ Home Ec/ Bible	2nd Principal/President of JC	Morioka
Kemp, Rosa-lyn E. (Reiff)	Miss	1942	2015	New York	1965–1968	1965–1969	Three-Year Term Missionary	Eng. Conv. Sr. High		
Livingston, Beth	Mrs.	1928	2015	Alabama	1952–1968	1966–1967	Missionary	Part-time/ English/Jr. College		Tokyo, Morioka, Rifu/ Shiogama

Personal Information						Service in Japan						
Names English	Title	Birthdate	Death	Home State	Dates: Japan	Dates: Shokei	Status	Subject	Special Notes	Other Places of Service
McCoy, Beulah M.	Miss	1915	2002	Rhode Island	1947–1979	1952–1979	Missionary	English/ Jr. High-Jr. College	Acting President	Soshin
McCullogh, Gertrude F.	Miss	1890	1985	Michigan	1948–1951	1949–1951	Missionary	English & Music/Jr. College		China
Mead, Lavinia	Miss	1860	1941	Minnesota	1890–1926	1890–1902	Missionary	Boarded Students/ Bible	Founder/ Principal	India, Osaka
Meline, Agnes Sofia	Miss	1886	1969	Nebraska	1919–1932	1926–1927	Missionary	English/ Honka		Soshin
Nelson, Mary	Mrs.	1913	1981	California	1978–1981	1978–1981	Special Service Worker	English/Jr. College		
Newbury, Georgia Maud	Miss	1888	1962	Washington	1921–1935	1924–1935	Missionary	English/ Honka		Taiwan
Nicholson, Goldie M. (Yasunaga)	Miss	1906	1995	Indiana	1932–1940	1935–1937	Missionary	English/ Honka/ Senkoubu		
Oglesby, Louella R.	Mrs.	1916	2007	Oklahoma	1979–1982	1979–1982	Special Service Worker	English/Jr. College		

| Personal Information | | | | | Service in Japan | | | | | |
Names English	Title	Birthdate	Death	Home State	Dates: Japan	Dates: Shokei	Status	Subject	Special Notes	Other Places of Service
Palmiter, Viola (Dalhberg)	Mrs.	1909	2003	Wisconsin	1974–1976	1974–1976	Special Service Worker	English/Jr. College		
Patten, Lora Mabel	Miss	1896	?	Indiana	1936–1940	1936–1939	Missionary	English/Koutobu		
Paulson, Gerda Christian	Miss	1871	?	Minnesota	1899–1905	1899–1902	Short-term Missionary (1902)			
Pawley, Annabelle	Miss	1890	1945	New York	1915–1938	1922–1923	Missionary	English/Honka		Soshin
Phillips, L. Adele	Miss			California?	1890–1893	1890–1891	Missionary	PreShokei/Boarded girls		
Pope, Henrietta	Mrs.	1911	2003	Illinois	1976–1979	1976–1979	Special Service Worker	English/Jr. College		
Post, Vida (Shouts)	Miss	1897	1989	New York	1920–1961	1949–1961	Missionary	English/High School		Hinomoto
Ray, Elizabeth	Miss	?				1939–1939		English/Honka		
Ross, Charles H.	Mr.	1879	1969	California	1910–1929	1928–1929	Missionary	Part-time/Honka		

Personal Information					Service in Japan					
Names English	Title	Birthdate	Death	Home State	Dates: Japan	Dates: Shokei	Status	Subject	Special Notes	Other Places of Service
Ross, Sadie	Mrs.	1884	1975	California	1910–1929	1928–1929	Missionary	Part-time/English/Domestic Sc		
Sanderson, Abbie G.	Miss	1893	1970	Maine	1954–1960	1955–1960	Missionary	English		China
Skevington, Florence	Miss	1898	1977	California	1927–1928	1927–1928	Missionary	English/Honka		China
Skevington, Gladys	Miss	1901	1985	California	1927–1928	1927–1928	Missionary	English/Honka		China
Smith, Ruth E. (Leonard)	Miss	1893	?	Ohio	1918–1926	1922–1924	Short Term Missionary	English/Physical Ed.		
Somers, Gladys Marir (Boynton)	Miss	1885	?	Colorado	1919–1921	1920–1921	Short Term Missionary	English/Honka		China
Stephens, Roberta L.	Miss			California	1977–2014	1979–1997	Missionary	Eng. Conv. Jr/Sr. Hi		
Sutherland, Jewell	Miss	1900	?	Illinois	1962–1963	1962–1963	Contract Worker	English		
Topping, Helen Fairlle	Miss	1889	?	New York	1911–1917	1911–1913	Short Term Missionary	English		

| Personal Information | | | | | Service in Japan | | | | | |
Names English	Title	Birthdate	Death	Home State	Dates: Japan	Dates: Shokei	Status	Subject	Special Notes	Other Places of Service
Tuxbury, Nina	Mrs.	1870	?	Colorado	1907–1917	1908–1910	Missionary			
Waddington, Lois Hampton	Mrs.			New Jersey	1952–1968	1967–1968	Missionary	Part-time/English/Jr. College		Hinomoto, Morioka
Ward, Ruth Clarisa	Miss	1890	1980	California	1919–1926	1921–1926	Missionary	Music/Honka		
Waterman, Gertrude M.	Miss	1908		Conneticut	1948–1976	1959–1976	Missionary	Early Childhood Ed./Jr. College		Mead Cntr-Osaka
Whitman, Marie Antoinette	Miss	1856	1917		1883–1917		Missionary			Sara Curtis School
Wilkinson, Jessie M. G.	Miss	1885	1954	Massachusetts	1919–1931	1925–1931	Missionary	English/Honka		
Wilson, Helen Louise	Miss	1903	1953	New York	1929–1935	1931–1934	Missionary	English/Honka		Soshin
Wilson, Jesse	Mr.	1892	1974	Texas	1921–1926	1924	Missionary			
Wilson, Louise	Mrs.	1890	1993	Texas	1921–1926	1924	Missionary	Part-time/English/Honka		

Bibliography

47th Class of Shokei Jogakuin. Interview of fifteen members by Roberta Lynn Stephens. Shokei Girls' High School, 28 August 2002. Archival Room. Shokei Gakuin Administration Office. Natori, Japan.

Allen, Thomasine. Interview by Elizabeth Hemphill, 1959. Tape recording. Board of International Ministries. Archival Collection of American Baptist Historical Society. Atlanta.

American Anthropological Association. "1800s–1850s: Expansion of slavery in the U.S. American Anthropological Association." http://www.msnbc.msn.com/id/24714472.

Annual Commencement. "165th Annual Commencement." Columbia University. 4 June 1919. https://babel.hathitrust.org/cgi/pt?id=mdp.39015055319514;age=root;view=image;size=100;seq=6;num=4.

Askew, Eddie. A Silence and a Shouting. London: The Leprosy Mission International 1982.

Bank of Japan. "Nihon Ginko hyakunenshi boshu inkai shu 'nihon ginko hyakunen shi shiryou shu'" ("Bank of Japan 100th Anniversary Committee, '100 Year History of the Bank of Japan'"). Nihon Ginko (Bank of Japan): 1986. Other related material came from http://www.boj.or.jp/announcements/education/oshiete/history/11100021.html.

Barton, Ruth Haley. Sacred Rhythms—Arranging Our Lives for Spiritual Transformation. Downers Grove, IL: InterVarsity, 2006.

Behr, Edward. Hirohito: Behind the Myth. New York: Villard, 1989.

Bender, Alice Covell to Roberta Lynn Stephens, January 1997.

Blake, I. George. Finding a Way Through the Wilderness. Indianapolis, IN: Central, 1983.

Board of International Ministries Collection. Correspondence. American Baptist Historical Society, Atlanta.

Brodbeck, Emma L. China Farewell. 3rd edition. Alhambra, CA: n.p., 1970.

"Cables: Incoming Cables: 1927–1935." Board of International Ministries. Archival Collection of American Baptist Historical Society. Atlanta.

"Cables: Outgoing Cables: 1923–1927." Board of International Ministries. Archival Collection of American Baptist Historical Society. Atlanta.

Chiba, Yugoro to A. F. Ufford and Hazel Shank, 10 November 1945. Board of International Ministries. Archival Collection of American Baptist Historical Society. Atlanta.

Clarence, Earl Frost. Heritage Quest Online. http://palmspringsbum.com/geneology/familygroup.php?familyID=13469&tree=Legends.

Custer, Mark Douglas, and Orlene Elizabeth Ehleys. "Custer Family Genealogy, Ball Genealogy." http://www.angelfire.com/tx4/custer/ball.html.

Daniels, Roger. "United States Immigration Acts of 1924, 1952, and 1965." *Kodansha Encyclopedia of Japan*. Tokyo: Kodansha, 1983.

Detzer, David. *Allegiance: Fort Sumter, Charleston, and the Beginning of the Civil War*. Orlando, FL: Harcourt, 2001.

"Epping Forest." Wikipedia. http://en.wikipedia.org/wiki/Epping_Forest.

Father of a student to M. D. Jesse, 12 August 1947. Board of International Ministries Correspondence File of Mary D. Jesse. Archival Collection of American Baptist Historical Society. Atlanta.

"The First Post-War Year." Distributed at the Foreign Missions Conference of North America. Board of International Ministries. Archival Collection of American Baptist Historical Society. Atlanta, n.d.

Fridell, Elmer. "Japan." 14 November 1947. *War Years Collection*. Board of International Ministries. Archival Collection of American Baptist Historical Society. Atlanta.

Fridell, Elmer, and C. H. Sears, eds. "Japan Statement." Board of International Ministries. Archival Collection of American Baptist Historical Society. Atlanta, 1947.

Frost, Earl Clarence. "de Jarnette and Allied Families in America (1699–1954)." Heritage Quest Online. San Bernardino, CA: EC&M, 1954. http://palmspringsbum.com/geneology/familygroup.php?familyID=13469&tree=Legends.

"Gakusei Kibou." In *Student Attendance Record Book*. Shokei Jo Gakuin High School Office. Archival Collection Shokei Jogakuin. Sendai, Japan. May 1951.

Gleanings Magazine. Vol. 2–26. 1911–1923.

Harper, Douglas. "American Colonization Society." http://www.slavenorth.com/colonize.htm.

Harris, Catherine Embree. *Dusty Exile: Looking Back at Japanese Relocation During World War II*. Honolulu: Mutual, 1999.

Hemphill, Elizabeth. "Transcription of Oral History Tape of Interview of Thomasine Allen, 1959, Biographical File of Thomasine Allen." Board of International Ministries. Archives of the American Baptist Historical Society. Atlanta.

———. *A Treasure to Share*. Valley Forge, PA: Judson, 1964.

Henshū Inkai (Editorial Committee). *ECHO no Hibiki* (*Reverberations of an Echo*) *LEVOL* 20 (March 1969) 24. Shokei Jo Gakko: Sendai, Japan.

Iglehart, Charles W. *A Century of Protestant Christianity in Japan*. Rutland: Charles E. Tuttle, 1959.

"J Sensei Kougou Heika Ni Gomenkai" ("J Teacher's Interview with the Royal Family"). *Shokei Shinbun* (*Shokei Newspaper*) 19, 22 July 1952. Archival Room. Shokei Gakuin Administration Office. Natori, Japan.

Japan Baptist Annual. Yokohama, Japan: Seishi Bunsha, 1907–1937. Archival Collection of American Baptist Historical Society. Atlanta.

Japan Missionary Fellowship of the American Baptist Foreign Mission Society and the Woman's American Baptist Foreign Mission Society, ed. *Out of the Ashes*. n.p., n.d.

Japan Reference Committee and Conference Minutes. In the Reference Committee & Conference File. Archival Collection. American Baptist Foreign Mission Society Office. Tokyo, 1916–1921. Collection moved to ABHS in 2009.

"Japanese Yen." Wikipedia. http://en.wikipedia.org/wiki/Japanese_yen#cite_note-11.

Jesse, Mary D. "Building Together For a Better Shokei." Speech given at the opening of Shokei Junior College. Sendai, Japan, 11 November 1950. Archival Room. Shokei Gakuin. Natori, Japan.

Kagawa, Toyohiko. *Christ and Japan*. Translated by William Axling. New York: Friendship, 1934.

Kodansha Encyclopedia of Japan, 1983.

Kusakabe, Tai Iikawa to Mary D. Jesse, 12 May 1948. Letters to Jesse Teacher File. Archival Room. Shokei Gakuin Administration Office. Natori, Japan.

Letter Collection. Archival Room. Shokei Gakuin. Administration Office. Natori, Japan.

Library of Congress Exhibition. "Colonization: The African American Mosaic." http://www.loc.gov/african/afam002.html.

Lincoln, Abraham. "First Inaugural Address of Abraham Lincoln, Monday, March 4, 1861." Lillian Goldman Law Library. The Avalon Project. http://avalon.law.yale.edu/19th_century/lincoln1.asp.

Mary Ball Washington Museum Library. Epping Forest Files. Genealogy and History Library. Information by email from info@mbwm.org.

Mary Hampton DeJarnette Jesse. Ancestry.com. https://www.geni.com/people/Mary-Hampton-Jesse/6000000037786971837.

Matsukawa, Yukiko. "The First Japanese Kindergartens." *International Journal of Early Childhood* 22 (1990) 32. https://doi.org/10.1007/BF03174595.

Matsumura, Yoshie. "Report of Shokei Jogakuin." Board of International Ministries. Archival Collection of American Baptist Historical Society. Atlanta, c. 1953.

McCoy, Beulah M. "Report." Board of International Ministries. Archival Collection of Archival Collection of American Baptist Historical Society. Atlanta, 21 June 1952.

"Minutes of the Shokei Jogakkou Board of Trustees." January–September 1949, March 1952 in the Board of Trustees Record Book. Archival Collection of Shokei Gakuin. Natori, Japan.

Missionary Register Cards. "Mary D. Jesse." Board of International Ministries. Archival Collection in Valley Forge, PA.

Mizzou Alumni Association. "No Manner of Harm." *Mizzou* 87:3 (1999) 10–11. https://hdl.handle.net/10355/54845.

Mutsumi no kusari (Chain of Friendship). Vol. 8–15. Sendai, Japan: Shokei Jo Gakuin, 1915–1935, special edition 1968. Archival Room. Shokei Gakuin Administration Office. Natori, Japan.

"National Mobilization Law." In *Japan: An Illustrated Encyclopedia*, 1060. 1st ed. Vol. 2. Tokyo: Kodansha, 1993.

"National Spirit Mobilization Movement." In *Japan: An Illustrated Encyclopedia*, 1063. 1st ed. Vol. 2. Tokyo: Kodansha, 1993.

Nouwen, Henri J. M. *The Genesee Diary: Report from a Trappist Monastery*. New York: Doubleday, 1976.

Paliden1952. "Leaves, Trees & Nuts, Ancestor Family Trees." http://trees.ancestry.com/tree/9767217/person.

"Preliminary Considerations for Post War Study on Japan." Board of International Ministries. Archival Collection of American Baptist Historical Society. Atlanta, 1945.

"Report of the Board of Trustees." Shokei Jogakko. Archival Collection of Shokei Gakuin High School. Sendai, Japan, 1938, 1939.

"Savitar—The MU Yearbook." Columbus, MO: E. W. Stephens Printing Company, 1904, 1905, 1906, 1907, 1910. http://digital.library.umsystem.edu/cgi/t/text/text-idx?sid=bb64f351790364f203aa3b52addbf2f3&g=&c=savitar&cc=savitar&tpl=browse.tpl.

Seventieth Anniversary Committee. *Shokei Jogakuin Nanajuu Nen Shi (The Seventy-Year History of Shokei Jogakuin)*. Sendai, Japan: Yoshi Masatori, 1962.

Severance, Henry Ormal. *Richard Henry Jesse, President of the University of Missouri, 1891–1908*. Columbia, MO: 1937.

Sleeth, Natalie. "In the Bulb There is a Flower." Hope Publishing, 1986. http://www. hopepublishing.com/html/main.isx?sitesec=40.2.1.0&hymnID=3983.

Stephens, Roberta L. "Between Heaven and Hell." *Kenkyuu Kiyou* (Research Journal) 3 (1996) 1–9.

"Student Volunteer Movement." http://en.wikipedia.org/wiki/Student_Volunteer_Movement.

Student Volunteer Movement for Foreign Missions. "The First Two Decades of the Student Movement—Report of the Executive Committee to the Fifth International Convention, Nashville, February Twenty-Eighth to March Fourth, Nineteen Hundred and Six (1906) 4." https://babel.hathitrust.org/cgi/pt?id=mdp.39015055319514;age=root;view=image;size=100;seq=6;num=4.

Tada, Keiko Yoshida. Telephone interview by Roberta Lynn Stephens. Sendai, Japan, 15 December 1998. Transcript not available.

War Years Collection. Board of International Ministries. Archival Collections. American Baptist Historical Society. Atlanta.

Watanabe, Hajime. *Covell*. Translated by Pat Wine, edited by David and Betty Covell. Tokyo: Kodansha, 2000.

Wayland, John W. *The Washingtons And Their Homes*. Virginia: Virginia Books, 1944.

Westcott, Brooke Foss. BrainyQuote.com. http://www.brainyquote.com/quotes/quotes/b/brookefoss194199.html.

Woman's American Baptist Foreign Mission Society. "Foreign Department and Finance Committee Minutes, 1916–1920." Board of International Ministries. Archival Collection of American Baptist Historical Society. Atlanta.

———. *Our Work in the Orient*. New York: Woman's American Baptist Foreign Mission Society, 1916–1917, 1920–1926.

———. "Sendai." *Sixtieth Annual Report* (1930–1931) 55.

———. *Thirty-Eighth to Seventy-Ninth Annual Report of the Board*. New York: Womans' American Baptist Foreign Mission Society, 1909–1950.

Wynd, William. *Seventy Years in Japan: Saga of Northern Baptists*. New York: American Baptist Foreign Mission Society, n.d.

Zukan Asahi Hen (Asahi Newspaper Editorial Committee). *Nedan no Meiji, Taisho, Showa Fuuzokushi* (*Genre History of Prices in the Meiji, Taisho and Showa Era*). Tokyo: Asahi Shinbun, 1981.

Index

Acock, Winifred, 17, 36, 39, 40, 49, 52, 66, 81, 84, 130, 165

African-Americans, 4

agriculture, 108, 120

Aikawa Takashi, 172

Aizawa Kei, 55

Akama Kyoko, 170

Akihito (son of emperor), 53

Allen, Thomasine, 8, 19, 21, 30, 31, 48, 50, 52, 53, 55, 56, 58, 59, 66, 87, 89, 127–29, 130, 133, 140, 141, 165

alumnae, alumnus, 6, 15, 18, 42, 65, 67, 68, 71, 72, 73, 74, 76, 84, 85, 92, 93, 102, 104 147, 151, 153, 158, 163, 167, 183, 184, 185, 186

American Baptist Foreign Mission Society (ABFMS), xiv, 4, 79, 138, 153

American Baptist Historical Society (ABHS), ix, xi, 13, 91

American Baptist Missionary Union (ABMU), xiv, 14

American Colonization Society, 4

Anderson, Ruby, 30

Ando Kensuke, 67, 69, 74, 81–89, 103, 106

anniversary, ix, x, 15, 21, 74, 75, 102, 112, 174–76, 178

Aoyama Gakuin, 45, 70, 113

army, 38, 64, 98, 120, 121, 129, 142, 143

Asama Maru, 134

Ashland, 76, 104, 105

Askew, Eddie, 28, 50

Atherton Baptist Homes, 178

Axling, William & Lucinda, 63, 130

Ayashi, 119, 120

Ball, Colonel Joseph, 3

Ball Colonel William, 3

Ball, Mary, xi, 1–3

baptism, baptized, xiv, 9, 40, 43, 45, 46, 63, 68, 70, 71, 81, 92, 97, 142, 146, 147, 154, 166, 170

Baptist Missionary Training School, 68, 86

Barton, Ruth Harley, 50

basic education, 24, 25, 35, 36

Benninghoff, Harry Baxter, 15, 92

Bible Women, xvi, 17, 21, 22,23, 24, 33, 96

Bixby, Alice, 37, 38, 54, 64, 68, 70, 75, 80, 90, 92, 99, 100, 101, 116, 118, 128, 129, 131–34, 140, 142, 165

Board of Trustees, 80, 93, 114, 150, 152, 153, 155, 156, 157, 165, 173, 174

Brodbeck, Emma, 56, 60, 130

Brown, Nathan and Charlotte, xvi

bunkers, 129

Buzzell Kan (House), 99 , 100 133, 148, 142, 147

Buzzell, Annie S., xvii, 14, 17, 29, 40, 43, 63, 72, 77, 85, 86, 99, 102

camouflage, 121

Camp, Evelyn, 43

camp, camping, 65, 129, 170

Cary, Lott, 4

Catholic, 118, 128, 131, 133

celebration, 15, 16, 69, 98, 102, 112, 147, 157, 158, 163, 165, 174–78
censor, 111, 132
chaplains (army), 138, 142
Chiba Shin, 54, 64, 83, 89, 107
Chiba Yugoro, 40, 137
Chigasaki, 122–124, 126, 127
China, 11, 52, 56, 59–61, 64, 92, 97, 98, 103, 108, 110, 111, 130
choir, 11, 37, 99, 165, 166, 181
Christian fellowship, xvi, 103, 136, 138, 146, 164
Christian ideal(s), 4, 103, 109, 163, 164
Christian schools, 16, 29, 102, 113, 115, 121, 128, 140, 143, 146
Christmas, 37, 47, 63, 95, 98, 132, 133, 147
church, churches, xiv, xv, 10, 14, 16, 19, 21, 23, 29, 33, 39, 41, 42, 43, 45, 47, 51, 57, 62, 68, 70, 76, 96, 98, 99, 100, 102, 103,104, 114–116, 118, 119, 129, 130, 132, 133, 134, 136, 139, 140, 142, 143, 147, 148, 161, 164, 165, 166, 167, 170, 172, 176, 178, 180
(American) Baptist Churches, ix, x, xiv, xv, 32, 39, 137, 165, 170, 173, 175
First Baptist Sendai, *Daiichi,* 39, 95, 165, 147
Hosanna Church, 36, 39,95, 143, 147
Holiness Church, 116
Non-Church, 92
North Star, Kita San Bancho, 36, 39, 68, 92, 143, 147, 170
Reformed Church in America 37, 39, 72, 128
Shinsei Church, 165
Shokei Church, 39, 166
Uchimaru Church, 17
United Church of Christ in Japan, 36, 39, 116, 137, 146, 165
Yotsuya Church, 81
Civil Information and Education, 150
Civil War, xiv, 4
Clause, Freda, 65, 68
Columbia University, 19, 131
Commission of Six, 139, 140

Committee on Relations (COR), 156
communists, communism, 42, 130
construction, xvii, 14, 61, 81, 97, 103, 136, 151, 156
Converse, Clara, 81
Covell, James, 38, 39, 127
Cuddeback, Margaret, 81, 82, 84, 86, 87, 106, 131, 141

Decoration of the Fourth Order, 175
democracy, democratic, 86, 119, 137, 149, 154, 164, 179
denomination, x, xiv, xvi, 10, 25, 115, 116, 140
Department of Education, 22, 24, 40, 82, 101, 102, 162
Dinsmore, Carlos, 47, 51, 52
divine guidance, 28, 47, 48, 158
Doll Festival , 69
domestic science (see home economics)
dormitory, xvii, 15, 24, 31–34, 35, 71, 92, 93, 127, 142, 144, 145, 146, 151, 156, 174
Downman, Rawleigh, 3

earthquake, 38, 82, 185, 186
Ella O. Patrick Home, x, 21, 23, 24, 45, 58, 61, 66, 183, 184, 185
emperor, 15, 70, 110, 113, 175
empress, 113, 175, 177
endowment, 63, 67, 73, 75, 83, 89, 90, 101, 103
entrance ceremony, 113, 114, 115
Epping Forest, 1–6, 8, 11, 104
evangelism, 10, 15, 17, 20, 21, 24, 30, 31, 45, 61, 63, 70, 96, 97, 98, 99, 102, 139, 154, 175
Exclusion Act, 42, 46
Executive Order 9066, 104

faculty, 31, 36, 42, 43, 61, 62, 70, 73, 75, 79, 83, 88, 89, 90, 96, 97, 168, 174, 176
faith, xii, xiii, 5, 6, 9, 19, 20, 29–31, 35, 43, 45, 46, 80, 81, 88, 127, 132, 138, 178, 179, 180
fascist, 110, 112

Fife, Nellie, 29, 65
fire bomb, 39, 126
First Peter 3:3–4, xvii
foreign secretary, xv, xvi, 58, 72, 73, 93, 140
Foote, John, 144, 166
Formosa, 85, 86
Fridell, Elmer, 137, 140, 174

Gifford, Ella May, 66
Goa (place for war-time prisoner exchange), 129, 134
Goble, Jonathan and Eliza, xvi
graduates, 22–24, 26, 29, 35, 36, 40, 62, 63, 67, 71, 73, 84, 85, 87, 93, 95, 96, 100, 102, 148, 157, 158, 162, 165, 167, 175, 176, 180, 183
Great Eastern Japan Earthquake and Tsunami, 185
Great Kanto Earthquake, 38, 82
Greater East Asia Co-Prosperity, 116
gymnasium, 20, 32, 54, 136, 151–59, 162, 166, 167

Hachiman Kokumin School, 138
Hashimoto, Junryo, 174
Haven, Marguerite, 36, 44, 45, 54, 55, 57, 59, 64, 66
Hinchman, Bill, 166
higher department (upper division).
    See also koutouka and senkouka, 25, 26, 29, 31, 32, 34, 35, 48, 73, 87, 92, 117, 150, 164
higher education, 24, 25, 35, 56, 83, 102, 123, 140, 161, 162
Hinomoto Girls' School, 36, 64, 73, 86, 87, 165
Hirai Nisaku, 111, 174
home economics, 24, 25, 48, 62, 120, 121, 162, 164
honka, 24, 25, 26, 35, 36, 39, 53, 55, 60, 61, 63, 70, 71, 82, 88, 121, 162, 165
Honma Shunpei, 63
hospital(s), 69, 71, 89, 95, 96, 98, 119, 142, 148, 169
Hughes, Grace Anne, 13, 14
Humphreys, Ethel, xv, 82, 84, 87, 93

hymn(s), xvii, 33, 63, 70, 138

Imai Saburo, 45, 80
Immigration Exclusion Act, 46
Imperial Dept. of Education, 40
Imperial Diet, 63
Indiana Baptist Convention, 47, 51, 52
Indiana Building, 51, 56, 61, 62, 65, 68, 147
International Ministries, xiv, 13
internment, internees, 104, 127, 134

Japan Committee, 139, 140
Japanese language, ix, x, xi, 14, 17, 18, 31, 37 52, 54, 58, 59, 64, 65, 98, 99, 102, 104, 109, 128, 129,164
Jenkins, Louise, 64
Jesse, Richard H., 4–7
Jesse, William H., 4–8
Jesse, William T., 3, 4, 5
junior college,, 22, 35, 41, 83, 150, 151, 161–63, 168, 169, 171, 172, 174, 175, 180, 181, 183
Kagawa Toyohiko, 14, 91, 108
Kahoku Newspaper, 177
Kanamori Giichi, 55, 64
Kanto Gakuin, xi, 21, 32, 35, 41, 43, 137, 172
Karuizawa, 58
Kato, Shizuyo, 53
Katsura Island, 170
Kawaguchi Ukichi, 64, 68, 74, 75, 77–80, 83
Kawai Michi, 45
Keisen Girls' School, 45
Kesennuma, 17, 148
Kikuchi Kazuko Sato, 125
kindergarten, 14, 16, 17, 20, 32, 41, 82, 100, 110, 120, 121, 127, 133, 157, 183
Kokura, 78, 80, 93
Kon Takeo, 63
koutouka.
    See higher department, 35, 36, 39, 40, 45, 51, 55, 60, 61, 62, 64, 65, 69, 70, 71, 73, 82, 161
Kuji, 59, 89, 127

Kuomoto (Pastor of North Star Church), 143
Kurihara Motoi, 102, 148

legacy, 2, 4, 20, 86, 161, 178–80
Lincoln, Abraham, 4, 5
Livingston, Ted, 170

MacArthur, Douglas, 138, 139, 143, 150
Maddry, Charles, 78, 80
Maine, Grace, xv, 60, 72, 73, 74, 75, 78, 79, 80
Manchuria, 67, 86, 97, 98, 148
Maruyama Yoshinaga, 55
Matsumura Yoshitoshi, 146, 174
Matsushima, 121, 170
McCoy, Beulah, 165, 176, 177, 182
McCulloch, Gertrude, 152, 153, 164, 166, 167, 170
McVeigh, Mabelle, xv, 38, 47, 57, 58, 59
Mead Christian Center, woman's seminary, xvii, 17, 37, 43, 84, 86, 88, 131
Mead, Lavinia, xvii, 17, 21, 29, 69
Meline, Agnes, 40, 45, 52, 54, 55, 56, 131
mission board, 14, 30, 48, 49, 71, 73, 74, 75, 99, 109, 129
Missionary Register Card, 13, 19, 53, 68, 101, 130
missionary residence, xvii, 21, 37, 66, 146, 156, 183
Miyagi Jogakkou, 37, 72
Mochizuki Masamitsu, xi, 32, 57, 74, 75, 92, 93, 94, 125, 145, 153
Monma Nobuo, 112
morals, ethics, 110, 113, 119, 164
Morigo Christian Camp, 170
Morioka, 14, 16, 17, 20, 59, 128, 133
Mount Aoba Yama, 112
Muraoka Tenshi, 63
music, 36, 37, 38, 44, 52, 54, 57, 63, 64, 68, 71, 101, 103, 126, 128, 146
Mutsumi no Kusari, 2, 15, 18, 43, 48, 72, 74, 76, 83, 143, 165

Nagamachi, 121

Nakai Takashi, 173
Nakase Takeshi, 107, 122, 123, 174
national anthem, 101, 111, 113
National Origins Quota, 46
National Spirit Mobilization Movement, 110, 111, 112
nationalistic propaganda, 111, 112
Naturalization Act of 1790, 46
New Order in East Asia, 97, 112, 116
Newbury, Georgia, 42, 43, 52–55, 56, 59, 60, 63, 65, 66, 69–71, 73–85, 87, 95, 130
Nicholson, Goldie, 86–89, 106
Northern Baptist Convention, xiv, 137
Nouwen, Henri, 160
Numazawa Masako, 144, 152
nurse(s), 71, 95, 96, 148, 169, 183

occupation, 92, 130, 138, 139
Odatsume Bunya, 138, 163, 173, 174
Oriental University, 55
Oshima Teiko Kudo, 123
Oshima Yoko, 123

Pacific War, x, 102, 108, 114, 115, 116
Patrick, Ella O., 21
Patten, Lora Mabel, 86, 88, 89, 96
Pawley, Annabelle, 30
Pearl Harbor, 116
physical education, 31, 111, 150, 151, 162
Post, Vida, 165, 170, 173, 181
Poston Concentration Camp, 104, 105
P.T.A., 42, 68, 119, 151–153, 155, 157, 163, 171, 173, 177

Quota Immigration Act, 42

Reference Committee, xvi, 14, 15, 20, 25, 37, 59, 75, 83, 156
religious program, 94, 95, 100, 165
repatriation, 129, 130, 131, 133
Rescript on Education, 120
revival, 29, 41, 43, 44, 55, 147, 161
Robin Club, 44
Rochester Theological Seminary, 41
Rockefeller Fund, 32
roots of faith, xiii, 20, 29, 71, 178, 180

Ross, Charles and Sadie, 36, 49, 54, 60, 64, 140, 173
Russo-Japanese War, 110

S.S. Gripsolm (Prisoner exchange ship), 134
Sandburg, Minnie (Sears, Minnie), xv, 55, 68, 69, 72, 73, 76, 77, 78, 152–57, 162, 168, 170–76
Sara Curtis Home School, 18
Sasaki Komei, 186
Sato Misao, 68, 107, 165, 167
Savitar, The, 7, 8
Sawano Jiro, 55
S.C.A.P, 139, 140
Schneder, Rev. David B., 94
school excursion, 115, 169
school-church, 29, 37, 39, 40, 43, 45, 63, 95, 146, 165, 166, 167
Schroer, Cornelia, 128
Sendai Station, 122, 143, 160, 177, 182
senkoubu. See upper division, 82, 89, 92, 100, 101, 110, 120, 121, 147, 150, 161
Shank, Hazel, xv, 100, 101, 105, 109, 137, 140
Shinsei churches, 165
Shinsei shadan, 153, 157
Shinto, 98, 110, 112, 113
Shiogama, 17, 121, 147
Shokei Gakuin, 61, 163, 183
Skevington, Florence and Gladys, 56, 59
Sleeth, Natalie, 1
Smith, Ruth, 31, 49
socialist, 42
Society of Friends, 74, 83, 90
Somers, Gladys, 30
Soshin Girls' School, 39, 44, 54, 56, 59, 64, 73, 81, 129, 130, 137, 165
Southern Baptist, xiv, 78, 79, 93
Student Volunteer Movement, 9
Sugawara Beauty Salon, 176
Sunday school, xvii, 16, 17, 21, 33, 39, 40, 57, 62, 69
Suzuki Akiko, 120, 126, 127
Suzuki Yo, 84, 85
Sympathy Week, 70

Tada Keiko Yoshida, 169
Tagajo, 121, 134
Taira, 17
Takahashi Shigeto, 92, 107, 135, 144, 171
Takano Michie, 55
Takayama, 65
Teague, Collin, 3
Teia Maru (Prisoner exchange ship), 129, 130
Tohoku University, 63, 95 162
Tono, 20, 72, 77, 85
Topping, Helen, 14, 16
Topping, Henry and Evelyn, 16
Triennial Convention, xiv
trustees, xvi, 37, 57, 80, 85, 93, 114, 150, 152, 153, 155, 156, 157, 165, 173, 174
Tule Lake Concentration Camp, 129

United Church of Christ (UCC), xii, 36, 39, 116, 137, 146
Uchigasaki Sakusaburo, 63
Uchimura Kanzo, 92
Uchimura Tatsusaburo, 63
uniform, 8, 31, 113, 121, 125, 168, 169
University of Chicago, 41, 55
University of Missouri, xi, 6, 7, 8, 9
upper division. See *senkoubu*, 29, 31, 32, 89, 92

Vacation Bible School, 70, 165
Virginia (state), xi, 1, 2, 3, 4, 5, 6, 9, 104, 105, 165

Wajima Yoshio, 64
Ward, Ruth, 30, 36, 129, 130
Waseda Hoshien, 15, 63, 92
Washington, George, 2, 3
Westcott, Brooke Foss, 136
White, E. M., 34
Wilson, Helen, 69
Wilson, Jesse, 151, 166
Woman's American Baptist Foreign Mission Society (WABFMS), xii, xiv, 20, 25, 37, 72, 75, 76, 78,79,84, 85–88, 102, 105, 130, 131, 140, 153, 155, 156, 165,166, 171

Wynd, William, 37

Yamada Chiyo, 44
Yanbe Tamotsu, 173

Yasumura Saburo, 37, 43, 88
YWCA, 8, 43–45, 47, 48, 55, 57, 69,
77, 96